Literature, Art and Slavery

Edinburgh Critical Studies in Atlantic Literatures and Cultures

Series Editors: Laura Doyle, Colleen Glenney Boggs and Maria Cristina Fumagalli

Available titles

Sensational Internationalism: The Paris Commune and the Remapping of American Memory in the Long Nineteenth Century
J. Michelle Coghlan

American Travel Literature, Gendered Aesthetics, and the Italian Tour, 1824–1862
Brigitte Bailey

American Snobs: Transatlantic Novelists, Liberal Culture and the Genteel Tradition
Emily Coit

Scottish Colonial Literature: Writing the Atlantic, 1603–1707
Kirsten Sandrock

Yankee Yarns: Storytelling and the Invention of the National Body in Nineteenth-Century American Culture
Stefanie Schäfer

Reverberations of Revolution: Transnational Perspectives, 1770–1850
Edited by Elizabeth Amann and Michael Boyden

Consuming Empire in U.S. Fiction, 1865–1930
Heather Wayne

Derek Walcott's Painters: A Life with Pictures
Maria Cristina Fumagalli

Literature, Art and Slavery: Ekphrastic Visions
Carl Plasa

Forthcoming titles

Emily Dickinson and Her British Contemporaries: Victorian Poetry in Nineteenth-Century America
Páraic Finnerty

The Atlantic Dilemma: Reform or Revolution Across the Long Nineteenth Century
Kelvin Black

Visit the series website at: www.edinburghuniversitypress.com/series/ECSALC

Literature, Art and Slavery

Ekphrastic Visions

Carl Plasa

Edinburgh University Press is one of the leading university presses in the UK. We publish academic books and journals in our selected subject areas across the humanities and social sciences, combining cutting-edge scholarship with high editorial and production values to produce academic works of lasting importance. For more information visit our website: edinburghuniversitypress.com

© Carl Plasa 2023, 2025

Grateful acknowledgement is made to the sources listed in the List of Illustrations and in the text for permission to reproduce material previously published elsewhere. Every effort has been made to trace the copyright holders, but if any have been inadvertently overlooked, the publisher will be pleased to make the necessary arrangements at the first opportunity.

Edinburgh University Press Ltd
13 Infirmary Street,
Edinburgh, EH1 1LT

First published in hardback by Edinburgh University Press 2023

Typeset in 11/13pt Adobe Sabon by
Cheshire Typesetting Ltd, Cuddington, Cheshire

A CIP record for this book is available from the British Library

ISBN 978 0 7486 8354 3 (hardback)
ISBN 978 0 7486 8357 4 (paperback)
ISBN 978 0 7486 8355 0 (webready PDF)
ISBN 978 0 7486 8356 7 (epub)

The right of Carl Plasa to be identified as the author of this work has been asserted in accordance with the Copyright, Designs and Patents Act 1988, and the Copyright and Related Rights Regulations 2003 (SI No. 2498).

Contents

List of Figures vi
Series Editors' Preface viii
Acknowledgements ix

Introduction: Reframing Ekphrasis 1

1. Adding to the Picture: New Perspectives on David Dabydeen's 'Turner' 11

2. Looking beyond 'Turner': William B. Patrick's 'The Slave Ship' 45

3. 'Slave-Ships on Fantastic Seas': The Art of Abolition 66

4. The Secret Afterlives of Dido Elizabeth Belle 95

5. African-American Ekphrasis and the 'Peculiar Institution' 129

6. *Icon*-versations: F. Douglas Brown, Jacob Lawrence and Frederick Douglass 166

Bibliography 208
Index 221

Figures

1.1	J. M. W. Turner, *Slavers Throwing Overboard the Dead and Dying – Typhon Coming On*, 1840.	12
2.1	*Description of a Slave Ship*, 1789.	54
3.1	Agnes Martin, *Islands No. 4*, c. 1961.	69
3.2	*Stowage of the British Slave Ship 'Brookes' under the Regulated Slave Trade Act of 1788*, c. 1788.	75
3.3	'Négrier Poursuivi, Jetant ses Nègres à la Mer' ('Slave Ship Being Pursued, Throwing its Blacks into the Sea'), undated.	86
4.1	David Martin, *Portrait of Dido Elizabeth Belle and Lady Elizabeth Murray*, c. 1779.	96
4.2	After Scipio Moorhead? *Phillis Wheatley, Negro Servant to Mr. Wheatley, of Boston*. Frontispiece to Phillis Wheatley, *Poems on Various Subjects, Religious and Moral*, 1773.	125
5.1	William Sidney Mount, *Bar-Room Scene*, 1835.	130
5.2	Thomas Satterwhite Noble, *Margaret Garner*, 1867.	136
5.3	Mathew B. Brady, *The Modern Medea – The Story of Margaret Garner*, 1867.	140
5.4	Thomas Satterwhite Noble, *The Price of Blood: A Planter Selling His Son*, 1868.	143
5.5	Thomas Gainsborough, *The Blue Boy*, 1770.	144
5.6	George Fuller, *The Quadroon*, 1880.	148
5.7	Gilbert Stuart, 'Edgehill' *Portrait of Thomas Jefferson*, 1805.	153
5.8	*Coffee after Dinner, Dean Hall Plantation, Berkeley County, South Carolina*, c. 1900.	158
6.1	Sixth-plate daguerreotype of Frederick Douglass, c. 1841.	168
6.2	Fra Angelico, *Cortona Altarpiece with the Annunciation*, c. 1432–3.	171
6.3	Sandro Botticelli, *Annunciation of Cestello*, 1488–9.	172

6.4	Jacob Lawrence, *Frederick Douglass* series, Panel 1, 1938–9.	175
6.5	Jacob Lawrence, *Frederick Douglass* series, Panel 2, 1938–9.	179
6.6	Jacob Lawrence, *Frederick Douglass* series, Panel 3, 1938–9.	183
6.7	Jacob Lawrence, *Frederick Douglass* series, Panel 10, 1938–9.	185
6.8	Jacob Lawrence, *Frederick Douglass* series, Panel 8, 1938–9.	190
6.9	Jacob Lawrence, *Frederick Douglass* series, Panel 21, 1938–9.	194
6.10	Jacob Lawrence, *Frederick Douglass* series, Panel 18, 1938–9.	198
6.11	Jacob Lawrence, *Frederick Douglass* series, Panel 32, 1938–9.	202

Series Editors' Preface

Modern global culture makes it clear that literary study can no longer operate on nation-based or exceptionalist models. In practice, American literatures have always been understood and defined in relation to the literatures of Europe and Asia. The books in this series work within a broad comparative framework to question place-based identities and monocular visions, in historical contexts from the earliest European settlements to contemporary affairs, and across all literary genres. They explore the multiple ways in which ideas, texts, objects and bodies travel across spatial and temporal borders, generating powerful forms of contrast and affinity. The Edinburgh Critical Studies in Atlantic Literatures and Cultures series fosters new paradigms of exchange, circulation and transformation for Atlantic literary studies, expanding the critical and theoretical work of this rapidly developing field.

Laura Doyle, Colleen Glenney Boggs and
Maria Cristina Fumagalli

Acknowledgements

Like Lewis Carroll's White Rabbit, this book is worryingly overdue, starting life more than ten years back and experiencing a number of conceptual reshuffles before settling into its final form. I am grateful to Michelle Houston, commissioning editor at Edinburgh University Press, for her faith, patience and understanding along the way; and to Matthias Bauer and Li-hsin Hsu for their encouragement at various points in the book's evolution, as well as to the anonymous reader at EUP for some useful insights. Katie Bramell and Stephanie Lampkin from the National Underground Railroad Freedom Center, Cincinnati, Ohio, went to heroic lengths in providing me with the photographic image of Thomas Satterwhite Noble's *Margaret Garner*; while Beth Bilderback from the South Caroliniana Library, University of South Carolina, offered invaluable contextual knowledge about the plantation photograph discussed in Chapter 5.

Thanks are also due to Cadan and Emmett for the at-a-glance perspicacity of their responses to some of the other images the book includes and for assistance with the finer points of virtual paperwork. My truest debt, as in all things, is to Betty J., who put me in the picture with regard to slavery several lifetimes ago and who has risen above the consequences with grace and humour ever since.

The following material is reproduced by permission:

Chapter 1: excerpts from 'Turner' in *Turner: New and Selected Poems*. Copyright © 2010 by David Dabydeen. Reprinted by permission of Peepal Tree Press.

Chapter 2: excerpts from 'The Slave Ship' in *These Upraised Hands*. Copyright © 1995 by William B. Patrick. Reprinted by permission of The Permissions Company, LLC on behalf of BOA Editions, Ltd., www.boaeditions.org.

Chapter 3: 'Islands Number Four' in *Words for Images: A Gallery of Poems*, edited by John Hollander and Joanna Weber, Yale University Art Gallery. Copyright © Elizabeth Alexander, 2001; used by permission of the author and first published in *Antebellum*

Dream Book by Elizabeth Alexander, published by Graywolf Press, Minneapolis, MN.

Chapter 4: excerpts from 'Dido Elizabeth Belle – A Narrative of Her Life (Extant)' in *Dat's Love* and first published in 1995 by Seren. Copyright © The Estate of Leonora Brito; *Dat's Love and other stories* / Library of Wales / edition published 2017 by Parthian Books; and excerpts from 'Dido' in *The Woman Who Gave Birth to Rabbits*. Copyright © 2002 by Emma Donoghue and used by permission of the author.

Chapter 5: 'The Price of Blood' in *Taboo: The Wishbone Trilogy, Part 1* by Yusef Komunyakaa. Copyright © 2004 by Yusef Komunyakaa. Reprinted by permission of Farrar, Straus and Giroux. All rights reserved; excerpts from 'Blood' and 'Enlightenment' in *Thrall: Poems* by Natasha Trethewey. Copyright © 2012 by Natasha Trethewey. Reprinted by permission of Mariner Books, an imprint of HarperCollins Publishers LLC. All rights reserved; and excerpts from 'Antebellum House Party' by Terrance Hayes in *Found Anew: Poetry and Prose Inspired by the South Caroliniana Library Digital Collections* edited by R. Mac Jones and Ray McManus. Copyright © 2015 by University of South Carolina Press. Reprinted by permission.

The first section of Chapter 1 is lightly revised from 'Towards a Bigger Picture: Transatlantic Ekphrasis in William B. Patrick's "The Slave Ship"', *The Wenshan Review of Literature and Culture*, vol. 11, no. 2, June 2018, pp. 1–33, while the rest of the chapter originally appeared, in slightly different form, in '"In Another Light": New Intertexts for David Dabydeen's "Turner"', *Connotations: A Journal for Critical Debate*, vol. 26, 2016–17, pp. 163–203. Chapter 2 features material first published in the article in *The Wenshan Review* already cited; section 1 of Chapter 3 and section 3 of Chapter 4 (on poems by Elizabeth Alexander and Honorée Fanonne Jeffers, respectively) are based on material initially included in 'Ekphrastic Poetry and the Middle Passage: Recent Encounters in the Black Atlantic', *Connotations: A Journal for Critical Debate*, vol. 24, no. 2, 2014–15, pp. 290–324.

For my mum

Introduction: Reframing Ekphrasis

Since the beginning of the new millennium there has been a noticeable upsurge in critical work on the visual archive of Atlantic slavery, resulting in a host of important studies. While most of these contributions are weighted towards images created during the era of slavery itself,[1] some have adopted a more historically far-reaching approach, exploring the ways in which such images live on beyond the original context of their production, circulation and consumption, returning imaginatively in different forms at different times and in different places. A signal instance of this latter trend is Cheryl Finley's *Committed to Memory: The Art of the Slave Ship Icon* (2018), a dazzling *tour de force* which examines how *Description of a Slave Ship* (1789), the abolitionist schema of the Liverpool slaver the *Brookes*, has been extensively reinterpreted and reinvented in 'the creative work of black artists and their allies in the twentieth century and today', as they slot into a 'visual genealogy' and practise what Finley dubs a 'mnemonic aesthetics' (5).[2] The present book shares this fascination with the afterlives which such visual materials have accrued to themselves, but places the critical accent on how that posterity has occurred and evolved in the context not of art but of literature. The book's focus, in specific terms, is on the transactions between a diverse selection of texts written between the mid-1990s and 2020 and a range of images that belong (with one exception) to British and American traditions. These images are taken from a period (between c. 1779 and 1939) which is of considerable historical significance, witnessing, as it did, several landmark events in the intertwined transatlantic histories of slavery and race – from the campaign for the abolition of the slave trade (1787–1807) to the American Civil War (1861–5) to the Harlem Renaissance

(1919–c. 1934).³ Many of the images are well-known – the diagram of the *Brookes* itself, for instance – but, with the obvious exception of David Dabydeen's 'Turner' (1994), the textual responses they have elicited are largely to be found languishing on the outskirts of the canon, having to date received little or no critical analysis. Yet whatever the status and degree of critical recognition conferred on them, these responses, taken together, are of vital moment as a means of identifying and analysing the ways in which slavery's visual culture continues to resonate within the realms of contemporary literary production.

In generic terms, all the texts examined here fall under the rubric of ekphrasis, a literary form that has a long history, stretching back to the classical age and the depictions 'of the shields of Achilles and of Herakles by Homer and Hesiod respectively' (Hollander 7). Despite its ancient provenance, however, ekphrasis has continued to attract much critical attention, especially since the advent of two studies produced just prior to the appearance of Dabydeen's long narrative poem: W. J. T. Mitchell's 'Ekphrasis and the Other', a journal-article originally published in *The South Atlantic Quarterly* in 1992; and James A. W. Heffernan's *Museum of Words: The Poetics of Ekphrasis from Homer to Ashbery* (1993).⁴ For Mitchell, the ekphrastic relationship is not informed by the sort of cordiality implicit in conventional figurations of poetry and painting as 'Sister Arts', but unfolds, rather, in terms of a certain antagonism wherein texts vie with visual images as potent but alien forms of representation that need in some way to be overcome. This is a position that Heffernan in turn adopts in his theorisation of the ekphrastic encounter, arguing, for example, that 'the poet's word seeks to gain mastery over the painter's image' (7).

Just as Heffernan builds on Mitchell, so his own work has exerted an enduring influence over the field, particularly his definition, 'simple in form but complex in its implications', of ekphrasis as '*the verbal representation of visual representation*' (Heffernan 3; italics in original), a statement routinely cited by other critics as a point of departure for their own approaches (Cheeke 24; Hedley, Halpern and Spiegelman 21; Kennedy 8).⁵ Yet for all its erudition and continuing relevance, Heffernan's book is not without its drawbacks, not the least of which is its privileging of literature by male authors (a trait also of Mitchell's work). Such androcentrism continues, by and large, to determine the field, although it has been directly and fruitfully challenged by *In the Frame: Women's Ekphrastic Poetry from Marianne Moore to Susan Wheeler* (2009), a collection of critical essays edited by Jane Hedley, Nick Halpern and Willard Spiegelman. This volume addresses the question of the ways in which the type of ekphrastic poetry produced by women might differ from that authored by men, even as what it ends up demonstrating, ironically, is the ways in which that poetry differs from itself, composed, as it is, of a dynamic plurality of practices and strategies.[6]

An additional irony of this otherwise valuable female-centred and feminist-orientated inquiry is that it corrects one critical blindness only to consolidate another, since – with the (predictable) exception of Rita Dove – all of the women writers it features are white, a racial bias in the formation of the ekphrastic field evident in Mitchell and Heffernan alike and in later criticism too.[7] This book itself happily accommodates ekphrastic texts by white male (and female) writers, but the vast majority of the authors with whom it deals are either black Caribbean, black British or African American (like Dove) – nine out of twelve to be precise (with seven in the latter category). Apart from the intrinsic value of their work, these Black Atlantic writers (five male and four female) have been deliberately chosen in order to counter the prevailing investment in what might be called white ekphrasis, shifting the angle of the critical gaze in a way that brings into view a more racially equitable, varied and complex picture of ekphrastic endeavour than has been available hitherto. The turn towards such writers (and their turn towards the resources of ekphrasis) becomes all the more charged and significant when the role of sight – that most 'despotic . . . of senses' (Wordsworth 475) – in the historical and ongoing domination and oppression of black subjects is taken into account, as manifested, for instance, in the general context of racial taxonomy and racial stereotyping by means of visual markers (hair and skin colour); the theatre of cruelty that is the slave auction; or the spectatorial violence of the post-slavery lynching ritual.

There has, of course, already been some critical acknowledgement of how writers have sought to transmute the visions of slavery that confront them into verbal form, the most prominent example being the multiple readings that have grown up around the aforementioned 'Turner', a major postcolonial Caribbean response to J. M. W. Turner's *Slavers Throwing Overboard the Dead and Dying – Typhon Coming On* (1840), more commonly known as *The Slave Ship*. Nonetheless, it is the argument of this book that the range of ekphrastic engagements with slavery's visual representation has been seriously underrecognised, thus closing off access to some particularly innovative and compelling literary works.[8] The book also argues that the ekphrastic texts it covers invariably exceed the images that are their cues, unlocking narrative possibilities the producers of those images could not have envisaged. It further proposes that such texts do not always or necessarily exist in the kind of antagonistic relationship to the visual that Mitchell and Heffernan both claim to be constitutive of the ekphrastic mode. As Elizabeth Bergmann Loizeaux puts it, writing back to Mitchell: 'While ekphrasis depends on the difference between word and image and can stage their representational contest and opposition, it also stages relations across difference. Otherness is not always "rival," even when it is "alien"' (15–16). The book's final claim is that the texts in question are rarely reducible to the straightforward or conventional dyadic structure promoted by Heffernan: rather, they disrupt his model by simultaneously drawing on, alluding to, revising or otherwise incorporating into themselves other sources that take verbal rather than visual form. In this sense, these texts often turn out to be ampler and more complex in their operations than Heffernan's succinctly serviceable thumbnail definition would seem to allow.

Nowhere is the braiding and enrichment of the intermedial with the intertextual more apparent than in 'Turner', and it is with this extended ekphrasis – daring, disturbing and lyrical at once – that the book's first chapter is concerned. Beginning with an outline of the historical incident inspiring the painting that inspires Dabydeen's poem – the atrocity aboard the *Zong* in 1781 – the argument moves on to situate the text in dialogue with John Ruskin's 'Of Water, as Painted by Turner' in *Modern Painters I* (1843) but, in a departure from other critics, places the emphasis not on the set-piece ekphrastic rendition of *The Slave Ship* with which 'Of Water' closes but earlier parts of that chapter's art-critical reflection, analysing how they come surreptitiously to inform Dabydeen's poetic vision.

While these elements of Ruskin's account of Turner have been sidelined in critical readings of 'Turner', two other intertexts have been much more significantly neglected. The first is *Macbeth* (1606), the Shakespeare play to which (ironically) Ruskin's ekphrasis on *The Slave Ship* twice alludes and the second Toni Morrison's *Beloved* (1987), another searching meditation on the Middle Passage and its devastations. 'Turner''s engagement with Morrison's novel is particularly noteworthy because it enables the poem to sidestep the Anglo-Caribbean lines of influence which most critics see in it – locating the text in relation to *The Tempest* (1611) or Derek Walcott's *Omeros* (1990), for instance – and moves it into a new relationship with the African-American literary tradition instead.[9]

According to Mary Lou Emery, 'More than any other in the European tradition, Turner's painting has catalysed a literary response from the Caribbean diaspora' (21), with leading examples besides Dabydeen's 'Turner' (and his own *A Harlot's Progress* [1999]) including Michelle Cliff's *Free Enterprise: A Novel of Mary Ellen Pleasant* (1993) and Fred D'Aguiar's *Feeding the Ghosts* (1997). Yet the violent dramas of Turner's masterpiece have also called forth responses from outside that diasporic orbit, a particularly sophisticated and intriguing case in point emanating from a white American context in the shape of William B. Patrick's 'The Slave Ship' (1994). In contrast to the Caribbean texts just adduced, this work has so far eluded criticism altogether, even as it amply rewards exploration and analysis, as Chapter 2 sets out to demonstrate, as a kind of lost or forgotten companion-piece to Dabydeen's much-feted and much better-known poem.

In Chapter 3, the book switches the focus away from ekphrases on *The Slave Ship* to consider the literary legacies of three abolitionist images from British and French traditions: *Stowage of the British Slave Ship 'Brookes' under the Regulated Slave Trade Act of 1788* (c. 1788); the previously mentioned *Description*; and 'Négrier Poursuivi, Jetant ses Nègres à la Mer' ('Slave Ship Being Pursued, Throwing its Blacks into the Sea'), an illustration thought to be from the early part of the nineteenth century and included in volume four of Charles van Tenac's *Histoire Générale de la Marine* (*General History of the Navy*) (1847–8).

In the afterword to *Committed to Memory*, Finley makes a rare and unexpected foray into the realm of ekphrastic criticism to examine the role which the second of these images plays in 'Islands Number Four' (2001), a poem by the African-American poet Elizabeth Alexander, and the chapter begins by offering its own reading of this short and somewhat cryptic text. At the same time, though, the chapter discusses the poem's dialogue with and debt to the *Stowage* print, something Finley's otherwise detailed analysis chooses, oddly, to ignore.

As the chapter proceeds to argue, this latter print provides the ekphrastic grist for two further writers: Honorée Fanonne Jeffers, another African-American poet, who uses it as the basis for a short poem in *The Age of Phillis* (2020), her reimagining of the life and times of Phillis Wheatley; and Matthew Plampin, a white British novelist, who reworks it in *Will & Tom* (2015), a serio-comic novel about Turner's early career. Yet if *Stowage* provides an unlikely bridge between Plampin on the one hand and his African-American contemporaries on the other, Plampin at the same time adds a different image into the mix in the shape of the *gravure* in Tenac. Within the fictional world that Plampin creates, that picture combines with *Stowage* to confront the young Turner with a series of unnerving visual experiences that in due course feed into the artist's much later production of *The Slave Ship*, as if they were part of that painting's own visual genealogy.

As is implicit in the chapter-sketches offered so far, one of this book's features is the manner in which it juxtaposes two (or sometimes three) perspectives on a single image, allowing for comparison and contrast of ekphrastic work both between and within different literary cultures and traditions: Dabydeen and Patrick on *The Slave Ship*; Alexander, Jeffers and Plampin on *Stowage*. This pattern is continued in Chapter 4, which examines three texts (two short stories and one short poem) that are as it were all latently secreted in *Portrait of Dido Elizabeth Belle and Lady Elizabeth Murray* (c. 1779), a painting highly unusual for its time in its sisterly juxtaposition of a young mixed-race woman and her white counterpart.[10] The first of the stories is 'Dido Elizabeth Belle – A Narrative of Her Life (Extant)' (1995) by Leonora Brito, self-styled 'black Cardiffian' (Brito, 'Staying' 44), while the second is 'Dido' (2002), by the white expatriate Irish author, Emma Donoghue. The poetic response that rounds out the chapter in a brief coda returns the book to Jeffers's *The Age of Phillis* and another of the poems in that volume, 'Portrait of Dido Elizabeth Belle Lindsay, Free Mulatto, and her White Cousin, the Lady Elizabeth Murray, Great-Nieces of William Murray, First Earl of Mansfield and Lord Chief Justice of the King's Bench'.

Despite their shared visual source, there are marked differences between these three texts, with Jeffers broadly maintaining a nuanced focus on the painting itself and its interracial dynamics, while Brito and Donoghue, for their parts, move quite extravagantly beyond the image that quickens their narratives, conjuring lives and possibilities for Dido radically removed from the scene in which she originally appears. In this way, their stories interweave history with fiction to fashion a hybrid narrative form that has affinities with Plampin's *Will & Tom*.

Up to this juncture, consideration of how African-American writers have used ekphrasis as a technique for addressing slavery's visual archive has been limited to just three poems (one by Alexander and two by Jeffers), all keyed to images intimately associated with a British slave-history. In Chapter 5, by contrast, the emphasis falls squarely upon the ways in which other African-American writers have turned the ekphrastic gaze towards images that either represent American slavery directly or are closely related to it and that were all created by white Americans between 1805 and c. 1900. Examples of such a turn are certainly infrequent, if all the more important precisely for that reason and provided here in a kind of ekphrastic gallery of six short texts by four authors: John Edgar Wideman, Yusef Komunyakaa, Natasha Trethewey and Terrance Hayes. Despite the different perspectives from which these writers approach the same visual archive, their engagements with slavery ultimately operate along comparable lines, often taking the images that inspire them in fresh directions, placing them in new contexts or using them to generate new narratives.

Like its predecessor, the book's sixth and final chapter is exclusively devoted to slavery and ekphrasis in an African-American vein, taking F. Douglas Brown's *Icon* (2018) as its field of inquiry. This small-press collection is notable for the culturally diverse mix of poetic genres it deploys (Kundiman, Golden Shovel, erasure, ghazal and of course ekphrasis, *inter alia*); its use of the Japanese presentational mode of PechaKucha; and its eclectic play of allusion, which runs a dizzying gamut from the Annunciation pictures of the Italian Renaissance to comic-book superheroes and from popular African-American dance-styles to the film musicals of the 1950s. In thematic terms, *Icon* is partly concerned with contemporary African-American experience, encompassing topics as heterogeneous as the transgenerational dynamics of Brown's own family relationships and the violent deaths of African Americans either in or as a consequence of police custody. Its overriding orientation, however, is not towards images produced from a white American perspective (as featured in Chapter 5) but the work of the African-American painter Jacob Lawrence and specifically, his *Frederick Douglass* series of 1938–9, created when Lawrence was between twenty-one and twenty-two years of age.[11]

Part of the distinctiveness of the thirty-two panels that make up that series is that they are themselves based on Douglass's own voluminous autobiographical writings and constitute a kind of reverse ekphrasis in which the visual represents the verbal rather than the other way around. Brown's conversation – or *Icon*-versation – with Lawrence is thus also a conversation with Douglass, to whose work he alludes on numerous occasions. In thus combining the intermedial and the intertextual, *Icon* brings the book full circle, returning it to the similarly double-stranded workings of 'Turner'.

As well as intervening in, diversifying and expanding the field of ekphrastic criticism, this book has a resonance that transcends a purely academic horizon. If the writers it encompasses have been captivated by images of slavery – whether from the eighteenth, nineteenth or twentieth centuries – it is surely not only because such materials are historically or aesthetically compelling in themselves but also because the structures of oppression they dramatise are at once strange yet familiar, removed yet immediate, speaking with an uncomfortable directness to the asphyxiating racial tensions and terrors of today, as spectacularly crystallised and embodied in the murder of George Floyd on 25 May 2020 (itself an event captured on video and swiftly circulated around the globe). These uncanny images may cross from visual to verbal mode, in other words, but such processes of transformation and renewal cannot disguise the startling continuities that still stubbornly obtain between the present and the past.

Notes

1. For a cross-section of such work see Wood, *Blind Memory*; Kriz; McInnis; Molineux; Lugo-Ortiz and Rosenthal; Cutter; and Fox-Amato.
2. Among other critics to have explored *Description* along similar lines are Francis; Trodd; and Bernier, '"SLAVE SHIP"'. For studies which examine the imaginative recreation and revisiting of other archival images see Stauffer, Trodd and Bernier 93–121; Bernier and Durkin; and Macaluso.
3. Most of the images the book discusses (primarily paintings, but also engravings and photographs) represent slavery directly, but some engage with it less obviously, even as, in these cases, slavery's presence remains constitutive: how, for example, would it be possible to understand Gilbert Stuart's 'Edgehill' *Portrait of Thomas Jefferson* (1805), featured in Chapter 5, without a knowledge of Jefferson's status as a slave-owner?
4. Mitchell's article later reappeared, with minor amendments, in his *Picture Theory: Essays on Verbal and Visual Representation* (1994). Another notable contribution to the ekphrastic debate at around this time is John Hollander's *The Gazer's Spirit: Poems Speaking to Silent Works of Art* (1995), a sumptuous anthology complete with a sweeping historical ninety-one-page introduction and 'commentaries' on individual texts that 'yield an expansive taxonomy of ekphrastic tropes and tactics' (Hedley 40).
5. Mitchell himself invokes this definition in *Picture Theory* (152).

6. For other book-length studies containing some discussion of the uses of ekphrasis by female poets see Loizeaux and Kennedy.
7. Like *In the Frame*, Loizeaux's book, for example, also includes a chapter on Dove, but otherwise has little to say about other African-American or black poets more generally, while Kennedy's excludes them altogether. See also Kennedy and Meek, in which the white (male) paradigm remains preeminent.
8. As well as a prose essay, these works include several fictional texts (a novel and two short stories), whose inclusion in the book pulls against the typical orientation of much ekphrastic criticism towards poetry. The seemingly automatic nature of the penchant for the poem as the object of analysis is suggested by Heffernan's unapologetic declaration that he 'has nothing to say about ekphrasis in fiction' (8). The fact that many of these works, whether poems or fictions, have not been taken up by critics but nonetheless provide powerful opportunities for reflecting on the relationships between ekphrasis and slavery bears witness, similarly, to the virtues of looking beyond well-trodden and canonical literary paths.
9. It is worth noting that the mid-1990s moment in which Dabydeen's 'Turner' was published was a particularly dynamic time for Black Atlantic poets using ekphrasis as a means of reflecting on the historical trauma of the transatlantic slave trade. This claim is evidenced by the appearance not only of Dabydeen's poem itself, but also Clarence Major's 'The Slave Trade: View from the Middle Passage' (1994) and Kwame Dawes's *Requiem: A Lament for the Dead* (1996). Major's poem surveys, engages and takes issue with a range of Western images of black subjects from the Renaissance to the abolitionist era, while Dawes's collection is inspired by the fifty-five drawings in Tom Feelings's *The Middle Passage: White Ships / Black Cargo* (1995) and the harrowing 'story in pictures' that they tell. The high incidence of such visually driven poems at this particular juncture may be purely a quirk of literary history, but invites reflection even so and can be seen, for example, as a literary counterpoint to the reimagining of the 'slave ship icon' (to recall the subtitle of Finley's book) taking place in the late 1980s and the 1990s in the realms of the visual arts, as manifested in the work of Howardena Pindell, Keith Piper, Willie Cole, Mary Evans, Betye Saar and others. It can also be suggestively contextualised in relation to the contemporaneous critical endeavours of Mitchell and Heffernan, for whom, as already observed, ekphrasis is a resolutely white rather than black phenomenon.
10. Once believed to have been by Johan Joseph Zoffany, the painting has been ascribed in recent research to the Scottish artist David Martin, or possibly Allan Ramsay. The case for the attribution to Martin (which this book follows) is made with convincing and literally forensic precision in 'A Double Whodunnit', series 7, episode 4 of the BBC's *Fake or*

Fortune? programme, first aired on 17 September 2018. For an argument in support of Ramsay as the portrait's creator – or indeed the idea that he began the picture and Martin completed it – see Gerzina 171–2.

11. As well as engaging with Lawrence's painterly rendering of Douglass's story, *Icon* enters into ekphrastic exchange with another of Lawrence's early works, the *Harriet Tubman* series of 1939–40. The latter is a close companion to the artist's Douglass project and begins by representing its eponymous heroine's life in and escape from slavery, before going on to dramatise Tubman's subsequent role as an agent in the Underground Railroad and eventual service as 'spy', 'scout' and 'if need be ... hospital nurse' for the Union 'cause' (Lawrence qtd. in Wheat 107) during the American Civil War. Yet while Brown gives some space to this slightly later series, he responds, in the end, to just six of its thirty-one panels in six poems of his own, as compared to twenty of the paintings in the sequence on Douglass.

Chapter 1

Adding to the Picture: New Perspectives on David Dabydeen's 'Turner'

Introduction

As noted in this book's introduction, David Dabydeen's 'Turner' takes its inspiration from J. M. W. Turner's celebrated painting, *The Slave Ship* (Fig. 1.1). This canvas was first exhibited at the Royal Academy in London in 1840 (the same year as the first World Anti-Slavery Convention) and is generally agreed to be based on the *Zong* massacre of 1781 (discussed shortly in more detail below), one of the most notorious episodes in the four-hundred-year history of the transatlantic slave trade.[1]

While Dabydeen readily appreciates *The Slave Ship* in aesthetic terms – he calls it Turner's 'finest painting in the sublime style' (*Turner* 7) and has more recently confessed his 'love' for the artist and the 'epic dimensions' of his art (qtd. in Macedo 187) – he is nonetheless perturbed by what he sees as the undercurrents to Turner's vision, as becomes clear from the preface's last paragraph: 'The intensity of Turner's painting is such,' Dabydeen concludes, that 'the artist in private must have savoured the sadism he publicly denounced' (8).[2]

Whatever the validity or otherwise of this assertion, the true villain of the piece, in Dabydeen's view, is not so much the possibly perverse artist as his admiring contemporary critic and apologist, John Ruskin, who not only gives a rapturous ekphrastic account of *The Slave Ship* in 'Of Water, as Painted by Turner', a chapter included in the first volume of *Modern Painters* (1843), but also came to own the picture when his father presented it to him on 1 January 1844 as a New Year's gift. For Dabydeen, the problem with Ruskin's reading

Figure 1.1 J. M. W. Turner, *Slave Ship (Slavers Throwing Overboard the Dead and Dying, Typhoon Coming On)*, 1840 (oil on canvas). Museum of Fine Arts, Boston, Henry Lillie Pierce Fund.

of *The Slave Ship* is that it emphasises artistic technique – 'dwelling on the genius with which Turner illuminate[s] sea and sky' – at the expense of the painting's egregious 'subject', the 'shackling and drowning of Africans' carried out in the name of financial self-interest. As Dabydeen suggests, such a reading is doubly problematic because it effectively renders Ruskin complicit with the actions he ignores: the atrocious historical truth of Turner's image is relegated to a casual comment in a 'brief footnote' in Ruskin's text, which, as Dabydeen ingeniously points out, seems 'like an afterthought, something tossed overboard' (*Turner* 7).

As if to mimic Ruskin's marginalising gesture, Dabydeen ejects from his preface the throwaway remark the footnote contains ('She is a slaver, throwing her slaves overboard. The near sea is encumbered with corpses' [Ruskin 572]), before proceeding in the poem proper to render slavery central by salvaging 'the submerged head of the African in the foreground of Turner's painting' (*Turner* 7) and magically reawakening it to speak the text's twenty-five cantos.[3] At the same time, he complicates the picture, so to speak, by introducing into his poem another resurrected castaway, in the form of a 'stillborn child tossed overboard from a future ship' (*Turner* 7–8). Like the slave-captain who condemns the poem's speaker to his watery fate, this miscreated figure is also named Turner, its role as all-but-silent auditor to the speaker's lengthy reverie making the text a kind of surreal dramatic monologue.

For most critics, Turner's painting and Ruskin's response to it provide the typical ambit within which Dabydeen's poem operates, and there have been numerous insightful analyses of the text along these lines.[4] As this opening chapter argues, however, to situate 'Turner' solely in relation to these particular coordinates is ultimately reductive, missing the ways in which the text draws on other materials that are just as important to the shaping of its intense and compelling imaginative vision.

In order to make this case, the chapter is divided into four sections, the first of which focuses on the *Zong* episode and its various consequences, providing contextual material relevant not only to Dabydeen's poem itself but also several of the texts to be discussed in the next three chapters, especially William B. Patrick's 'The Slave Ship'. The chapter then proceeds to look beyond Ruskin's critically privileged reading (or writing) of *The Slave Ship* to earlier parts of his reflections on Turner in 'Of Water' and explores the ways in which they enter Dabydeen's poem and ripple its surfaces. It goes on from this, in its third and fourth sections, respectively, to more extended examinations of 'Turner''s links with two further works – Shakespeare's *Macbeth* (1606) and Toni Morrison's *Beloved* (1987) – neither of which has to date received anything more than the most fleeting critical attention as intertexts for Dabydeen's poem.[5]

While it thus expands the sense of 'Turner''s intertextual range and the concomitant ways in which the poem can be read against its author's grain, the chapter has a secondary significance, relating, in particular, to *Macbeth* and *Beloved*. By excavating *Macbeth*'s unacknowledged presence in 'Turner', the chapter reveals something new about how Dabydeen imagines the atrocity aboard the *Zong* and brings out, more broadly, the distinctiveness of his project, since, in so many writings of the Middle Passage – from Robert Hayden and Edward Kamau Brathwaite to George Lamming and Barry Unsworth – it is *The Tempest* that is invariably the dominant Shakespearean intertext that is invoked and reworked.[6] By bringing *Beloved*'s role in the poem to light, the chapter at the same time enables an appreciation of 'Turner' not just as an example of the empire writing back to the metropolitan centre (whether Turner, Ruskin, Shakespeare or a combination of all three) but also as a text that overruns the borders of the Anglophone Caribbean literary tradition to which it is more often than not confined.

1. Transition on the *Zong*: From 'Conduct so Shocking' to 'Poetical Language'

The tragedy aboard the *Zong* began on 18 August, when the slaver, under the command of Captain Luke Collingwood, set sail from Accra, on the coast of Africa, for Black River, Jamaica, carrying a cargo of some 442 slaves and a crew of seventeen, together with Collingwood's first mate, James Kelsall, and one passenger, Robert Stubbs, erstwhile governor of the slave-fort at Anomabu. Although Collingwood had made several previous slave-trading voyages as ship's surgeon, this was his first assignment as ship's master, and his inexperience in such a position, coupled with his ill-health, resulted in a state of generalised mismanagement – of the *Zong*'s course, provisions and chain of command alike. By 27–8 November, more than three months into its journey, the *Zong* had lost its bearings: it was at this point sailing away from Jamaica (which it had mistaken for Saint-Domingue, then rival Caribbean territory held by France) and was in a state of distress, with sixty-two African captives already dead and many more struggling with disease and illness. Under the era's maritime insurance law, owners who lost slaves from such causes during the Middle Passage were not eligible to receive financial compensation, but could be so remunerated if it could be proven that their slaves' deaths were in some way necessary. Aware of this protocol, Collingwood duly ordered the drowning of 132 of the sickest Africans under his charge, dispatching them into the Atlantic in parcels of fifty-four, forty-two and thirty-six across a period of several days beginning on 29 November. The captain legitimated his actions by claiming that they were carried out in order to protect the slaver's water supplies, which were allegedly running perilously low, a claim later exposed as false. This murderous subterfuge prepared the ground for the *Zong*'s owners (the Liverpool-based Gregson syndicate) to seek indemnities from the ship's underwriters at a rate of £30 *per capita*. In addition to those whom Collingwood deliberately drowned, the final death toll included a further ten slaves who refused the role of victim allotted them by choosing to drown themselves.

The owners' case eventually came to court on 6 March 1783 at London's Guildhall, where proceedings were attended by an anonymous eyewitness who reported on the trial in a letter addressed 'To the Printer of *The Morning Chronicle*' and published in that newspaper some twelve days later. As the letter recounts, 'The narrative' of the shipboard massacre 'seemed to make every person' present at the hearing 'shudder', even as its sensational horrors were evidently insufficient to prevent the 'Jury, without going out of Court', from finding against the insurers. This decision leaves the letter-writer both scandalised and more broadly fearful for the corrupting effects it is likely to have upon the British nation at large, as it threatens to 'sink' even 'the most flourishing kingdom in anarchy and ruin'. It also outraged the insurers themselves, who petitioned for a new trial, their appeal heard (and upheld) later in the year by Lord Mansfield, Lord Chief Justice of England from 1756 to 1788.

As the letter continues, its writer's sense of moral outrage and national anxiety is overtaken by a different mood. Struck by the courage of one of the slaves who ends his suffering in suicide, the author becomes gripped by his own desire for compensation, though this is of a type altogether different from and more refined than that desired by Gregson and company:

> I wish some man of feeling and genius would give poetical language to one of those brave fellow's (sic) thoughts, whose indignation made him voluntarily share death with his countrymen . . . . With what noble disdain would he animate his sentiments, with what resignation

would he consider himself, when plunging into the ocean, as escaping from brutes in human shape, to throw himself on the unsearchable mercy of his Creator. What a tender adieu would he bid his family and country! What a parting look would he cast on a glorious world, on the sun and heavens, disgraced by such a scene. What dreadful imprecations would he utter against such monsters, and against the barbarous, unfeeling country that sent them out, or wished to profit by their trade.

Here the compensation sought is not pecuniary but imaginative, as the letter-writer longs for 'some man of feeling and genius' capable of not only salvaging the desperate 'thoughts' of a self-destructive slave but also articulating them in 'poetical language'. In one sense, the wish for the advent of a poet who can function as empathetic spokesman for the suicidal slave, who in turn represents his 'countrymen', is something the epistolary author himself fulfils, as his own text fleetingly assumes a suitable elevation of tone and becomes populated with 'tender adieu[s]', 'parting look[s]' and Biblical evocations of the 'Creator''s 'unsearchable mercy'.

As critics have noted, this document is important from a historical perspective, for two reasons. First, as Seymour Drescher points out, it is something of a rarity, being the only account of the trial to have been carried by the London press of the day (576). Secondly, as James Walvin argues, it was to have 'profound and unexpected consequences' (104): it drew to light the monstrous truth of the slave trade in a way that was harnessed by prominent antislavery figures, including Olaudah Equiano and Granville Sharp, as part of their efforts to bring the barbarous traffic to an end (Walvin, *Zong* 104–6). Ultimately, indeed, it was a factor in the formation, in 1787, of the Society for Effecting the Abolition of the Slave Trade, of which Sharp was one of twelve founding members.[7]

What has not been critically observed about the letter, however, is that it also has a literary significance, broadly looking forward to the responses to the *Zong* affair, as it came to be called, that Dabydeen (and Patrick) have elaborated and which implicitly share the letter-writer's faith in poetry as a resource for reckoning with atrocity.

2. Ruskin's Role in 'Turner'

What Dabydeen construes as Ruskin's insouciance towards that atrocity and the bodies drowning in *The Slave Ship* has its correlate in the Victorian art critic's comments on two other of Turner's productions, the 1835 'vignette to "Lycidas"' (Ruskin 566) and *Hero and Leander* (1837), a picture on which Dabydeen's poem draws in cantos XII to XIV. While both of these paintings are responses to narratives in which drowning plays a central part, Ruskin approaches them, once again, primarily in terms of technique, resolutely evaluating the degree to which Turner's art is able (and occasionally unable) to reproduce particular watery effects. Just before embarking upon the reading of *The Slave Ship* which crowns 'Of Water', Ruskin likens 'hold[ing] by a mast or a rock' in order to witness a storm at sea at close quarters to 'a prolonged endurance of drowning which few people' (including Ruskin himself) 'have courage to go through' (571), even, it seems (as his technical approach to Turner's paintings suggests), in the second-hand context of pictorial representation.

Equally, though, the 'endurance of drowning', or some kind of perilous watery submersion, at least, is something to which Ruskin is strangely attracted, especially in 'Of Water''s opening sections. This is evident, in the first instance, in his observations on the difficulties that artists inferior to Turner have in 'giv[ing] a full impression of surface' to '*smooth water*': 'If no reflection be given, a ripple being supposed,' Ruskin writes, 'the water looks like lead,' whereas, 'if reflection [is] given, [the water], in nine cases out of ten, looks *morbidly* clear and deep, so that we always go down *into* it, even when the artist most wishes us to glide *over* it' (537; italics in original). This sense of falling into the water rather than skimming across it is also an effect produced by the work of artists who fail to grasp the principle that the reflection of objects (Ruskin's example is 'leaves hanging over a stream') is not 'an exact copy of the parts of them which we see above the water, but a totally different view and arrangement'. By naïvely 'giving underneath a mere duplicate of what is seen above,' Ruskin observes, such artists 'are apt to destroy the essence and substance of water, and to drop us through it' (542). Needless to say, such errors and the hazards they offer potential viewers are avoided by the 'master mind of Turner' (544), whose technique is so exquisite and secure it not only delights but also protects the critic. Commenting on the water in Turner's *Schloss Rosenau* or 'Château of Prince Albert' (1841), as he calls it, Ruskin states: 'we are not allowed to tumble into it, and gasp for breath as we go down, we are kept upon the surface, though that surface is flashing and radiant with every hue of cloud, and sun, and sky, and foliage' (539).

Ruskin's comments on reflection are not confined within the frame of art but extend to include the natural realm the artist strives to capture, together with the organisation of the eye as it switches focus between different objects. As Ruskin notes, it is this organisation that is constitutive of perception and determines how things are either seen or not seen, a point he explains and illustrates, in his chapter's very first paragraph, by taking the reader turned beholder 'to the edge of a pond in a perfectly calm day, at some place where there is duckweed floating on the surface, not thick, but a leaf here and there' (537). On this dreary brink, he tells us:

> You will ... see the delicate leaves of the duckweed with perfect clearness, and in vivid green; but, while you do so, you will be able to perceive nothing of the reflections in the very water on which they float, nothing but a vague flashing and melting of light and dark hues, without form or meaning, which to investigate, or find out what they mean or are, you must quit your hold of the duckweed, and plunge down. (538)

With the insistence that the reader-spectator relinquish his or her visual grip on the 'duckweed' and 'plunge down' in order to 'perceive ... reflections', Ruskin's optical experiment here echoes the subaquatic language informing his treatment of such natural phenomena as they appear in the context of art.

By the end of his chapter, Ruskin has moved a long way off from this tranquil if potentially threatening rural site and into the stormy and corpse-laden Atlantic of *The Slave Ship*, from which Dabydeen rescues and reanimates his poem's speaker. Yet Ruskin's pond nonetheless resurfaces on several occasions in the course of 'Turner', where it is transformed into one of the principal elements out of which the speaker's evocation of his African boyhood is forged. The first instance of this occurs at the beginning of canto II, where the often neologising speaker compares the impromptu watery descent of the 'stillborn' that he witnesses to the event of 'a brumplak seed that bursts buckshot / From its pod' and 'fall[s] into the pond / In the backdam of [his] mother's house' (10). Just as 'pond' dehisces from 'pod', so this initial scene is developed and expanded in canto III. Here the dangerous if merely metaphorical immersions of the Ruskinian spectator become actively literalised by the speaker's more daring exploits in a 'pond' that is all his own:

> When I strip,
> Mount the tree and dive I hit my head
> On a stone waiting at the bottom of the pond.
> I come up dazed, I float half-dead, I bleed
> For days afterwards. (12)

Like the 'savannah' that 'climb[s] and plunge[s] all day', the memory described in these lines is built around the youthful delights of a repetition that seems unending – 'Diving from a branch into water, swimming / About, climbing again for another go' (12) – but that is suddenly stopped. Yet even as the carefree rhythm of 'Mount[ing]' and 'div[ing]' comes abruptly to an end, the memory of its curtailment lingers on, like the bleeding that continues 'For days afterwards'. It recurs, for instance, in canto XII, when the speaker 'drag[s] [him]self / To the bank of the pond' and it is his head that is this time imagined as a bloody 'pool / And fountain' (22). Or again, there is the example of canto XVIII, when the 'waves slapping [the] face' of the stillborn reawaken the speaker's recollection of his own 'mother's hands summoning [him] back / To [him]self, at the edge of the pond' (31), a phrase that simultaneously involves a summoning back of Ruskin.

Intertextual ripples of Ruskin's pond are discernible not only in the African landscape the speaker describes but also in the complementary English realm etched in canto XVI and that he can only surmise, basing his 'knowledge' on the 'Pictures' adorning the wooden wall of Turner's cabin as his 'ship / Plunges towards another world we never reached' (27). In his comments about the 'water . . . in the foreground' to the *Schloss Rosenau*, Ruskin describes the sensation of 'glid[ing] over it a quarter of a mile into the picture before we know where we are' (539), and a similar sense of dislocation, in which spectator becomes participant, characterises the speaker's encounters with these wall-paintings, as he migrates into the shifting scenes that they depict of village life as lived in Turner's England. As these scenes take shape, it soon becomes evident that, like Ruskin's text, they too raise questions about visibility and invisibility – what, or rather who, can and cannot be seen – while at the same time giving these issues a distinctly racial slant:

> I walk along a path shaded
> By beech; curved branches form a canopy, protect
> Me from the stare of men with fat hands
> Feeling my weight, prying in my mouth,
> Bidding. The earth is soft here, glazed with leaves,
> The path ends at a brook stippled with waterflies,
> But no reflection when I gaze into it,
> The water will not see me. (27)

As he pursues his imaginary 'path', Dabydeen's mental traveller is at first not only an unseen figure sheltered and 'shaded' by a 'canopy' of 'curved branches' but also one who enjoys such womb-like enclosure and concealment because it defends him against the commoditising (and covertly sexual) 'stare' of the white 'men' who are attracted to him and might like him to do their furtive 'Bidding'. Yet at the point where the path 'ends', the speaker's invisibility becomes less a boon than a burden. In the case of Ruskin's pond, the absence of reflection the spectator experiences can be resolved in the blink of an eye, but in Dabydeen's 'brook' the situation is different: such absence is less an ephemeral perceptual effect than a trope for the constitutive failure of the white gaze to recognise the black subject in anything other than stereotypical terms.

This figurative blindness is subsequently replicated *en masse* by the 'villagers' among whom the speaker wanders and, in particular, an old woman 'with silver / Hair' who, in contrast to the corpulent-handed male bidders, does not so much stare at the speaker as 'through' him. It is even to be seen in the window of the 'butcher's shop' that will not countenance the speaker's own visage, supplanting it with the gruesomely suspended carcasses of 'goose and pheasant', while radiantly welcoming 'other faces' (27). This sense of how the visual field accommodates the white subject but excludes the black is climactically underscored when the speaker enters the villagers' place of worship and finds himself in the presence of another butchered and hanging body. Although the body in question here is that of the crucified Christ, it is mistaken by him as belonging to a less exalted master. As the speaker puts it, what he 'behold[s]' on entering the local church and becoming 'accustomed' to its melancholy 'gloom' (28) is not God's Son but the hallucinatory figure of the slave-ship captain who has cast him seaward:

> Turner nailed to a tree, naked for all to see,
> His back broken and splayed like the spine
> Of his own book, blood leaking like leaves
> From his arms and waist. (28)

Such hallucinatory misrecognition is perhaps appropriate, given the speaker's struggle for acknowledgement among the local populace – 'The elders and the young' alike – with his own sense of invisibility and forsakenness paralleled in the disappearance of Christ's image beneath Turner's. It can also perhaps be read, despite the 'cry' of 'pity and surprise' (28) that the hallucination induces, as wish-fulfilment, as Turner suffers amid the church's obscurity in reprisal for the unseen horrors endured by the 'grown-ups [who] cried in the darkness' of his 'hold' (27).

As previously observed, Ruskin's most direct acknowledgement of such horrors in his description of *The Slave Ship* is confined to a vague footnote, yet Ruskin finesses his own insight even at that safe remove, primarily by transferring the responsibility for the slaves' sufferings from the human to the inanimate. After all, in his anthropomorphising phrase, it is the feminised 'slaver' itself (or herself) rather than the male master or slave-captain that appears both to own the slaves and to engage in the act of jettison: to recall Ruskin's offhand phrase, 'She is a slaver, throwing her slaves overboard.'

These evasive rhetorical tactics are evident not only in the asterisked footnote that so exercises Dabydeen but also in the main body of Ruskin's account, where they take the form of the pathetic fallacy. At the climax to his appreciation of Turner's 'canvas', Ruskin writes:

> Purple and blue, the lurid shadows of the hollow breakers are cast upon the mist of night, which gathers cold and low, advancing like the shadow of death upon the guilty ship as it labours amidst the lightning of the sea, its thin masts written upon the sky in lines of blood, girded with condemnation in that fearful hue which signs the sky with horror, and mixes its flaming flood with the sunlight, and, cast far along the desolate heave of the sepulchral waves, incarnadines the multitudinous sea. (572)

In this powerful ekphrasis, the guilt in question is guilt on the move, as Ruskin ascribes it to the 'labour[ing]' vessel rather than captain and / or crew, just as it is the 'ship''s 'thin masts' that are 'girded with condemnation'.

Such guilt would be merited well enough in the general run of things but assumes additional intensity when it is remembered that the specific historical incident to which Turner's painting looks back is that of the *Zong*, in which, as Sharp observes, '132 innocent human Persons' were subjected to 'Wilful Murder' (qtd. in Lyall 301). Yet just as Ruskin only admits to the guilt entailed in the slave trade (and this episode particularly) by displacing it from human to non-human, so he admits to its murderous nature only through the detour of allusion, drawing his blood-red deeps from *Macbeth*, a play in which guilt and murder interlock. As the self-questioning Macbeth soliloquises:

> Will all great Neptune's ocean wash this blood
> Clean from my hand? No – this my hand will rather
> The multitudinous seas incarnadine,
> Making the green one red. (2.2.59–62)

In this anxious moment, the links between guilt and murder that Ruskin does not explicitly articulate become overt, along with the limitations they impose upon Macbeth's destructive powers. He may be able to commit multiple murders (when he speaks these lines he has already just dispatched King Duncan and in so doing also 'murder[ed]' the 'innocent sleep' [2.2.36]), but what he cannot destroy is the torturing sense of the sinfulness of his actions (even as he will go on to perpetrate further murders). As the lines conclude, Macbeth's vocabulary changes dramatically from the polysyllabic Latinate phrase in which Ruskin revels – 'multitudinous seas incarnadine' – to the monosyllabic Anglo-Saxon of 'green one red', yet Macbeth's own homicidal trajectory swiftly takes him in the opposite direction, carving out a course from a single initial murder to a profusion of subsequent killings.

As Marcus Wood has demonstrated in some detail, the intertextual 'dialogue' between Ruskin's description of *The Slave Ship* and *Macbeth* extends far beyond the borrowing of a single phrase and 'runs deep' (*Blind Memory* 65). Equally, though (and this is not something Wood addresses), there is an even profounder dialogue between Shakespeare's text and Dabydeen's, as the next section of this chapter endeavours to show.

3. 'Turner' and *Macbeth*

One of the ways in which such a dialogue is manifest is in terms of the language of cleansing and staining that marks the passage from Shakespeare's play just cited. The first signs of the presence of that language emerge in the poem in the context of the speaker's account of his pastoral childhood in Africa. In canto II, for instance, he recalls how 'each morning' (10) he and his two sisters 'Brush [their] teeth clean' (11) with 'twigs' from the 'chaltee tree' (10) and then weave games around one of the family cows that involve 'decorat[ing] its heels with the blue and yellow / Bark of hemlik'. While this aestheticising mischief is forbidden by the speaker's less than playful father, who sends the children 'off to school' (11), the latter himself observes a different set of daily rituals that nonetheless runs along similar lines, as illustrated in canto IV. Here the father prays at 'Dawntime' and 'Washe[s] his fingers', 'tongue' and 'face', 'in a sacred bowl / Repeatedly', before 'smear[ing] / His forehead with green dye' and setting out for the 'savannah' (13). Such rituals in turn parallel those carried out by the enigmatic village elder and 'magician' (11), Manu, though, in this case, they are connected not so much to prayer as divination. In canto XVII, for example, Manu 'darts his hands out' at the 'ancient ingredients' in one of the 'sacred bowls' arranged around him, 'Scoops up red jelly, daubs it on his face [and] / Howls' (29) before the future visions of white violence and black counter-violence that are opened up to him.

Perhaps the most striking manifestation of this pattern occurs in an incident in canto III, in which it is the speaker's own hand rather than that of his father or Manu that becomes central. This time, however, the hand engages in a deed neither prayerful nor prophetic but innocently (and humorously) transgressive:

> I dream to be small again, even though
> My mother caught me with my fingers
> In a panoose jar, and whilst I licked them clean
> And reached for more, she came upon me,
> Put one load of licks with a tamarind
> Stick on my back, boxed my ears; the jar fell,
> Broke, panoose dripped thickly to the floor. (12)

Although the memory recalled at this point is a painful one, its sweetness makes it just as difficult to resist as the contents of the 'jar' themselves. Given its trivial nature, the self-indulgent crime the speaker commits here is hardly comparable to the macrocosmic evil unleashed by Macbeth, yet Dabydeen's image of manual transgression is not without a residual Shakespearean flavour, faintly recalling *Macbeth*'s description of how the play's increasingly embattled protagonist 'feel[s] / His secret murders sticking on his hands' (5.2.16–17). The image further links 'Turner' to *Macbeth* in terms of the irony intrinsic to the speaker's decision to clean his fingers by licking them. While this action rids those fingers of both the syrup for which they reach and (by implication) whatever guilt this induces, it does so in a way that merely compounds the crime, since it reproduces the oral gratification that the speaker is seeking in the first place. The suggestion is that the speaker's own self-cleansing exercises bear the traces of the very misdemeanour they should eradicate, just as Shakespeare's 'multitudinous seas' are turned red by the very hand Macbeth hopes they will purify. The sense of a sin whose extirpation is not straightforward is captured both by Dabydeen's use of assonance (the quadruple 'ick'-sound stretched across five lines) and the ways in which the punishment the speaker's mother inflicts on him only works as a reminder of the clinging pleasures of his original offence ('load of licks' and even 'Stick').

These processes of cleansing and staining are not restricted to the scenes of childhood the speaker delineates but feature significantly in the account he gives of his Atlantic experience, where they take on a more sinister dimension, are organised differently depending on race and performed by the sea itself. As becomes evident, the speaker's posthumous ordeals amid the 'endless wash and lap / Of waves' (10) bring him into contact with other dead figures besides the stillborn child, including the men and women who are 'spew[ed] off the edges' of the 'different sunken ships' he witnesses in the course of his surreal aquatic trials. Although these temporary 'companions' (13) are white, he boldly reimagines them as black and blesses them with seductive African names – 'Adra, Zentu, Danjera' – in order to make them seem more 'familiar', even as the sea conducts its own unpredictable programme of transformations: it lovingly 'decorates' the women's countenances with 'festive masks' made of 'salt crystals' before it 'strips them clean' of 'flesh' (15) completely. The sea carries out a similar divestiture of the white male figures of canto XIV, as it not only 'soothes and erases pain from the faces / Of drowned sailors' with 'an undertaker's / Touch' but also liberates them entirely from their bodies and the rough histories inscribed upon them, 'unpast[ing] flesh from bone / With all its scars, boils, stubble, marks / Of debauchery' (25).

When it comes to black bodies, however, the sea's cleansing work is both less extreme and less certain, as suggested by the self-contradictory utterances in canto IX:

> the child
> Floats towards me, bloodied at first, but the sea
> Will cleanse it. It has bleached me too of colour,
> Painted me gaudy, dabs of ebony,
> An arabesque of blues and vermilions. (19)

Here it is difficult to be persuaded of the redemptive future the speaker envisages for the 'bloodied' child – the utopian possibility of a clean break with the past, as it were – because of his own history, in which the sea 'bleache[s]' his skin only so that it can make it into a kind of *tabula rasa* or blank canvas on which it 'Paint[s]' its 'gaudy' hues, restoring the tell-tale 'dabs of ebony' which, he claims, it has removed.

Ultimately, the issue of whether the speaker's skin is bleached or colourfully painted is irrelevant, since the dilemma he confronts goes deeper than this. Dabydeen makes this point in his preface, where, in a prefiguring of the contradictions just noted, he observes how, despite the sea's best efforts at whitening the black body, the speaker 'still recognises himself as "nigger"' – sees himself, that is, in terms of the degrading stereotypes to which blackness has been historically reduced. As the preface also points out, the catalyst to this recognition is the child, who exposes the speaker's 'desire to begin anew in the sea' as a forlorn hope and thwarts his 'creative amnesia' with the indelible stains of 'grievous memory' (7):

> 'Nigger!' it cried, seeing
> Through the sea's disguise as only children can,
> Recognising me below my skin long since
> Washed clean of the colour of sin, scab, smudge,
> Pestilence, death, rats that carry plague,
> Darkness such as blots the sky when locusts swarm. (21)

As the speaker responds to this brutal address, echoed at four further junctures in the poem (twice in canto XVIII and twice again in canto XXV), he returns the poem to *Macbeth* and the problem of the aftermath to Duncan's killing.[8] In Shakespeare's tragedy, the royal blood that stains the hands of the murderous double-act at the play's centre can be physically removed but comes back to haunt them in the hallucinatory shape of 'thick-coming fancies' (5.3.37) that cannot be staunched any more than a 'rooted sorrow' can be 'Pluck[ed] from the memory' (5.3.40) or the 'written troubles of the brain' 'Raze[d] out' (5.3.41). In 'Turner', similarly, the speaker's body can be 'Washed clean' of its blackness but he himself cannot escape the radically demeaning associations with which it is encrusted and that are here couched in an overtly Biblical and increasingly apocalyptic language, ranging from 'sin, scab [and] smudge' to a 'Darkness' that, in another staining metaphor, 'blots the sky when locusts swarm'.

Macbeth's decision to kill Duncan is partly motivated by a desire to take his place as king but also by a need to reaffirm his own masculinity. This is so particularly in relation to his wife, who fears that he is 'too full o'th' milk of human kindness' (1.5.16) to realise his ambitions and taunts him with the opinion that his initial determination to 'proceed no further in this business' (1.7.31) is unmanly. While such goading peeves Macbeth into telling his 'dearest partner of greatness' (1.5.10) that he 'dare do all that may become a man' (1.7.46), her own involvement in their destructive enterprise is predicated, ironically, on the very sort of gender-betrayal of which she accuses him, as exemplified when she commands the 'spirits / That tend on mortal thoughts' (1.5.39–40) to 'unsex' her and 'Come to [her] woman's breasts / And take [her] milk for gall' (1.5.40, 46–7).

Such gender-instability, in which the wavering Macbeth is 'quite unmanned' (3.4.74) and his more resolute spouse defeminised, is consonant with the ontological and linguistic ambiguities of *Macbeth* as a whole, where 'nothing is / But what is not' (1.3.142–3), the dead seem (in the shape of Banquo) to 'rise again' (3.4.81) to unnerve and persecute the living and the play's corps of witches, particularly the self-proclaimed three 'Weird Sisters' (1.3.32), 'palter with us in a double sense' (5.7.50). This feature of *Macbeth* is paralleled in 'Turner', where, to come back to the preface, the 'sea ... transform[s]' the poem's speaker and 'complicate[s] his sense of gender' (7) to such an extent that he wishes to 'mother' (8) the 'piece of ragged flesh' (21) that drifts towards him.[9] Yet the speaker is not the only male mother in Dabydeen's poem, the other being the slave-ship captain, Turner, and it is by reading the vicissitudes of this strange (and ultimately monstrous) figure in the light of *Macbeth* that it is possible to discern further signs of Dabydeen's intertextual debt to Shakespeare.

In Shakespeare's play, Lady Macbeth is prepared not just to be unsexed in pursuit of her goals, but, as the disturbing image of breastmilk turned to gall implies, even to violate maternal duties. Nowhere does this become clearer than in the still more unsettling vision she invokes early on in the play in order to convince her husband of the depth of her resolve:

> I have given suck, and know
> How tender 'tis to love the babe that milks me;
> I would, while it was smiling in my face,
> Have plucked my nipple from his boneless gums
> And dashed the brains out, had I so sworn
> As you have done to this. (1.7.54–9)

This shocking volte-face has its correlate in the equally volatile maternal disposition of Turner. As the speaker recollects, in one of his earliest flashbacks, this androgynous personage seems at first improbably benign and bountiful, as evidenced in the moment of the departure from Africa etched in canto IV:

> His blue eyes smile at children
> As he gives us sweets and a ladle from a barrel
> Of shada juice. Five of us hold his hand,

> Each takes a finger, like jenti cubs
> Clinging to their mother's teats, as he leads us
> To the ship. (13–14)

Here Turner provides the 'children' he is in fact enslaving with oral gratification in the form of 'sweets' and 'shada juice', offering them the 'fingers' of a 'hand' they grasp as eagerly as 'jenti cubs / Clinging to their mother's teats'. Yet once his ship is underway, Turner's features alter dramatically: his 'smile' shrinks 'like a worm's / Sudden contraction' in canto VIII and 'strange words [are] spat' from the 'gentle face' that had once 'so often kissed ... / His favoured boys' (18). By canto XIV, Turner's transformation from tenderness to cruelty is complete, as he severs the bond with the speaker with a similarly high-handed violence to that with which Lady Macbeth sunders her ties to her trusting 'babe'. At this point, Turner's fingers are mysteriously devoid of maternal comfort, irrevocably tensed instead into a 'hand gripping' the speaker's 'neck, / Pushing [him] towards the [ship's] edge' and finally letting him 'fall towards the sea' (25). If Turner's maternal mutability is comparable to that of Lady Macbeth, it is also suggestive of his resemblance to *Macbeth*'s witches: as Macbeth understands at the end of the play, these 'juggling fiends' (5.7.49) are not to be relied upon (they 'keep the word of promise to our ear / And break it to our hope' [5.7.51–2]), just as Turner 'curl[s]' the speaker 'warmly to his bed' (18) only to consign him, finally, to 'the waters' and the 'flush / Of betrayal' (25).

Macbeth's realisation of the witches' unreliability emerges specifically in relation to the various predictions about his future that they make, and it is these that provide one final link between Shakespeare's play and Dabydeen's poem. For all its preoccupation with the past, 'Turner' is, like *Macbeth*, itself a text with an eye trained on the future, articulating such concerns, as already suggested, chiefly through the figure of Manu, who routinely holds 'daedal / Seed[s]' 'up to the sky / For portents of flood [or] famine' (31) and is able to foresee both Turner's coming and the 'lamentation in the land' (29) that it will bring. But as well as broadly echoing *Macbeth* in this way, 'Turner' engages with the prophecies in Shakespeare's play in a more detailed manner by weaving them into its own narrative. This can be seen on at least two occasions, the first of which is in the poem's dramatic opening canto, where the speaker reprises the marred origins of the child he comes to adopt:

> Stillborn from all the signs. First a woman sobs
> Above the creak of timbers and the cleaving
> Of the sea, sobs from the depths of true
> Hurt and grief, as you will never hear
> But from woman giving birth, belly
> Blown and flapping loose and torn like sails,
> Rough sailors' hands jerking and tugging
> At ropes of veins, to no avail. Blood vessels
> Burst asunder, all below-deck are drowned.
> Afterwards, stillness, but for the murmuring
> Of women. The ship, anchored in compassion
> And for profit's sake (what well-bred captain
> Can resist the call of his helpless
> Concubine, or the prospect of a natural
> Increase in cargo?), sets sail again,
> The part-born, sometimes with its mother,
> Tossed overboard. (9)

Here the child's abortive condition is underscored both by the truncated first sentence (made all the more jarring by the poem's far more usual pattern of fluid enjambment) and the way in which the canto as a whole closes back on itself, recalling its first word in its last, 'Stillborn' in 'dead' (9). Such permanent immobility contrasts sharply with the slaver's more temporary 'stillness', enacted in the parenthesis that encloses the 'well-bred captain' and his Siren-like if 'helpless / Concubine' and briefly suspends the poem's narrative movement, before, that is – like the 'anchored' 'ship' itself – the verse 'sets sail again'.

Considered simply in terms of content, 'Turner''s own imaginative parturition is indeed a moment of 'cleaving', as mother and child are separated one from another by the twinned agonies of labour and death. Approached from a Shakespearean perspective, however, the opening entails a cleaving in the directly opposite sense of the word, as the poem once again latches itself onto *Macbeth* and, in particular, the prophecy spoken by the '*Apparition*' of a '*bloody child*' (4.1; stage direction, italics in original) that 'none of woman born / Shall harm Macbeth' (4.1.94–5). While such a statement causes Macbeth to assume that he is physically invulnerable and 'bear[s] a charmèd life' (5.7.42) during his final confrontation with Macduff, the security it gives him turns out to be false when Macduff discloses that he is the mature embodiment of such a seemingly impossible progeny. As he tells Macbeth, he himself 'was from his mother's womb / Untimely ripped' (5.7.45–6), a condition that connects him, intertextually at least, to Dabydeen's 'part-born', torn in turn from its mother's 'belly', albeit 'to no avail', by 'Rough sailors' hands'.

The appearance of *Macbeth*'s equivocal ghost-child is followed by that of another spirit, in the form of '*a child crowned, with a tree in his hand*' (4.1; stage direction, italics in original), who states that Macbeth will 'never vanquished be, until / Great Birnam Wood to high Dunsinan Hill / Shall come against him' (4.1.107–9). Such a prophecy once again seems to bode well, since, as its hearer reasons, it is surely not possible either to 'impress the forest' or 'bid the tree / Unfix his earthbound root' (4.1.110, 110–11) and advance towards his stronghold. Like the previous vision of the bloody child, however, the spectre of its tree-bearing counterpart also proves, in the end, to be untrustworthy: Birnam does indeed in a sense become mobile when its branches and foliage are deployed by the forces opposed to the 'abhorrèd tyrant' (5.7.10) as a means of camouflaging their march in his besieged direction. Yet the route of this 'moving grove' (5.5.38) does not end when Malcolm arrives at Dunsinan and instructs his men to 'throw down' their 'leafy screens' (5.6.1), but extends into Dabydeen's poem and the pictures of Turner's England into which the speaker transports himself in fantasy. Here it is not only that, as noted earlier, the speaker imagines 'walk[ing] along a path shaded / By beech' (and in this way enjoys his own version of those Shakespearean 'screens'), but that the surrounding bushes and trees are themselves imbued with motion:

> [Turner] held a lamp
> Up to his country, which I never saw,
> In spite of his promises, but in images
> Of hedgerows that stalked the edge of fields,
> Briars, vines, gouts of wild flowers: England's
> Robe unfurled, prodigal of ornament,
> Victorious in spectacle, like the oaks
> That stride across the land, gnarled in battle
> With storms, lightning, beasts that claw and burrow
> In their trunks. (27)

As well as celebrating the beauties of the English countryside, these lines offer an implicit homage to the nation's naval preeminence (which includes its role in the slave trade) and in so doing are pervaded by a subtle irony. The 'oaks / That stride across the land' may seem, like the 'stalk[ing]' 'hedgerows', to be 'Victorious in spectacle' and to have won the 'battle' against the natural world, but ultimately will be cut down to provide the 'timbers' for the ship in which their own 'images' are displayed. In this respect, they share the predicament of the seemingly untouchable Macbeth himself, defiantly 'Hang[ing] out [his] banners' on his castle's 'outward walls' (5.5.1) just moments before the announcement of Lady Macbeth's death sets life at naught and he thereafter receives the messenger's seemingly equally absurd and certainly ominous 'report' that Birnam is on the 'move' (5.5.31, 35).

Macbeth's contribution to 'Turner' is an important if critically unheralded one, yet Dabydeen's poem is imaginatively reliant also on *Beloved* and it is the poem's (similarly unexplored) dialogue with this novel – another great contemporary engagement with slavery and the Middle Passage – that provides the focus for this chapter's final section.

4. African-American Connections: 'Turner' and *Beloved*

The relationship between 'Turner' and *Beloved* is evident in numerous respects, the first of which concerns the manner in which each text sets out to retell the story of slavery from the slave's perspective. In the case of Morrison's novel, the story she rewrites appears in a newspaper article by the Reverend P. S. Bassett published in *American Baptist* on 12 February 1856 and revolves around the fugitive slave, Margaret Garner, who, in January of that year, had cut the throat of her two-and-a-half-year-old daughter and attempted to murder her three other children, in order to prevent them from suffering the horrors of slavery as she herself had done.[10] In the case of Dabydeen's poem, however, the immediate source of inspiration is not an ephemeral if compelling piece of abolitionist journalism but the more culturally enduring and elevated painting of Turner's *The Slave Ship*, an image that is itself a kind of retelling too.

In rearticulating the story of the slave-mother and the baby girl she kills (respectively renamed in her novel as Sethe and the eponymous Beloved), Morrison's overriding concern is to develop a sense of the slave's inner life, something which, she argues, is largely occluded in both the white archive of which Bassett's article is a part and the tradition of the African-American slave narrative, on which *Beloved* also draws. As Steven Weisenburger puts it, '*Beloved* returns to us a slave mother who was always not only the subject of others' obscurely coded stories about her, but far more significantly herself a thinking and feeling subject' (10). A comparable point might be made about the project of 'Turner', as Dabydeen similarly delves into the psychic processes of his own 'subject' and plots their rhythms. These are typically recursive, with the poem obsessively looking back to particular events (the child's fall into the sea and its offensive cry of '"Nigger"' or the speaker's plunge into his pond) and underscoring this tendency by means of a widespread pattern of verbal self-echoing, more often than not involving the initial lines of individual cantos: the first line of canto II ('It plopped into the water and soon swelled' [10]) is repeated almost verbatim in that of canto IV ('It plopped into the water from a passing ship' [13]), with the time between these two textual moments taken up by an extended digression back into the realms of the speaker's African past. These aspects of Dabydeen's poem constitute another of its links to *Beloved*: Morrison's text is similarly both fixated on a selection of emotionally charged events and marked by a narrative whose movement is constantly disrupted by the sudden and insistent return to (or of) past memories.

In both texts, though, such memories tend not to be directly available to consciousness but are repressed, requiring the intervention of others in order to bring them back to life. In *Beloved*, this process is primarily undertaken by the ambiguous Beloved herself, who, throughout the text, plays a double part as the reincarnation of Sethe's dead daughter, on the one hand, and of her African mother, a survivor of the Middle Passage, on the other. In 'Turner', by contrast, it is the 'creature that washe[s] towards' the speaker who rekindles memory, 'waken[ing]' him to the 'years' he had 'forgotten' and 'burning [his] eyes / Awake' with its 'salt splash' (17). Such reawakening partly stimulates in him a regressive 'lust' for the sensory delights of home, ranging from 'the smell / Of earth and root and freshly burst fruit' to the 'taste of sugared milk',[11] but also occasions recollections that are bound up with the Atlantic crossing and that are hence more typically 'obscene'. But however violent the fluctuations of memory's mood in 'Turner', the moments when its revival is self-consciously announced in the text are, appropriately enough, moments in which the intertextual memory of *Beloved* is also activated, as in canto XI. As the speaker indicates at this point, the instant of memory's return coincides with that in which the child is first jettisoned from the slaver – 'It broke the waters', he states, 'and made the years / Stir, not in faint murmurs but a whirlpool / That sucks [him] under' (21) – just as Dabydeen's language is here pregnant with the metaphorical patterns in *Beloved*, as used, specifically, during the scene in which Sethe first sets eyes on her 'girl come home' (201). In this episode, as Sethe gets 'close enough to see'

Beloved's 'face' and begins to recall the history she has forgotten, she is overwhelmed by the impulse to empty her 'bladder', a process of seemingly 'endless' discharge that the novel likens to the unstoppable rush of 'water breaking from a breaking womb' (51).

'Turner' and *Beloved* not only both use birth as a metaphor for the renaissance of the past but also include scenes in which birth is featured as a literal event and that exist in a complex interplay of difference from and similarity to one another. This is a point that can be developed by returning to the *in medias res* account of blighted labour with which 'Turner' begins and comparing it to the equally critical but ultimately triumphant narrative of birth in *Beloved*. The latter unfolds as the nineteen-year-old Sethe, six months into term with her fourth child and second daughter, attempts to escape from slavery on the Sweet Home plantation by crossing the Ohio River to freedom in Cincinnati, using a stolen boat with 'one oar, lots of holes and two bird nests' (83). In 'Turner''s first canto, it is the mother who is abandoned by her child: she 'sobs from the depths of true / Hurt and grief', sunk beneath her tears in a way which oddly parallels the plight of the stillborn submerged in blood and later water. In the scene in Morrison, conversely, the identity of the bereaved is less fixed and has the potential to be assumed by either mother or child as their fortunes shift. At one stage, it appears that it will be Sethe's fate to be the one bereft, as her daughter's delivery stalls and she seems to be 'drowning in [her] mother's blood' as 'river water, seeping through any hole it chose . . . spread[s] over Sethe's hips' (84), while, at an earlier juncture, it is the daughter herself who is threatened with bereavement. This prospect arises when the exhausted Sethe concludes that she cannot complete the flight from Sweet Home and is condemned 'to die in wild onions on the bloody side' (31) of the Ohio, her body little more than a 'crawling graveyard for a six-month baby's last hours' (34). In the event, neither of these scenarios comes to fruition, largely because of Amy Denver, whose last name Sethe transforms into her newborn's first in recognition of both the selfless ministrations of this impoverished 'whitegirl' (76) and, more broadly, the interracial alliance they represent: '"That's pretty. Denver. Real pretty."' (85).

In facilitating the 'magic' and 'miracle' (29) of Denver's nativity, the dextrous Amy succeeds where Dabydeen's rough-handed midwives fail, but there are other differences between the two birth scenes also. When Amy is 'walking on a path not ten yards away' and hears Sethe's 'groan' at the thought of 'herself stretched out dead while [her] little antelope lived on – an hour? a day? a day and a night? – in her ... body', she 'stand[s] right still' (31), her sudden stasis not dissimilar to that of Dabydeen's slaver. Yet while the slaver's course is interrupted primarily 'for profit's sake', Amy halts on compassionate grounds, just as her 'dreamwalker's voice' (79) encourages in the 'antelope' a sustaining 'quiet' (34) radically at odds with the 'stillness' befalling its intertextual companion. That said, there is perhaps at least some sense in which Amy too profits from the exemplary kindness of her actions: in rescuing Denver from engulfment and Sethe from death, she at the same time masters two of her own past traumas – the vision of the 'drowned' 'nigger' who 'float[s] right by [her]' when she is 'fishing off the Beaver once' (34) and her 'mama''s demise 'right after' (33) she is born.

While it would be wrong to overstress this last point, it is an important one even so, not least because it suggests an element of congruence rather than difference between the scenes in question, since, in 'Turner' too, the boundaries between compassion and profit are not always clear or stable. In the captain's case, the type of profit at issue is economic, but, for the poem's speaker, profit takes an affective or a psychological form, as the discarded child not only becomes his 'bounty' and 'miracle of fate' but also bestows on him the 'longed-for gift of motherhood': by adopting or appropriating the child, the speaker is able symbolically to reenact the very relationship with his own mother that the slave trade has severed, thus initiating his own version of the quest for a lost maternal love – that 'clamor for a kiss' (275) – that so consumes Morrison's novel. In this respect, the naming of the stillborn as 'Turner' is entirely apposite, as it is indeed turned from being 'mere food for sharks' into the resourceful speaker's 'fable' (9) while simultaneously turning him from male to female.

The speaker's identification with his own mother is partly a matter of timbre and storytelling, as, for instance, in the moments when he considers how best to address 'this thing' that is at once 'drawn' to him and 'yet / Struggling to break free': 'Shall I call to it in the distant voice / Of my mother' (33) he muses, wondering later if he should also 'suckle / It on tales of resurrected folk' (34) to satisfy its hunger for the 'mirage / Of breast' it is 'seeking' (33). More typically, though, identification is a matter of bodily action and, in particular, the embrace. As 'Birds gather from nowhere to greet' this 'morsel of flesh', 'Screaming their glee [and] flapping cruel wings' (18), the speaker responds to this terrifying congregation with his own countermovement: while in canto XXV he might be unable to defend himself from the rapacious Yeatsian 'Wings of Turner brooding over [his] body', 'white [and] enfolding' (41),[12] he can guard the child from the 'vengeful' creatures that encircle it, not only by softening them with 'Gentle names – Flambeau, Sulsi, Aramanda' (19) – but also by 'gather[ing] it in with dead arms' (26). Here the ambiguity of this phrase intertangles the two pairs of limbs to which it simultaneously refers (the speaker's and the child's) in a way which also intertangles Dabydeen's poem with *Macbeth* once more and its own comparison of battling armies to 'two spent swimmers that do cling together / And choke their art' (1.2.8–9). But the loving gesture by which the speaker cradles the stillborn also recollects the salvific maternal embraces that bless his early years, played out in a seemingly prelapsarian Africa prior to Turner's catastrophic advent. On one occasion during this phase of the speaker's life, his mother 'buries [him] in the blackness / Of her flesh' when 'fevers starch [his] blood' (18) and, at another time, she 'catch[es]' and 'pin[s]' him 'tightly, always, / To her bosom' when he 'crie[s] out in panic / Of falling' from her lap while 'tugg[ing]' too firmly at her 'silver nose-ring' (23). And she is also there in the wake of the diving accident discussed earlier, 'pluck[ing] . . . up' her son from the side of the pond where he lies injured and carrying him to safety with 'huge hands' (22).

Yet even as the speaker fondly clasps the child to himself in a way that reenacts how he was once embraced maternally, there are points in the poem in which his relationship to his mother appears to be ominously fractured, even before it is ruptured once and for all by Turner's arrival and the initiation into the Middle Passage which this sets in train. One way in which this is illustrated is in the resurfacing memories of 'harvest-time' (26) in Africa:

> We trooped into the fields at first light,
> The lame, the hungry and frail, young men
> Snorting like oxen, women trailing stiff
> Cold children through mist that seeps from strange
> Wounds in the land. We float like ghosts to fields
> Of corn. All day I am a small boy
> Nibbling at whatever grain falls from
> My mother's breast as she bends and weaves
> Before the crop, hugging a huge bundle
> Of cobs to her body, which flames
> In the sun, which blinds me as I look up
> From her skirt, which makes me reach like a drowning
> Man gropes at the white crest of waves, thinking it
> Rope. I can no longer see her face
> In the blackness. The sun has reaped my eyes. (26)

As these lines indicate, the process of gathering the 'corn' brings mother and child into comforting proximity, yet at the same time is shadowed by a sense of growing distance. No longer a suckling imbibing milk but a 'small boy', the speaker must be content with 'Nibbling at whatever grain falls from / [His] mother's breast', even finding his place there taken by 'a huge bundle / Of cobs', which themselves quietly oust the 'jenti cubs / Clinging to their mother's teats' in canto IV. Such exile is crucially augmented by the way in which this bundle 'flames / In the sun', its brightness blinding the speaker as he looks 'up' to his labouring mother and discovers her faceless. As his 'eyes' are thus 'reaped', the speaker suffers a quasi-Oedipal trauma that both parallels the 'strange / Wounds' marking the misty 'land' and links him to those 'lame' figures 'trooping into the fields'. Equally, by likening these infirm workers and their companions to floating ghosts and then comparing his own predicament to the floundering delusions of a 'drowning / Man' who 'gropes at the white crest of waves, thinking it / Rope', the speaker anticipates the moment when Turner suddenly metamorphoses from good mother to bad and flings his charge into the sea.[13]

Alongside the mutual preoccupation with the mother–child bond – how it is severed by the institution of slavery and how it can be restored – there are two further elements of common ground between Dabydeen's poem and *Beloved*, the first of which emerges from the parallels between Turner and the figure of Morrison's schoolteacher. Throughout *Beloved*, the latter not only manages (and torments) the slaves on the Sweet Home plantation after the death of the relatively humane Mr Garner but also places them under constant surveillance, 'Talking soft and watching hard' (197) as he 'wrap[s]' his 'measuring string' (191) around their heads and bodies and instructs his two 'nephews' (36) in the art of correctly tabulating Sethe's 'human' and 'animal' 'characteristics' (193). While Dabydeen's Turner does not engage in quite the same coldly pseudoscientific studies, he nonetheless shares the faith in the Western rationalism that underpins them and seeks to inculcate a similar belief in his own slaves: as the speaker puts it in canto II, 'since Turner's days' he has 'learnt to count, / Weigh, measure, abstract, rationalise' (10). But Turner also uses his reasoning powers as an equally chilling means of calculating both the quantity and value of the black bodies that he plans to jettison. In canto XII, he is to be found 'sketch[ing] endless numbers' (22) and 'multiplying percentages' (23) in his ledger:

> He checks that we are parcelled
> In equal lots, men divided from women,
> Chained in fours and children subtracted
> From mothers. When all things tally
> He snaps the book shut. (23)

Although economic rather than anthropometric or anthropological in spirit, this sinister volume consolidates the intertextual link with *Beloved* by recalling the 'notebook' (37) in which Morrison's soft-voiced sadist records his observations of the Sweet Home slaves, even extending these to include the scene in which Sethe is euphemistically 'nurse[d]' (6) by his 'boys' (36) during her pregnancy, 'one sucking on [her] breast' and 'the other holding [her] down' (70).

The prospect of having 'her daughter's characteristics' listed 'on the animal side of the paper' is one of the main motives precipitating both Sethe's escape from schoolteacher's regime and her apotropaic slitting of Beloved's throat just one month later when he comes to reclaim her. But an equally powerful influence upon Sethe's actions is the thought of the daughter's inevitable rape under that same dispensation, her 'private parts invaded', as Sethe surmises, by a 'gang of whites' (251). This aspect of *Beloved* – white male sexual violence towards the black subject – constitutes the second of the additional elements in the intertextual dialogue between Morrison's novel and Dabydeen's poem and can be brought into initial focus by considering the speaker's accounts of his two sisters, as they appear in cantos XXII and XXIII, as the poem draws to a close.

As even the most cursory reading of *Beloved* suggests, the sexual fate Sethe fears for her 'beautiful, magical best thing' (251) is, by contrast, part of the daily round for numerous other black females in the novel, one case in point being Ella, a woman whose 'puberty' is 'spent in a house where she [is] shared by father and son'. Ella designates the latter with the oddly nondescript soubriquet, '"the lowest yet"' (256), but it is arguable that Dabydeen's Turner himself qualifies for such an unenviable accolade, particularly with regard to his treatment of the speaker's younger sister, who, by a curious coincidence, is Ella's virtual namesake:

> Afterwards [Turner] will go to Ellar, the second-born,
> Whom he will ravish with whips, stuff rags
> In her mouth to stifle the rage, rub salt
> Into the stripes of her wounds in slow ecstatic
> Ritual trance, each grain caressed and secreted

> Into her ripped skin like a trader placing each
> Counted coin back into his purse. Her flesh is open
> Like the folds of a purse, she receives
> His munificence of salt. By the time he has done
> With her he has taken the rage from her mouth.
> It opens and closes. No word comes. It opens
> And closes. It keeps his treasures.
> It will never tell their secret burial places. (39)

In these graphic (if not pornographic) lines, Ellar is subjected to a form of bodily suffering that is powerfully eroticised and can be read as a figurative rape or even the grotesque preparation of the victim for literal violation. Turner 'ravish[es]' her with 'whips' and then massages 'salt' into her 'wounds' in a process that merely produces further pain for her but pleasure for him and whose ritualised and entrancing nature is reciprocated in the rhythms of the text. These are strikingly repetitive, as the reader not only twice suffers receipt of the same harrowing information about Ellar's abuse but is also mesmerised by the kaleidoscopic recycling and echoing of individual words, images and phrases. As Frantz Fanon comments in *Black Skin, White Masks* (1952), 'We know how much of sexuality there is in all cruelties, tortures, beatings' (159), and this episode fully confirms his view, even exploiting the traditional associations between money and semen stirred up in the image of salt as a 'coin' placed inside Ellar's purse-like 'flesh'.

Yet it is not only the traumatised Ellar, but also her elder sister, Rima, who is exposed to the 'munificence' of Turner's sexual cruelty, albeit in a way that is neither at first glance obvious nor indeed to be expected from her story as the speaker tells it. As that story starts, Rima – referred to, in another curious intertextual coincidence, as the speaker's 'beloved'[14] – is an 'extravagant' and 'wayward' figure, with little respect, even 'as a child', for the structures of patriarchy, denying her father's rule, trampling on her brother's mock-'battleground' and 'Talk[ing] above the voices of the elders'. As the story ends, however, she seems to have been punished by the patriarchal order she defies, dying in 'childbirth', with the 'village idiot whom she / Married out of jest and spite' looking on. Although respected in death and accordingly 'bur[ied] . . . / In a space kept only for those who have / Uttered peculiarly' (37), the possibility remains that Rima's enemies will pursue her into the afterlife, filling it with terrors that require a collective female prophylaxis to keep them at bay. As the speaker anticipates:

> And the women will come
> Bearing stones, each one placed on her grave
> A wish for her protection against kidnapping,
> Rape, pregnancy, beatings, men, all men:
> Turner. (37–8)

While *Beloved*'s murderous 'motherlove' (132) would appear to be an effective means of exempting the black female from the predations of the white man, the strange and disturbing implication of this peculiar utterance is that such drastic steps are not guaranteed to succeed in every case and that death itself may be no refuge.

Together with its emphasis on the sexual violence white males inflict upon black females, *Beloved* acknowledges how these 'men without skin' (210) also visit such violence upon the black male. This is encapsulated most clearly in the account of the morning rituals Paul D suffers while on the coffle in Georgia, in which he and other slaves are forced to fellate their white male guards once 'Chain-up [is] completed'. As well as forcing upon the reader an unwelcome taste of this metaphorical 'breakfast' in America, the slaves' chained and 'Kneeling' (107) posture links them to the statuette Denver encounters as she leaves the residence of the novel's erstwhile abolitionists, the Bodwins, the 'white brother and sister who . . . hated slavery worse than they hated slaves' (137). Though not an image of a slave at least, this figurine is nonetheless strongly expressive of ongoing racial inferiority amid the Reconstruction era of the early 1870s in which the novel's present action takes place. The artefact represents a black subject posed 'on his knees' atop a 'pedestal' bearing the legend '"At Yo Service"' and moulded in caricature: he has 'eyes' 'Bulging like moons . . . above [a] gaping red mouth' filled with 'coins', with these features set within a 'head thrown back farther than a head could go' (255). Equally, though, as much as it links them to this florid sign of a racism still unchallenged even among progressive whites, the slaves' position on the chain gang quietly looks beyond the sublunary horizons of the white world that oppresses them. As they kneel in the morning 'mist', the slaves suggest a prayerfulness which in turn suggests 'obedience' neither to the 'hammer at dawn' (107) nor the grunting guards but to a higher master, in the shape of 'Jesus' (108), whose redemptive presence is registered in this scene, albeit faintly, by the cooing of the distant 'doves' (107).

Such sexual abuse and humiliation as is dramatised in *Beloved*'s coffle-episode is an important feature of 'Turner' also. For much of the poem, it is something only hinted at, as, for example, in those 'fat hands' of canto XVI, 'Feeling' the speaker's 'weight' and 'prying in [his] mouth'; the *double entendre* with which the physical spaces of Turner's slaver become fused with the more intimate recesses of his boys' anatomy as he kisses them in 'quiet corners' and 'Unseen passages' (18); or, again, in the image of Turner's 'creased mouth / Unfolding in a smile' as he 'enter[s] / His cabin, mind heavy with care' and 'beholds / A boy dishevelled on his bed' (23). In the course of the poem's penultimate canto, however, Turner's violations of his boys become more overt, even as, at this point, they are metaphorical in nature rather than literal and carried out in the name of other impositions:

> Turner crammed our boys' mouths too with riches,
> His tongue spurting strange potions upon ours
> Which left us dazed, which made us forget
> The very sound of our speech. Each night
> Aboard ship he gave selflessly the nipple
> Of his tongue until we learnt to say profitably
> In his own language, *we desire you, we love
> You, we forgive you*. He whispered eloquently
> Into our ears even as we wriggled beneath him,
> Breathless with pain, wanting to remove his hook
> Implanted in our flesh. The more we struggled
> Ungratefully, the more steadfast his resolve
> To teach us words. He fished us patiently,
> Obsessively, until our stubbornness gave way
> To an exhaustion more complete than Manu's
> Sleep after the sword bore into him
> And we repeated in a trance the words
> That shuddered from him: *blessed, angelic,
> Sublime*; words that seemed to flow endlessly
> From him, filling our mouths and bellies
> Endlessly. (40; italics in original)

As so often in the text, Turner is Protean here, his identity shifting dramatically from one guise to the next. Throughout the canto, he is most obviously aligned, once again, with Morrison's schoolteacher, giving his reluctant pupils lessons in English that leave them 'dazed' and forgetful of their own 'speech'. Yet the master who ferries his charges across the Lethe that leads from their language to his is also an overbearing mother-figure, his 'tongue' a 'nipple' 'spurting strange potions' in a way that extends the repertoire of mammary images both in Dabydeen's poem itself and in *Macbeth* and *Beloved*. This role is no sooner assumed, however, than it is usurped by Turner the paedophile, implanting his 'hook' in the 'flesh' that 'wriggle[s]' beneath him and is 'Breathless with pain'. These two identities – of Turner as tyrannical mother and as suffocating abuser – coalesce in the ironically terminal description of Turner's 'shudder[ing]' 'words' 'flow[ing] endlessly' into his young slaves' defenceless 'mouths and bellies', like breastmilk or semen or a mix of both.[15]

As noted earlier, the speaker behaves towards the stillborn child who navigates the fluctuating course of his monologue as his mother formerly behaved towards him: the care he gives it recapitulates the care he once received, thus allowing him to restore his past and vicariously regain a love otherwise lost. Equally and more troublingly, however, the speaker's treatment of the child also possesses a family resemblance to that which he experiences from Turner, as becomes clear at the start of the poem's final canto:

> 'Nigger,' [the child] cries, loosening from the hook
> Of my desire, drifting away from
> My body of lies. I wanted to teach it
> A redemptive song, fashion new descriptions
> Of things, new colours fountaining out of form.
> I wanted to begin anew in the sea
> But the child would not bear the future
> Nor its inventions, and my face was rooted
> In the ground of memory. (41)

Like Turner's, the speaker's 'desire' (significantly figured here as a 'hook') is to 'teach' the child, though he is evidently not as adept in this enterprise as his mentor. In the one case, the pupils capitulate to their instructor in a state of 'exhaustion' so 'complete' that all they can do is chant back the hypnotic and idolatrous 'words' they hear – '*blessed, angelic, / Sublime*' – but, in the other, the student will not be so brainwashed, rejecting what he is taught as a 'body of lies' and ultimately emerging, indeed, as the true pedagogue. In that bleakly authoritative '"Nigger,"' what the child demonstrates to the speaker is that the wish 'to begin anew in the sea' – breaking away from their common history – is impossible. This is a point Dabydeen underlines by once more resorting to the device of internal echo and recycling here the selfsame phrase as first appears in the preface, as if the poem is unable to break free from its own origin.

It is the realisation of history's inescapability that prompts the speaker himself to follow the child's scornful lead and turn against the authority of his own narrative, rejecting his autobiography as no more reliable or authentic than the hope for a future sealed off from the preface's 'memory of ancient cruelty' (8). His final utterance is, accordingly, a resounding palinode:

> No savannah, moon, gods, magicians
> To heal or curse, harvests, ceremonies,
> No men to plough, corn to fatten their herds,
> No stars, no land, no words, no community,
> No mother. (42)

Among this catalogue of negations, the most significant for this chapter is the speaker's claim that he has 'no community'. In one respect, this is all too poignantly true, especially given the fact that he has just been abandoned by his unwilling confidant, who 'dips / Below the surface' of the sea they share and 'frantically ... tries to die' (41). From an intertextual perspective, however, the claim is anything but persuasive, since 'Turner' is rich with community, engaging in a play of call and response with a wide array of other voices.

Conclusion

To recall 'Turner''s preface one last time, this chapter enables work on Dabydeen's poem to 'begin anew', taking the critical debate beyond the frame of reference that the preface sets up (and that 'Turner''s critics have largely endorsed), raising questions about the interpretative authority writers can (or cannot) exert over their own creations: it directs attention to parts of Ruskin's 'Of Water' that are rarely if ever considered in readings of Dabydeen's poem and more significantly, to *Macbeth* and *Beloved*, texts whose importance to an understanding of 'Turner' has been similarly 'submerged' in the critical seas that have washed over the text in the years since its publication.[16]

As stated in the introductory chapter, one of the cardinal aims of this book is to bring into focus a number of black-authored ekphrastic texts about slavery that have to date been largely overlooked. The book draws these materials increasingly into view from Chapter 3 onwards, but in the next chapter makes a brief detour from this path to consider an instance of white-authored ekphrasis, William B. Patrick's 'The Slave Ship'. This poem has itself been consigned to the critical periphery but, it is argued, provides an important complement to Dabydeen's work.

Notes

1. According to Baucom, 'art historians agree' (268) on the role this incident plays in shaping *The Slave Ship* but, as Slapkauskaite notes, are 'unable to fully substantiate their claims' (318), a point similarly made by McCoubrey 321–2. Whatever the exact truth of the matter, it is abundantly clear that, within the imaginative compass of Dabydeen's poem, the *Zong* episode and Turner's painting are fully intervolved.
2. Although Dabydeen does not support this provocative claim, it is worth noting that in 1805 Turner participated in a failed tontine scheme to purchase the Dry Sugar Work pen near Spanish Town, Jamaica. This speculative involvement in slavery of course long predates the composition of *The Slave Ship* (and could even be paradoxically used to argue as much against imputations of the artist's 'sadism' as for them), but would surely resonate with Dabydeen, who was born and brought up for much of his childhood on a sugar plantation in Guyana. For a thorough and balanced account of Turner's part in the tontine venture and his relationship to slavery and the slave trade more generally, together with the bearing that both have on his work, see Smiles.
3. 'Turner''s drive to retrieve that which is marginal or overlooked, transmuting absence into presence, silence into voice is quite typical of other texts, whether poetic or fictional, in which Dabydeen uses ekphrasis as a technique with which to negotiate the visual memory of slavery. In 'Dependence, or the Ballad of the Little Black Boy', the final poem in *Coolie Odyssey* (1988), Dabydeen renarrates Francis Wheatley's *A Family Group in a Landscape* (c. 1775) in the first-person voice of the silhouetted slave looking in from the left-hand edge of a domestic gathering which includes and excludes him at one and the same time. Similarly, in *A Harlot's Progress*, the personage endowed with new centrality is the young black page occupying the lower right-hand corner of the second plate in the 1733 series of Hogarthian engravings from which Dabydeen's novel derives its title.
4. See, for example, the essays by Frost, Gravendyk, Härting, Slapkauskaite, Wallart and Ward. For a departure from this normative critical approach, see Boeninger, who sets Dabydeen's poem in an interesting relationship to Walcott's *Omeros* (1990). For another such departure, see Jenkins, who not only locates 'Turner' in the tradition of the 'maritime epic' that includes *Omeros* but also defines Dabydeen's poem as 'a sustained rewriting' (78) of Eliot's *The Waste Land* (1922).
5. In Tlostanova's essay on 'Turner', for instance, *Macbeth*'s intertextual presence in Dabydeen's poem is restricted to a single phrase, in which she detects 'vaguely Shakespearean echoes' (90). The phrase in question is 'the idiot witter / Of wind through a dead wood' (39), which

Tlostanova presumably construes as an echo of Macbeth's despairing rejection of existence as 'a tale / Told by an idiot' (5.5.26–7). For its part, *Beloved* is more frequently cited in critical readings of 'Turner' (Craps 136n; Härting 80n; Jenkins 79; Mackenthun 178), even as such citations remain radically undeveloped. Dabydeen himself mentions Morrison's novel approvingly in the course of reflecting on his own poem during a 1994 interview with Kwame Dawes, but, similarly, does not elaborate the links between the two texts (Grant 201–2).

6. As is widely recognised, Dabydeen participates also in the reworking of *The Tempest*, both in 'Turner' and, more explicitly, in earlier poems (in *Slave Song* [1984] and *Coolie Odyssey*) that move away from the Middle Passage and into the terrain of the plantation. As he notes, however, his formative encounter with Shakespeare's late romance was of an unusual kind, occurring not in a direct reading of the play but in the mediated shape of an exposure to William Hogarth's *Scene from Shakespeare's* The Tempest (c. 1735). For Dabydeen's commentary on his imaginative relationship with this picture, see his 'Hogarth and the Canecutters' (2000) in Macedo 80–5.

7. For a more detailed account of the *Zong* massacre, together with its legal, social and historical significance, see the symposium of articles in *Journal of Legal History* and Walvin, *Zong*. For a useful collocation of legal and other documents pertaining to the *Zong* case and, especially, the insurers' petition for the second trial (thought never to have taken place), see Lyall 239–374.

8. At the same time, as several critics have noted, these moments of violent interpellation echo Chapter Five of Fanon's *Black Skin*, in which he famously dramatises the devastating 'occasion' when he is obliged to 'meet the white man's eyes' (110) during his time as a medical student in Lyon. As it turns out, the 'eyes' in question are not a 'man's' but belong to a child who is out walking with its mother on a 'white winter day' (113) and who, like 'Turner''s stillborn, repeatedly engages in acts of exclamatory violence, escalating from '"Look, a Negro!"' (111) to '"Look at the nigger!"' (113). On this point, see Craps 65 and Falk 191. See also Döring, who was the first to recognise and explore Fanon's relevance for 'Turner' (Döring 158–9).

9. The gender-transformations that befall 'Turner''s speaker occur not just in the poem itself, but in the preface that announces them. The preface refers to the speaker as 'he' (7), even as, in *The Slave Ship*, the figure is female (Costello 209; Stephen May 112; McCoubrey 344, 345). Dabydeen is well aware of this, as evidenced in an interview with Karen Raney in 2010: 'in my "Turner" poem, I make the character male, but don't forget: in the Turner painting it's a female who's drowning; it's a female figure who's being devoured by those sexual, phallic, monstrous . . . fish' (qtd. in Macedo 194).

10. Bassett's account of these harrowing events is included in Harris, Levitt, Furman and Smith 10. The episode in discussed in greater detail in Chapter 5.
11. This particular remembered delight is no doubt one that would also appeal to Morrison's Beloved, whose appetite for such foodstuffs is seemingly boundless: 'sweet things were what she was born for. Honey [and] the wax it came in, sugar sandwiches, the sludgy molasses gone hard and brutal in the can, lemonade, taffy and any type of dessert Sethe brought home from the restaurant' (55).
12. On the resonance of this image with Yeats's 'Leda and the Swan' (1923), see Jenkins 79.
13. The 'drowning / Man' to whom the speaker compares himself here is another subtle reminder of 'Turner''s historical foundation in the events aboard the *Zong*. As Sharp notes, 133 slaves were originally to have been jettisoned from the slaver, 'but one Man was saved by catching hold of a Rope which hung overboard' (qtd. in Lyall 301n).
14. This incidental link to *Beloved* is also noted by Jenkins 86n.
15. Like the image of Turner's 'white enfolding / Wings' discussed above, these lines bear traces of Yeats's 'Leda and the Swan', in which 'the staggering girl' is subjected to the 'shudder in the loins' of the sonnet's feathery and tyrannical god.
16. As it conducts that latter double-exchange with Shakespeare's Renaissance tragedy and Morrison's late twentieth-century novel, 'Turner' encourages consideration of the links between these two texts, both of which pivot, after all, around different types of murder and the guilt that springs from them and feature supernatural agencies (to suggest only two of the most obvious commonalities). The conversation that might be going on between those two ostensibly disparate texts is a topic for another occasion, but its existence perhaps accounts for their copresence as central elements in Dabydeen's remarkable poetic project.

Chapter 2

Looking beyond 'Turner': William B. Patrick's 'The Slave Ship'

Introduction

By a curious coincidence, 'The Slave Ship' was first published in *The Southern Review* in the same year as 'Turner' and subsequently included in Patrick's *These Upraised Hands* (1995). This collection not only places 'The Slave Ship' at its mid-point and uses a repeated line from the text as its title but also bears the image of Turner's violent seascape on its front cover, creative and editorial decisions which combine, ironically, to advertise the poem's preeminence within the volume overall, if not the wider spheres of critical reception and debate.

It is not this chapter's purpose to speculate on why 'Turner', written by a black Caribbean author, has been granted such critical prestige while 'The Slave Ship', written by an author who is a white American, remains critically invisible, nor is the concern to adjudicate between the aesthetic merits of these two poems, which would seem to have been composed entirely independently of one another. The aim, rather, is to bring the transatlantic encounter between Patrick's poem and Turner's *'magnum opus'* (Howley 4; italics in original) into sustained critical focus, thus providing a new slant on the corpus of ekphrastic texts that – to a greater or lesser degree – take Turner's painting as their interlocutory ground. At the same time, the chapter serves as a reminder that the institution of the transatlantic slave trade with which both poets deal via Turner is just as much a part of a Euro-American as a Caribbean (or African) diasporic history and in need of interrogation from that perspective too.

1. Setting the Scene: Conflicting Visions in 'The Slave Ship'

As well as being written from a white rather than a black perspective, Patrick's poem offers an approach to *The Slave Ship* (and the *Zong* massacre) quite different from Dabydeen's, particularly in terms of structure. 'Turner' is a posthumous utterance, spoken by the drowned slave whom Dabydeen magically rescues and revives from the tumult of the artist's Atlantic, but Patrick's text has a more intricate arrangement, juxtaposing two figures who could hardly be further apart from one another, whether historically, geographically, ideologically or linguistically. The first of these, located in the late 1780s at the start of the abolitionist era, is an officer of the British Royal Navy whose three-year sojourn in Africa affords him direct experience of the slave trade. Although he does not personally participate in or profit from it financially, the officer firmly supports the institution, outlining his observations and opinions in a letter (that takes up less than a quarter of the poem) addressed to a 'dear friend' (51) domiciled in England. 'The Slave Ship''s second and textually dominant figure, by contrast, is implicitly situated in the end-of-millennium period when the poem was published and spends his time exploring and commenting on Turner's painting as he gazes at it in the Museum of Fine Arts in Boston, where it is currently housed. Thus cast in the role of art critic or art expert, he adds another chapter to the chequered history of the reviews *The Slave Ship* has stimulated ever since its early Victorian debut. The discourses of these two figures are each split into six sections presented alternately, with the art critic interrupting the naval officer and vice versa in a series of stops and starts that spans the historical divide between them. This patterning creates a sense of textual discontinuity commensurate with the scene of violent bodily disintegration that Turner's painting so powerfully sets forth.

Alongside the historical and geographical differences between naval officer and art critic, there are ideological conflicts too, with the latter disturbed and repelled by an institution the former condones. This radical antipathy has its curious and striking corollary in the different types of grammatical dispensation characterising the two figures' respective contributions to the text. In the shorter epistolary pro-slave trade parts of the poem belonging to the naval officer, punctuation is conventional and syntax unremarkable, and no sentences go beyond six lines in length, with the majority not exceeding three. This preferred pattern of bite-sized grammatical units lends an air of order to these sections and is designed to make the buying and selling of slaves seem innocuous and banal – something that passes without notice – while also being tailored to the 'childish heart' (51) the naval figure condescendingly ascribes to his (probably female) correspondent. In the anti-slave trade ekphrasis that takes up the lion's share of the poem, conversely, the laws of grammar are all but abandoned: all commas and full stops are vanquished, together with other routine marks of punctuation, such that it is only possible to identify where sentences begin and end by virtue of the capitalised words that appear sporadically at the start of particular lines. These devices work as improvised orientation points for an otherwise potentially flummoxed reader, just as italics are used to demarcate the places where a voice other than that of the art critic occasionally enters the text. Such a disturbance of grammatical norms can be read as a kind of linguistic signature for the poem's art expert, while also providing an empathetic textual acknowledgement of the visual disorder that marks *The Slave Ship*. At the same time, it seems well-suited to the dystopian value system governing the *Zong*, where the act of jettisoning slaves is indistinguishable from the discarding of a civilised morality.

As the allocation of textual space implies, Patrick's poem is much more energised and engaged by the art critic's fluid commentary than the slavish orthodoxies of thought and expression that regulate the naval officer's letter, and this imaginative weighting is reflected accordingly in the ensuing discussion. This begins with a brief overview of the epistolary sections of the poem, before going on to a much more detailed analysis of its more challenging and substantial ekphrastic elements.

2. African Apologia

As the poem's headnote indicates, the letter composed by 'The Slave Ship''s officer-figure is not wholly of Patrick's own invention but a pastiche of an archival document, in the relatively obscure shape of Lieutenant John Matthews's *A Voyage to the River Sierra-Leone, on the Coast of Africa* (1788) and it works, like the colonial memoir it recalls, to endorse the slave trading 'methods' (51) used by 'European coastal / dealers' (56), extolling them as providential.[1] Because they are 'much less severe / than the natives' own' benighted system of 'slavery' (51), the letter claims, such methods leave the

Africans whom their 'greedy' 'tribal kings' (56) sell to white traders in a condition that is ultimately 'more fortunate than most comprehend' (51).

As his discourse proceeds, it becomes increasingly apparent that the poem's officer-figure is ironically at odds with the close acquaintance to whom he writes. This implicit tension becomes explicit in the closing paragraph of the officer's letter, in which he expresses a sarcastic gratitude for the anti-slave trade 'essays' (61) his friend has thoughtfully sent him and which are the original stimulus to what the officer calls his 'last response' (51): 'I daresay you favor the brand of writer / who harps on the grave inhumanity / of our Slave Trade, while summering near Dover' (61), he testily remarks, using a trope that, in this context, has an unsettling connotation. By selecting the term 'brand', the officer obliquely signals his animosity towards the newfangled abolitionist texts the friend so pointedly prefers to read. He perhaps even hints at an exasperated desire to subject those texts' vacationing authors to the same suffering as is inflicted upon the slaves for whom they campaign and which he has regularly observed with such cool detachment during his tropical posting: 'When sales are through, buyers mark the [slaves] / they own, scalding each owner's unique mark / into chests or backs with an incandescent iron' (59).

In a final twist, it could even be said that the officer is at odds with himself, as his argument is marred by internal contradiction. In the same valedictory paragraph, he gruffly complains that 'slaves' are no better than 'beasts' (61) – 'links in Nature's / chain, at best' (61–2) – and that the slave trade 'save[s] these creatures from certain death in their [own] country' (62). Yet such claims do not pass muster when set against earlier disclosures which suggest that induction into the slave trade, far from enabling captured Africans to avoid death, in fact makes such a fate more likely:

> Then [the slavers] beat [the slaves] toward the beach
> with hide whips and most, glimpsing an ocean
> for the first time, will beseech
> the slavers to kill them there, or will clutch
> howling at the sand until the native Krumen
> drag them to the transport boats. Inasmuch
> as the slaves think whites are new kings, who would sell
> them to cannibals, they will jump
> to waiting sharks or, with their chains, try to strangle
> themselves. Some captains report that Ibos
> have hanged themselves at their first sight of Barbados. (59)

3. In and Out of the Frame: 'The Slave Ship' as Augmented Ekphrasis

As noted earlier, punctuation is reduced to a vestigial presence in the poem's six ekphrastic sections, but reappears as an ingenious if equally residual part of the picture they describe. In the second section, for example, the art critic at one point trains his eye upon the mysteriously buoyant shackles located in the middle foreground of *The Slave Ship* and likens the 'disembodied / iron loops' he beholds there to 'magenta question marks' (54).

In being drawn to these dubious shackles, floating 'for no reason / in the / quiet center' (54) of Turner's painting, the picture's late twentieth-century respondent follows *The Slave Ship*'s nineteenth-century reviewers in both Britain and America, several of whom also directed attention to these particular and peculiar items, which they regarded, like the painting as a whole, as artistically questionable and derisively so at that. One of the first to note and mock these fetters as anomalous was William Makepeace Thackeray, after viewing Turner's painting on its first appearance at the Royal Academy. Writing in *Fraser's Magazine* for June 1840 under the improbable soubriquet of Michael Angelo Titmarsh, Thackeray identifies these 'chains that will not sink' as part of a painting that itself seems to float irresolutely somewhere between the 'sublime' and the 'ridiculous', leading him to exclaim: 'Ye gods, what a "middle passage!"' (731). Mark Twain, satirising *The Slave Ship* in *A Tramp Abroad*, some eight years after the work was sold to John Taylor Johnston in 1872 and brought to America, similarly dismisses 'The most of the picture' as a 'manifest impossibility', partly supporting his argument by reference, once again, to those 'iron cable-chains'. These, as the errant Turner must surely know, belong with other 'unfloatable things' and not atop a sea that looks like 'glaring yellow mud' (157).[2]

For the anonymous reviewer writing in *Blackwood's Edinburgh Magazine* in September 1840, some three months on from Thackeray, *The Slave Ship* is a fanciful achievement too: it is a 'dream of the colour pots' and an 'unaccountable performance' 'out of all rule and measure' and the 'floating' chains themselves are 'quite miraculous'. Yet even as this reviewer's interpretation of these objects is in line with that of Thackeray and Twain, he ends his commentary by suggesting a more sympathetic reading, in which the unsinkable chains assume a tentative symbolic value. Is Turner's treatment of these things that 'water wouldn't swallow' intended to be 'poetical', the reviewer wonders, a metaphor, in other words, for how the memory of slavery remains difficult to digest and simply 'won't go down' (380).

This symbolic interpretation of what the contributor to *Blackwood's* calls 'slavery's chains' (380) implies a potential for serious reflection on the historical substance of Turner's painting, but it should be clear from the foregoing examples that nineteenth-century reviewers were primarily interested in the technical flaws of the work and that it was these, rather than *The Slave Ship*'s troubling content, that defined the source of their outrage. The emphasis on artistic technique rather than the pressing matter of history is also evident in Ruskin's assessment of the picture, as discussed in this book's opening chapter, the difference being that Ruskin extravagantly praises rather than condemns Turner's artistry, albeit in a way that Dabydeen finds problematic. For the latter, Ruskin's investment in technique is a strategy of deflection and distraction, a means of seeing one thing in order not to see something else, and the same may also be the case for the painting's other (less enthusiastic) reviewers.[3]

By contrast, no one could accuse the art critic in Patrick's poem of trying to block out the violent realities of Turner's painting, at first glance, at least. He plunges into them with the very first words he utters in the text, dragging the reader with him:

>   These upraised hands
>   and this one leg
>   upside down in the right foreground
>   the one exposed
>   mid-thigh to toe
>   as it slides down surrounded
>   by white fish
>   with bulging black eyes
>   and perfect hunger in their eager
>   upturned tails
>   these few extremities
>   easily mistaken for fish or waves
>   and caught
>   for this one instant
>   between the onrushing diagonal rain
>   and the torrential sea
>   that accepts
>   everyone
>   even this ship on the left
>   with its blood-red empty masts
>   tipping back

Looking beyond 'Turner': William B. Patrick's 'The Slave Ship'

> these evanescent strokes
> are people
> already almost completely under
> the burnt umber and white-lead foam
> flecked with hovering gulls
> (52)

This opening excerpt from the first segment of the art critic's discourse reverses the privileging of technique over content defining nineteenth-century responses to *The Slave Ship*, but possesses technical features of its own (aside from the down-swirling syntax) that are worthy of comment and designed to reflect rather than avoid the atrocious scene Turner depicts. If the poem's figuration of the 'iron loops' as 'question marks' briefly textualises Turner's image, so here Patrick's text assumes a more permanent visual quality: its lines are organised in a mutually centred pattern and varied in length in such a way as to approximate the shape of that topsy-turvy leg, as it 'slides down' into Turner's 'torrential sea', its inflated size causing the 'eyes' of the 'fish' encircling it to become gleefully enlarged in response, as they 'bulg[e]' with surprise and delight.

Perhaps what is most notable about these lines, however, is that while they may be centred relative to one another, they are manifestly off-centre relative to the page on which they are printed, giving the appearance of having been pulled towards the page's right, with the three longest lines in fact stretching far enough to touch the margin. This typographical displacement occurs across all the ekphrastic segments of the poem and serves as a concrete reminder of the art critic's sympathy towards the black figure in the early stages of being devoured by that company of monstrous fish crowding into the 'right foreground' of Turner's canvas. It also operates as a visual articulation of his ideological distance from the naval officer, whose pro-slave trade letter is delivered, throughout the poem, in verse conventionally aligned with the margin on the page's left.

The lines just cited clearly demonstrate that the art critic in Patrick's poem is much more willing and able than his nineteenth-century predecessors to face and embrace the terrible history *The Slave Ship* recollects. Yet as a closer look at his portions of the poem reveals, the situation is not quite as straightforward as that, as he too is at times driven to disavow the truth of what he sees. Such a denial is evident, for example, in the contradictory trajectories involved in his description of that flamboyantly protrusive object, the slave's leg: even as the art critic attests to how the limb is descending into the

Atlantic, his eye traces a line that moves in the opposite direction, from 'mid-thigh to toe'. Similarly, although he begins his account of *The Slave Ship* by immediately confronting the reader with a vision of the flotsam and jetsam of the slaves' body parts, it is not until much later that this anatomical detritus is resolved into the form of 'people', as if he cannot countenance the drastic depersonalisation to which the slave trade reduces its victims.

Considered in this light, it would appear that the art critic has a little more in common with *The Slave Ship*'s earlier reviewers than one might at first have supposed, an impression strengthened when his own recurrent emphasis on Turner's painterly techniques is taken into account. Before the slaves' randomised and broken bodies emerge as 'people', for example, they are, after all, just 'evanescent strokes' administered by the painter's brush, just as the 'foam' that has almost submerged them is an effect compounded from 'burnt umber' and 'white-lead'. Later on in the poem, the 'waves' of Turner's sea are described, comparably, in terms of the technique that produces them – they have been 'knife-smoothed' (54) by the artist – and 'painting' itself is defined, later still, as an abstract rather than a representational pursuit, an ongoing investigation of the interplay 'between form / light / [and] color' (60). It is as if, in these textual moments, 'The Slave Ship''s art critic raises up his own metaphorical hands against Turner's picture in a bid to shield himself from its terrifying visual assault.

As he strives to come to terms with the miscellaneous 'fragments of sky ship sea or human body' (60) with which Turner's painting confronts him, the art critic also mixes them with his own visions, augmenting what is commonly perceptible to the naked eye in *The Slave Ship* with sights that are not, and even imagining voices and sounds that, by definition, cannot be apprehended by the act of looking. In so doing, he starts to draw his silent companion (and the reader) back into the time before the moment the painting captures – that of 'sunset on the Atlantic' (Ruskin 571) – endowing the slaves on the point of being swallowed up by Turner's ocean with a short history just as oppressive as their imperilled and crepuscular present. This process begins in the lines that complete the first part of the art critic's ekphrasis:

> These bodies
> you cannot see
> were chained sideways
> ass to face

> alive or dead this morning
> in the slippery hold you also won't see here
> The blood
> squeezed from their bodies
> steamed up through
> gratings
> and became this swollen sky
> that sweeps up here
> to the left
> upper corner
> Before the first ominous red of morning
> a small boy
> who dreamed of the moon
> over his empty village
> woke up
> crying
> *Kickeraboo Kickeraboo*
> We are dying
> We are dying
> (52–3; italics in original)

As his insistent, 'you cannot see' and 'you also won't see' would suggest, the art critic seems privileged (or burdened) with a capacity for imaginative vision that is lacking in his less gifted companion, who can only 'see' the 'blood / squeezed from [the slaves'] bodies' when it is viscerally and vicariously transformed into the paint on Turner's canvas. Yet in one sense, the fearful vision into which the art critic voyages is not a private one somehow unique to him, since the 'bodies' he claims to see 'chained sideways' in the 'hold' recall those featured in *Description of a Slave Ship* (1789) (Fig. 2.1). This diagram (which will be discussed in more detail in the next chapter) was created as part of the abolitionist campaign and rapidly became a kind of public property, appearing, in different versions, on both sides of the Atlantic, in pamphlets, books and newspapers, as well as on posters put up in taverns and coffee houses.[4]

But if it is this image of the *Brookes* that informs the art critic's vision in the first six lines of this passage, it is eyewitness accounts of conditions aboard that iconic slaver that become important in the last nine, as the vision first shifts to the figure of the 'small boy', 'dream[ing] of the moon / over his empty village' and then takes on a hauntingly auditory element, as the moonstruck child awakens into the nightmare of his overcrowded Atlantic dungeon. Here the boy's cry of '*Kickeraboo Kickeraboo*', translated by the art critic

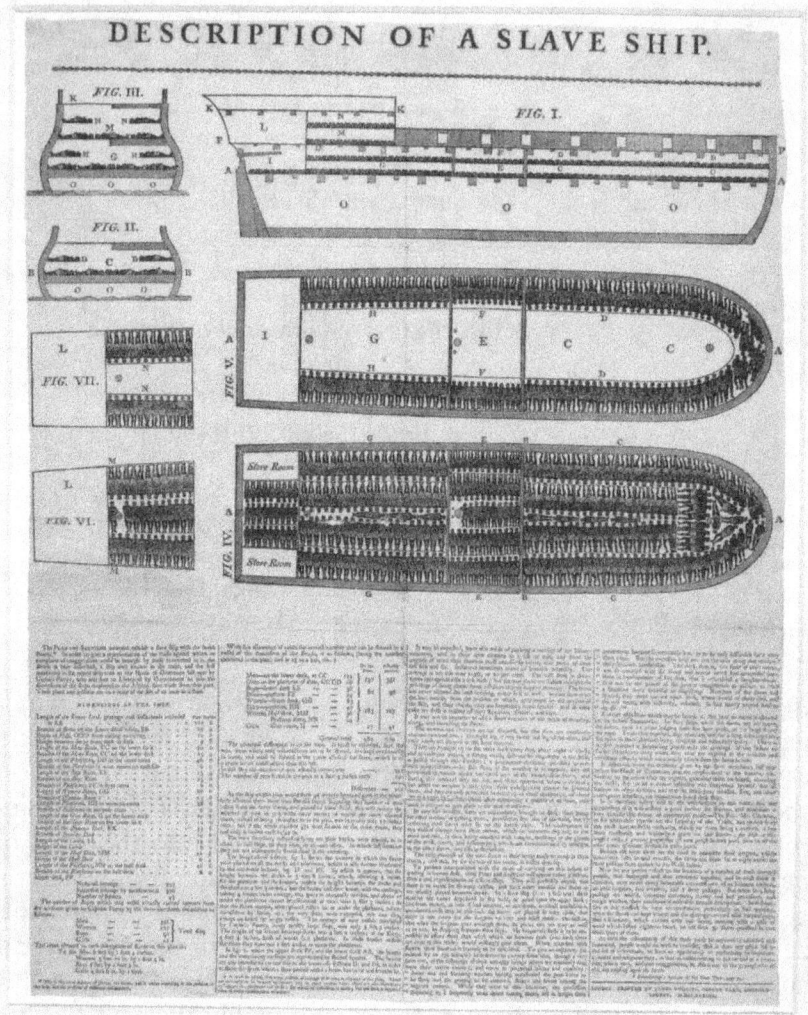

Figure 2.1 *Description of a Slave Ship*, 1789. Princeton Rare Book Collections.

as 'We are dying / We are dying', repeats not only itself but also the testimony of Thomas Trotter, surgeon aboard the *Brookes* during one of its voyages in 1783. Appalled by the black suffering he witnessed on this trip, Trotter became a fervent abolitionist and gave an account of his experiences before a Parliamentary Select Committee, set up in 1790 to gather information about the slave trade. In the course of this statement, Trotter recalls how, during the voyage, he had:

seen the slaves drawing their breath with all those laborious and anxious efforts for life, which is observed (sic) in expiring animals, subjected by experiment to foul air, or in the exhausted receiver of an air pump; [and] also seen them, when the tarpawlings (sic) have inadvertently been thrown over the gratings, attempting to heave them up, crying out, 'Kickeraboo, kickeraboo,' i.e. 'We are dying.' (*Abridgment* 37)

The strange word that so catches Trotter's ear and echoes in Patrick's poem (sometimes also spelt with an 'a' as 'kickaraboo') is 'presumed to be a black pronunciation of the phrase "kick the bucket"' (Green 317). The word appears in fledgling traditions of blackface minstrelsy, as, for example, in a song composed and originally published by the theatre manager and writer Charles Dibdin the Younger in his *Christmas Gambols*, just five years after Trotter gave his evidence. This is the song's first verse, as reproduced in George Hogarth's *The Songs of Charles Dibdin* (1842):

> Poor negro say one ting – you no take offence,
> Black and white be one colour a hundred years hence;
> For when massa Death kick him into the grave,
> He no spare negro, buckra, nor massa, nor slave.
> Then dance, and then sing, and the banjer thrum
>   thrum,
> He foolish to tink what to-morrow may come;
> Lily laugh and be fat, do best ting you can do, –
> Time enough to be sad when you kickaraboo. (165–6)

As W. T. Lhamon, Jr points out, this song provides 'an early instance of the slave's meditation on the master's death, and its meaning . . . . and appeared many times in Atlantic songsters' (436n).

Together with providing a helpful gloss on Dibdin's song, Lhamon's brief comments can be brought usefully to bear on the significance of 'Kickeraboo' as it features in the Atlantic soundscape that Patrick's text evokes.[5] Although the word sounds plaintive and despairing enough at first (as it does in Trotter's report), Dibdin's song suggests that it is not just a slaves' lament for their own mortality, but a celebratory recognition of how, in the end, both slave and master, 'negro' and 'buckra', are subject to the higher power of 'massa Death', who blindly overrides the hierarchical differences created by the artifice of race. Such a reading expands the first-person plural of 'We are dying', transforming it into an unsegregated grammatical 'grave' which can happily accommodate 'white' as well as 'Black' and, like Turner's sea, 'accepts / everyone'.

In the second and longest section of his commentary on *The Slave Ship*, the art critic's temporal retreat from the murderous Atlantic sunset depicted in Turner's painting extends beyond the fateful morning on which the boy's cry is heard to encompass earlier phases in his voyage. In such periods, the ship on which the boy is captive follows the grim rhythms of grim routines, starting by bringing its slaves up from hold to deck:

> Most mornings
> they were danced on deck
> in ankle chains
> like this one in the right foreground
> still attached
> to flesh
> ....
> Some would order the men in irons up
> *Jump*
> some would shout
> or
> *move your feet*
> though those with swollen ankles
> might bleed to death
> from dancing
> and the sailor with the cat-o'-nine-tails
> be flogged then
> A toothless woman might bang
> an upturned kettle
> and the fool who signed on at Liverpool
> to play bagpipes
> on the Guinea slaver
> for a quarter-percent share
> might try a reel
> to make the crew forget what they all do
> as the dancers
> sing their own words for
> sorrow
> for child
> ....
> and the sea would sing
> on quieter mornings
> to the dancers
> silently
> across these purple waves
> *Come home*

> *I am the way home*
> *Come home*
> (54–5; italics in original)

The ritual of '"Dancing the slave"' (Fabre 36) that these lines dramatise (and whose passive construction tells its own story of compulsion) is widely documented in eyewitness reports on the Middle Passage.[6] As Geneviève Fabre explains, the official purpose of this euphemistic measure was to provide African captives with exercise after the cramped conditions they would have endured in the hold overnight, although, as she notes, it is, in effect, just 'another kind of confinement' (35) and part, moreover, of a 'deliberate scheme to ensure subordination by destroying former practices, to curb any attempt at recovering freedom of movement, action, or thought' (36).

In addition to creating a torturesome disciplinary theatre for slaves' physical activity, these dance routines provided an important means of entertaining the crew, to such an extent indeed that, to cite Daniel P. Mannix and Malcolm Cowley, on whom Patrick here directly draws, 'Slaving captains ... advertised for "A person that can play on the Bagpipes, for a Guinea ship"' (114). In Patrick's poem, however, the 'slave ship dance' (Fabre 34) – complete with that 'upturned kettle' (Mannix and Cowley 114) that Patrick also borrows from his source – is not just a form of amusement for bored sailors, but at the same time carries out a collective psychological function. Specifically, it enables them briefly 'to forget what they all do' (Patrick 55), a phrase whose catch-all imprecision seems to enact the very oblivion to which it refers, effacing, in particular, the sexual violation perpetrated upon female slaves – 'the women they wanted' (Patrick 54) – which was also a routine part of the slave trade. For the 'dancers' themselves, conversely, it is recollection rather than forgetting that is paramount, as the slaves combine enforced movement with vocal expression, 'sing[ing] their own words for / sorrow / for child' as a way of preserving the memory of the land from which they have been exiled.

As Fabre further explains, in these shipboard rituals, 'the basic principles of many performances to come were set'. These include 'the blending and interplay of dance, song, and music; the call-and-response pattern between dance and music, between voice and instrument, body and song, and mostly between leader-caller and the assembly of dancers' (40). Yet here that pattern is reversed, as it is the dancers brought together on the deck who launch the initial call and the solitary sea that hearkens to and answers their sorrow songs with its seductive '*Come home . . . Come home*'. Such a Siren-like appeal is one some slaves were all too willing to answer, choosing to commit suicide not only in order both to end their suffering and regain control over their bodies but also in the belief that such an act would secure a jubilant return to Africa (Piersen 151). From this perspective, the crew's injunction to '*Jump*' takes on a new and ironic resonance, unwittingly sounding less like a dance-instruction than a more abrupt and abrasive version of the sea's fetching chant.[7]

'The Slave Ship''s third and fourth ekphrastic sections switch the focus back to the morning immediately preceding the massacre that Turner's painting depicts, while at the same time developing the suicidal theme by connecting it to that of bodily consumption. In section three, the poem also makes a spatial return from the dancing deck to the 'slippery hold', following the slave ship's enigmatic 'surgeon' as he is 'sent down / amidships' (56) to fulfil his daily medical programme. This infernal descent into 'heat / [and] noxious vapors', 'blood and mucus', prompts the surgeon to recall 'a slaughterhouse / he had worked in as a boy' (57), even as it is itself an intertextual recollection of *An Account of the Slave Trade on the Coast of Africa* (1788), written by Alexander Falconbridge, who, like Trotter, was a slave-ship surgeon turned abolitionist. But as well as recalling this text – an important source for these middle sequences of the art critic's discourse, in particular – 'The Slave Ship' significantly revises it: written under the auspices of the abolitionists, Falconbridge's *Account* is sympathetically disposed to his African charges, describing them as 'poor sufferers' (28) and regretfully conceding that 'Almost the only means by which [a] surgeon can render himself useful to the slaves, is, by seeing that their food is properly cooked, and distributed among them' (29). In Patrick's poem, however, the scene is very different, as the surgeon 'force-feed[s]' the slaves, starting with the 'tallest men', assisted in his endeavours by 'Two cutlass-armed sailors'. These menacing if ambiguous figures – armed with cutlasses or with cutlasses for arms? – thrust 'moldy plantains / awash in palm oil' (56) as well as 'mashed yams filled with maggots' (57) into the mouths of the slaves who resist eating.

Whether the surgeon performs his actions willingly or under duress is unclear, but, either way, they end in irony when he begins to suffer the ill-effects of the insanitary atmosphere to which his duties expose him:

> Just before
> the surgeon . . . fainted
> by the ladder
> and had to be dragged up
> the slave closest
> bit into his foot and held on so hard
> a toe came away
>
> (57)

Yet if the surgeon here becomes an object of consumption and dismemberment for the slaves who otherwise will not eat, the irony of the irony is that they themselves are destined to be devoured piecemeal by the pop-eyed fish that flounce and swish towards *The Slave Ship*'s viewer much earlier, with 'perfect hunger in their eager / upturned tails'.

In the course of his observations on slaves' diet, Falconbridge addresses the claim, made in 'favour of the captains in this trade, that the sick slaves are usually fed from their tables', but dismisses it by pointing out that the typical number ill at any one time is far too great to make such a custom practicable, even were 'a captain *disposed*' to adopt it, stating that just 'Two or three perhaps may be fed' (29; italics in original) in this way. This latter remark provides the cue for the grotesque breakfast laid out before the reader in the short fourth instalment of the art critic's ekphrasis, in which Luke Collingwood, previously introduced to the reader as simply 'the Captain' (54), is now properly named, along with his first mate, James Kelsall:

> On this morning
> Collingwood is awake
> sitting at his carved table
> easing pork chops down with English brandy
> Two slaves
> a woman
> he remembers giving beads to afterwards
> and a strong Fulani
> with a nose broken the first day out
> for trying suicide
> both weak
> from dysentery or scurvy
> bound to chairs
> are being fed from the Captain's table
> *Note this*
> he is saying to Kelsall

> as a sailor
> drains a tankard of rum into the man's mouth
> held open
> with a pair of hot tongs
> *Jamaican rum*
> Collingwood goes on
> *what we reserve for dashing Susu kings*
> Nothing
> *is too good*
> *for our guests on the Zong*
> (58–9; italics in original)

In this vignette, Collingwood's homely ability to 'eas[e] pork chops down with English brandy' sets him in stark opposition to the 'strong Fulani', who continues the quest for his own death (begun 'the first day out') by refusing to drink, such that his 'mouth' has to be kept open by 'a pair of hot tongs' while '*Jamaican rum*' is 'drain[ed]' into it – a coercive scenario similar to one sketched out in Falconbridge, where 'coals of fire, glowing hot' are 'put on a shovel, and placed so near [slaves'] lips, as to scorch and burn them' (23). The broken-nosed Fulani's resistance to the rum that is offered him is significant as the sign of a spirit that is precisely unbroken, but accrues additional meaning given the role the beverage plays in sustaining the transatlantic economy: manufactured as a 'product of slave labor' (Nesbitt 1) on the plantations of the Caribbean, rum finds its way to the African coast, where it is used, as Collingwood observes, for the purpose of '*dashing Susu kings*', who in turn furnish more slaves for those plantations, as the cycle of supply and demand renews itself.

In each of the four ekphrastic sections considered so far, the art critic exhibits an imaginative ability to enter narrative worlds located beyond the picture's immediate temporal frame that his silent auditor cannot emulate: watching the slaves being 'danced on deck'; following the surgeon into the carceral spaces of the ship's hold; and observing Collingwood at his macabre breakfast, where even the 'carved table' appears to be a victim of violence (albeit an aesthetic one). In the penultimate part of his discourse, however, the art critic returns to the time of the painting itself, but only in order, once again, to veer off towards the things that are 'not shown' in the picture and may or not in fact be present at all amid the deliberate indistinctness of Turner's 'mist and vapor and symbolic blood' (60). The most significant of these invisible presences take the form of the slaves gathered for jettison:

Looking beyond 'Turner': William B. Patrick's 'The Slave Ship'   61

>   somewhere in here then
>   perhaps
>   in a huddled line
>   starting at the stern rail
>   and coiling along the foam-battered
>   starboard side
>   are what remain of
>   135 pairs
>   of open eyes
>   we have simply not found yet
>   (60–1).⁸

What is noticeable here is how, though 'open', the eyes do their best to avoid the sights around or rather beneath them. They 'try not to notice / the swirling vortical curves / waiting below', just as, in a synaesthetic shift quite typical of the art critic's discourse from here on, they 'try', also 'not to hear / the half-finished / screams' of their companions as they are 'swallowed up in frenzied splashing' (61).

As the art critic moves into the final section of his discourse, his increasing concern, by contrast, is not to supplement what can be seen in Turner's painting with his own visionary or speculative flights but, in another approach, to transform it. Focusing squarely on the visible, he declares:

>   What you can see here
>   is the dream
>   beginning
>   the dream of the living
>   left on board
>   the ship
>   . . . .
>   You can see
>   these upraised hands
>   straining still
>   in the vaporous air and ochre light
>   leaving one final sign
>   Look
>   there is nothing hidden now
>   Look
>   they are waving
>   calling
>   to the ones
>   left listening on deck
>   or floating in the dark hold

>   They are waving
>   to the gathering mist of jib
>   and skewed masts
>   reeling off sideways
>   They are waving
>   to Collingwood and Kelsall
>   *Go ahead*
>   *these hands say*
>   *cross into the white foam of your future*
>   *Go ahead*
>   *you will be left with*
>   *yourselves*
>   *and the full memory of our eyes*
>   *burning*
>   *in all of our*
>   *children's*
>   *eyes*
>   They are waving
>   to us
>   They are waving
>   as they start home
>   (62–3; italics in original)

As much as they look back to the beginning of the art critic's observations on *The Slave Ship*, 'these upraised hands' that wave and call in the selfsame synaesthetic gesture resonate also with the evocation of the singing sea at the end of the poem's second ekphrastic fragment, echoing the watery inducement to the dancing slaves to '*Come home*' via the bittersweet channels of suicide. Yet the critical difference is that the hand-waving slaves in Turner's sea have not heroically willed or chosen their own demise but, if not dead already, are dying as a result of having been thrown overboard. The art critic claims 'there is nothing hidden now', but the opposite is the case, as his reading of the 'final sign' left by the gesticulating slaves works to mask the truth of Turner's painting. That truth is itself underwritten by the manuscript-verse Turner attached to his picture when it first went on display. Here the artist-cum-poet's lines ironically link the hands in the sea with those of the sailors on board the ship, themselves 'straining' to secure the vessel against destruction:

> Aloft all hands, strike the top-masts and belay;
> Yon angry setting sun and fierce-edged clouds
>   Declare the Typhon's coming.
>   Before it sweep your decks, throw overboard

The dead and dying – ne'er heed their chains.
Hope, Hope, fallacious Hope!
Where is thy market now? (qtd. in Ziff 341)

In reading the slaves' hands in the tendentious way he does, the art critic aligns himself with other evasive figures, from the slaves not-yet-jettisoned to the historically unanchored Ruskin. Equally, though, the vigour with which he asserts the veracity of his own reading, with his 'What you can see here', 'You can see' and double 'Look', lends him a certain resemblance to the naval officer from the poem's epistolary sections, similarly bent upon imposing his pro-slave trade views upon his 'dear' but sceptical 'friend'. Ultimately, though, it would appear that the art critic himself is unpersuaded by his own interpretative sleight of hand – the hermeneutic transformation of Turner's painting that he attempts – describing it, after all, as a 'dream' and even attributing it not to himself but to the 'living / left on board / the ship'. The dream in the sense of the ideal (in this case, a triumphant return to Africa) is also a dream in the sense that it is an illusion, a death wish, or, to use the terms of Turner's verse, a pathetic and 'fallacious Hope'.

Conclusion

Just as the art critic urges his unidentified companion, in this flurry of departures and farewells, to 'Look' at and interpret the slaves' 'hands' before they vanish altogether, so this chapter concludes by proposing that looking at 'The Slave Ship' – a poem currently hovering on the verge of its own critical extinction – is a valuable project. This is so not only in terms of what such a project reveals about the text itself but also with regard to how recognition of Patrick's poem helps circumvent the prevailing critical assumption that Dabydeen's 'Turner' is the only poetic work in which the legacy of *The Slave Ship* lives on.[9] Study of 'The Slave Ship' is of still wider benefit and significance when the relative infrequency with which contemporary white writers have tackled the subject of the Middle Passage (ekphrastically or otherwise) is borne in mind.[10]

Notes

1. The engagement with the archive of colonial history that Patrick's use of this particular source represents is also evident in the two poems

appearing in *These Upraised Hands* on either side of 'The Slave Ship' – 'In the New World' (37–50) and 'The Island of Birds' (64–71).

2. The complicated sequence of events resulting in the sale of *The Slave Ship* is documented in Stephen May 156–85. May also devotes some space to the painting's American reception – which largely mirrors the puzzlement and mockery of the earlier British response – but for more detail see Walker; and McCoubrey 349–52. Although Twain's low opinion of *The Slave Ship* did not change, it should be seen in the context of a larger appreciation of Turner's almost supernatural artistic power, which seems to hold him captive. As Twain comments, in his own footnote to his critique of the painting:

> Months after this was written, I happened into the National Gallery in London, and soon became so fascinated with the Turner pictures that I could hardly get away from the place. I went there often, afterward, meaning to see the rest of the gallery, but the Turner spell was too strong; it could not be shaken off. However, the Turners which attracted me most did not remind me of the Slave Ship. (158)

3. While Dabydeen's critique of Ruskin's reading of *The Slave Ship* has exerted a strong influence on numerous critics, it has also been challenged, most trenchantly by Frost, who sees Ruskin's response as in fact morally engaged by the picture's subject matter rather than blind to it. See Frost 382–6.

4. For a thorough analysis of the evolution of the image of the *Brookes* and the part it played during the political struggles of the abolitionist era, see Rediker 308–42.

5. As Skeehan argues, such a 'soundscape' is composed not only from the sounds made by slaves' voices (and bodies) but also 'the material conditions of their imprisonment – instruments of labor, chains, and the ship itself'. As well as necessarily eluding the written record of the slave trade, it is invariably linked, she argues, to slaves' strategies of resistance to their oppression.

6. These include the account by Trotter, which notes that, although the practice is 'general in the trade', it was only 'used' on the *Brookes* when 'exercise became absolutely necessary for [slaves'] health' (*Abridgment* 38).

7. The sailors' rough command perhaps also carries an echo of 'Jump Jim Crow', a blackface song-and-dance routine whose composition is credited to Thomas Dartmouth 'Daddy' Rice in the late 1820s. As Olson notes, Rice's choreography for this act 'borrowed heavily from African American dancing' and this was a feature that 'distinguished [it] from previous blackface routines and probably accounted for [the] act's great popularity', on both sides of the Atlantic. It is thus, as Olson adds, an 'early example of the exploitation of African American culture by Anglo American (sic) popular entertainers' (399).

8. In setting the number of the drowned at 135, Patrick adds three victims to the more usually cited but not necessarily more accurate figure of 132, which itself conflicts dramatically with the figure of 'one hundred and fifty ... negro slaves' (Lyall 242) given during the King's Bench hearings, held in May 1783, to consider the insurers' request for the retrial. This deadly uncertainty in the mathematics of the archive is compounded by the fact that 'some time after the ship arrived in Jamaica in December 1781, the *Zong*'s logbook went missing, and all formal record of the killings on that ship – and what had preceded them – simply vanished' (Walvin, *Zong* 140).
9. Two other shorter poems that challenge that assumption in interesting ways are Douglas Kearney's '***SWIMCHANT FOR NIGGER MERFOLK (AN AQUABOOGIE SET IN LAPIS)***' (2009) and R. T. Smith's 'Turner's *Slave Ship*' (2014). While critical ink is yet to be expended on Smith's poem, Kearney's text has been discussed by Shockley 796–806. Although she compares this poem with the more sustained (and radical) experimentation of Philip's *Zong!* (2008), Shockley does not go so far as to read it ekphrastically, even as Kearney himself has suggested both its affinities with the ekphrastic genre and its recourse to a visual poetics. See 'MAST', Kearney's blogpost for 24 January 2011. Kearney does not name *The Slave Ship* as a source or stimulus for '***SWIMCHANT***', but there are many connections between poem and painting.
10. The key exception to this pattern, in the decade when Patrick's poem appeared, is Unsworth's *Sacred Hunger* (1992), an epically scaled historical novel which is itself inspired by the story of the *Zong*.

Chapter 3

'Slave-Ships on Fantastic Seas': The Art of Abolition

Introduction

In 'Hayden in the Archive' (2010), Elizabeth Alexander looks back affectionately to the earlier African-American poet whom her poem's title honours, imagining him absorbed in the painstaking (and painful) labour of researching the transatlantic slave trade:

> Stoop-shouldered, worrying the pages,
> index finger moving down the log,
> column by column of faded ink.
>
> Blood from a turnip, this
> protagonist-less
> Middle Passage.
>
> Does the log yield lyric?

Here the question with which these lines conclude is rhetorical: the anonymised 'log' over which Hayden stoops and broods does indeed 'yield lyric', in the polyphonic late Modernist shape of 'Middle Passage' (1966), one of the most innovative and sophisticated poems to confront the historical catastrophe at its heart.

For others writing after 'Middle Passage' it is not so much the textual as the visual dimensions of the slave trade's archive that provide the occasion for utterance, as demonstrated in the poems by David Dabydeen and William B. Patrick discussed in the previous two chapters; and in those by Alexander herself and Honorée Fanonne Jeffers that are the focus, respectively, for this chapter's first two sections: 'Islands Number Four' and 'Illustration: "Stowage of the British Slave Ship 'Brookes' under the Regulated Slave Trade Act of 1788."'[1] But while Dabydeen and Patrick take J. M. W. Turner's *The Slave Ship* as the principal ekphrastic cue for their poems, Alexander and Jeffers look variously to earlier materials, in the form of the seemingly ubiquitous *Description of a Slave Ship* (1789), itself evoked, if only briefly, in Patrick; and the cognate print, *Stowage of the British Slave Ship 'Brookes' under the Regulated Slave Trade Act of 1788* (c. 1788), from which Jeffers, of course, takes her poem's title.

While it begins by exploring Alexander and Jeffers's responses to these prints, the chapter moves on, in its third and longest section, to analyse Matthew Plampin's *Will & Tom* (2015), a densely plotted and tonally mercurial novel about Turner's early career, in which 'terror' is often 'transformed into / Comedy' (Dabydeen 25) and vice versa. In this 'dark farce' (Plampin 60), Plampin gives the *Stowage* print an important role, imagining how it might have come athwart Turner's path at a point in his life when he is in the process of trying to establish himself professionally, in this case by undertaking a commission at Harewood House, an English stately home constructed in the mid-1700s. But as well as engaging, like Alexander and Jeffers, with this visual material, Plampin integrates into his novel another equally compelling abolitionist image, in the form of the illustration (mentioned in this book's introduction) that appears in Charles van Tenac's *Histoire Générale de la Marine* (*General History of the Navy*) (1847–8), where it is captioned 'Négrier Poursuivi, Jetant ses Nègres à la Mer' ('Slave Ship Being Pursued, Throwing its Blacks into the Sea'). As Handler and Steiner observe, this image 'accompanies a description of an incident that occurred at an unspecified date, but apparently sometime after abolition of the slave trade, near the Indian ocean island of Bourbon (present-day Reunion)' (66n) and is thus strictly speaking an anachronistic presence in Plampin's text. Even so, as both this image and the *Stowage* print appear and reappear across the course of Plampin's narrative, they at once plunge Turner into a crisis of witnessing and contribute to the vision of the Middle Passage which will eventually manifest itself in *The Slave Ship*.

1. Looking Beyond the Visible: Elizabeth Alexander's 'Islands Number Four'

Elizabeth Alexander's 'Islands Number Four' was originally commissioned for *Words for Images: A Gallery of Poems* (2001), a book which, as one of its editors, Joanna Weber, puts it, 'bring[s] poets who were once students back to the . . . campus' at Yale University to 'interact' with the 'objects' (ix) housed in that institution's Art Gallery. One such object is Agnes Martin's *Islands No. 4*, an abstract expressionist painting produced c. 1961 and positioned in the book on the right-hand page directly opposite Alexander's poem (Fig. 3.1). This small work (it is just 37.8 centimetres square) features twelve 'oval capsules', each traversed either six or seven times by the 'horizontal line' that, as Weber explains, is one of Martin's hallmarks and 'encased in a grid' in such a way, Weber continues, as to resemble 'an archipelago of islands organized as neatly as if they were in an ice cube tray' (82).

Alexander responds to this thought-provoking minimalist picture in her poem's enigmatic first stanza:

1.

Agnes Martin, *Islands Number Four*,
Repeated ovals on a grid, what appears
To be perfect is handmade, disturbed.
Tobacco brown saturates canvas to burlap,
Clean form from a distance, up close, her hand.
All wrack and bramble to oval and grid.
Hollows in the body, containers for grief.
What looks to be perfect is not perfect.

Odd oval portholes that flood with light. (italics in original)

As the poem continues, however, it becomes clear that Alexander is doing something more daring and complex than simply providing an ekphrastic gloss on another's artistic creation, stepping outside the frame of what is directly visible to make an engagement with an image that the reader cannot see on the page and that, on the face of it, could hardly be further removed from Martin's. This ghostly image is that of the *Brookes*, abruptly introduced at the beginning of stanza two:

2.

Description of a Slave Ship. 1789:
Same imperfect ovals, calligraphic hand.
At a distance, pattern. Up close, bodies
Doubled and doubled, serried and stacked
In the manner of galleries in a church.

'Slave-Ships on Fantastic Seas': The Art of Abolition   69

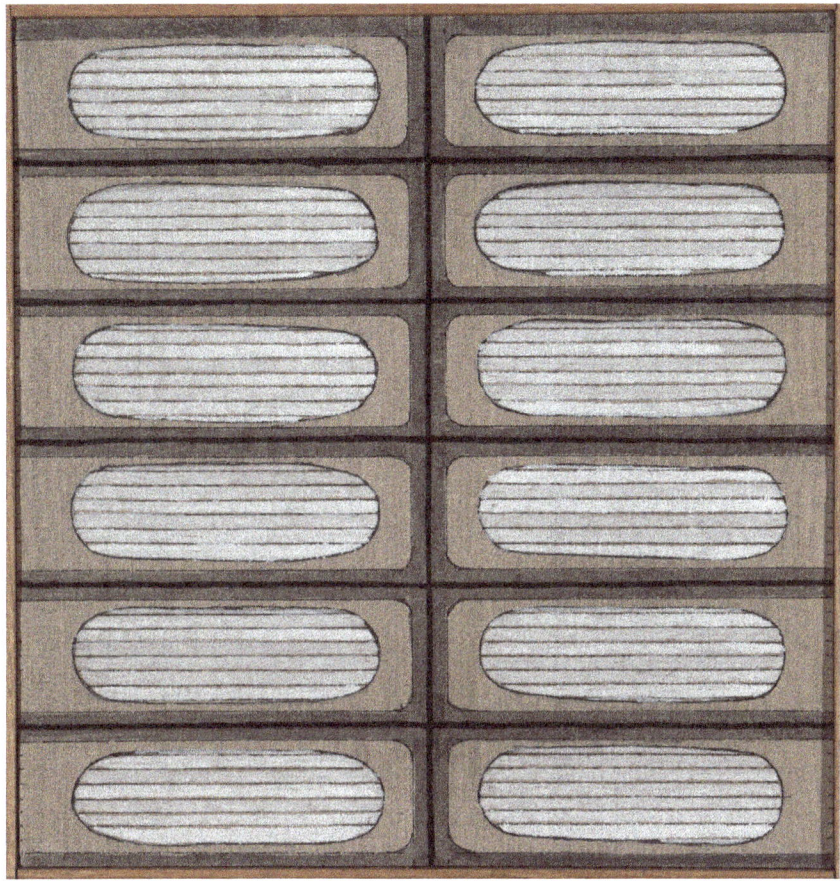

Figure 3.1 Agnes Martin, *Islands No. 4*, c. 1961 (oil on canvas). Yale University Art Gallery, Gift of the Woodward Foundation. © Agnes Martin Foundation, New York / DACS 2021.

In full ships on their sides or on each other.
Isle of woe, two-by-two, spoon-fashion,
Not unfrequently found dead in the morning.
Slave-ships, the not-pure, imperfect ovals,
Portholes through which they would never see home.
The flesh rubbed off their shoulders, elbows, hips.
Barracoon, sarcophagus, indestructible grief
Nesting in the hollows of the abdomen.
The slave-ship empty, its cargo landed
And sold for twelve ounces of gold a-piece

Or gone overboard. Islands. Aftermath. (italics in original)

On more considered inspection, however, the differences between these two images – the seen and the unseen, the modern and the archival, Martin's painting and *Description* – prove to be not quite so pronounced. Such an effect is curiously appropriate, given that it is brought about by the way in which, in Alexander's poem, the meanings of the two images themselves change as the distance from which they are contemplated is reduced.

In the case of Martin's picture, the regimented set of 'repeated ovals on a grid' of which it is composed initially gives the impression of 'clean form from a distance' but, when observed 'up close', reveals the traces of its production and, in particular, the artist's 'hand' – the shaping instrument which at once 'disturb[s]' the mechanical symmetries of the 'canvas' and sullies them with the touch of the human. Such subtle adulterations of the depersonalised effect for which the artist seems to strive are registered, in Alexander's text, by the poem's own play of subtly imperfect repetition. This begins with the poem's title (reappearing in italics in the first line), which quietly alters Martin's *Islands No. 4* to 'Islands Number Four' and is continued in the minor discrepancies of phrase that, for instance, revise 'what appears / To be perfect is handmade' into 'what looks to be perfect is not perfect'. But as well as detecting the presence of Martin's hand behind the apparent geometrical purities of 'oval and grid', the poem's speaker begins to invest the elusive images she sees with her own humanising meaning: Martin's gridded ovals are interpreted as 'hollows in the body' which are subsequently refigured as 'containers for grief', before finally turning into mysterious 'portholes that flood with light'.

The terms in which the speaker constructs the twelve abstract forms populating Martin's picture might seem somewhat arbitrary, but become less so when apprehended from the perspective of the poem's second stanza, in which, as already noted, the text shifts its ground from the realms of abstract art to those of *Description* and the slave trade. Here the speaker once more gains insight into the visual materials with which the poem deals at this point by means of an interpretative double take. When first observed 'at a distance', the image of the *Brookes* appears to feature the 'same imperfect ovals' as characterise Martin's work and to be organised in terms of a similar 'pattern'. Yet when examined 'up close', these forms show themselves in fact as captured African 'bodies' brusquely crammed into the different apartments of the slaver's lower deck – 'doubled and doubled, serried and stacked', as Alexander puts it – with the adult male slaves chain-hyphenated together, 'two-by-two', for good measure.

Martin's painting, in other words, provides the speaker with a way of approaching the representation of the slave ship while the latter provides a reciprocal frame of reference for interpreting the painting and understanding the speaker's response to it: the painting, it thus emerges, is haunted not only by the vestigial trace of the artist's hand but also by the spectral memory of a disturbing history, with the two images in the poem entering into dialogue with one another. In this way, Martin's work lends strange weight to Marcus Rediker's own haunting description of 'the slaver' as a kind of 'ghost ship sailing on the edges of modern consciousness' (13).

It would be an exaggeration to claim that the respective parts of the poem to which these images are assigned are held together with anything like the same force as the shackled figures in *Description*, but they are certainly suggestively interlinked all the same. One way in which Alexander forges the connections is by verbal association, with several of the terms used in the first stanza obliquely looking forward to the second by means of their resonances either with the nautical world more proper to the *Brookes* ('wrack', 'portholes', 'flood' and the punning 'canvas') or with plantation labour ('tobacco' and 'burlap'), while another is repetition. As noted above, the repetition with slight differences of phrases is an important aspect of the poem's first stanza but ultimately something that pervades it as a whole, as particular formulations are reworked: 'up close, her hand' becomes 'up close, bodies', for instance and 'hollows in the body, containers for grief' becomes 'indestructible grief / Nesting in the hollows of the abdomen'. This mosaic of phrasings and rephrasings is complemented both by the poem's phonetic order, which is dominated by the long and short 'o'-sound and by its lineation, with the last line of each stanza cut adrift from the block of verse that precedes it.

The image of the *Brookes* that Alexander invokes is far more overtly charged politically than Martin's *Islands* and absorbs more of the poem's imaginative energy (receiving some sixteen lines as opposed to nine), not least because it raises a number of questions about the interplay between verbal and visual modes of representation in which Alexander is herself interested. The image was originally produced and circulated by William Elford and the Plymouth Chapter of the British Society for Effecting the Abolition of the Slave Trade in November 1788 but quickly reappeared in several further editions published the following year in London, Philadelphia and New York and was copied and distributed by the thousand. While these four versions of the image are all accompanied by an extensive written commentary, what is striking about the most widely reproduced London version is the way in which it recalibrates the ratio of visual materials to verbal. This iteration of the print endows those visual materials with a much greater technical sophistication and complexity than is manifested by its three cognates, offering some seven views of the slaver (rather than the single view to which the other broadsides are restricted) and it also significantly reduces the amount of space available on the page for the written text. Emphasis on the visual dimension of the *Brookes*'s representation is even more extreme today: the image is now routinely used (or overused) by publishing houses to promote and sell books about the slave trade by novelists, historians and literary and cultural critics but invariably appears in this commercial context shorn of writing altogether (even as, ironically, what it advertises is precisely textual).[2]

Perhaps one way of accounting for the privileging of the visual in these ways is in terms of the assumption that images are ultimately more powerful than words as a means of conveying the trials the slaves underwent during the Middle Passage. Such an assumption is one which Alexander's poem will significantly challenge, but it certainly appears to underpin Thomas Clarkson's narrative of how the image of the *Brookes* both came about and was subsequently refined. As he tells it in *The History of the Rise, Progress, and Accomplishment of the Abolition of the African Slave-Trade by the British Parliament* (1808):

> The [Plymouth] committee also in this interval brought out their famous print of the plan and section of a slave-ship; which was designed to give the spectator an idea of the sufferings of the Africans in the Middle Passage, and this so familiarly, that he might instantly pronounce upon the miseries experienced there. The committee at Plymouth had been the first to suggest the idea; but that in London had now improved it. As this print seemed to make an instantaneous impression of horror upon all who saw it, and as it was therefore very instrumental, in consequence of the wide circulation given it, in serving the cause of the injured Africans, I have given the reader a copy of it in the annexed plate. (111)

Here it is noticeable that Clarkson, writing in the immediate aftermath to the slave trade's abolition in 1807, defines the recipient of the 'copy' of the 'famous print' he is discussing as a 'reader', whereas, when he reminisces about the preabolitionist period when the print was an instrument of political change, he uses a different nomenclature. In this more urgent context, the recipient is a collective 'spectator', exposed 'so familiarly' to the 'sufferings of the Africans in the Middle Passage' that 'he' 'instantly' becomes an authority able to 'pronounce upon' their 'miseries', receiving an 'impression of horror' that is, once again, 'instantaneous'.

There is no doubt that the image of the *Brookes* is a shocking one, confronting its beholder with a vision of the slave trade which it is hard to forget. Yet as much as it purveys 'horror', the image to some degree also screens or detracts from it, particularly with regard to those endlessly duplicated 'bodies' to which Alexander's text alludes. While these are so arranged in *Description* as to give the viewer an overwhelming sense of the Middle Passage's claustrophobic atmosphere, they seem strangely self-contained, especially with regard to the corporeal secretions that would be released during the Atlantic voyage. Yet even as this sense of sickening bodily discharge is thus expelled from *Description* in visual terms, it is communicated verbally in the personal abolitionist testimony of the ex-slave-ship surgeon, Alexander Falconbridge, whom *Description* quotes in the fourth and final column of the written text: 'The deck, that is, the floor of [the slaves'] rooms,' Falconbridge recalls, 'was so covered with the blood and mucus which had proceeded from them in consequence of the flux, that it resembled a slaughter-house.' Word supplements image, filling out its lack.

Together with their aura of self-containment, the enslaved bodies that *Description* renders visually appear surprisingly whole and vigorous, as if somehow uncorrupted by the often fatal illnesses to which they would normally be prone and which, as *Description* lists them, not only include the 'flux' (or dysentery), but also 'small-pox, measles . . . and other contagious disorders'. These impressions are corrected, however, both by *Description*'s written text and Alexander's poem, with its near-verbatim incorporation of three fragments of that text, using a similar collage technique to that deployed in Hayden's 'Middle Passage' and combining this with an italicised type perhaps suggestive of the sideways position slaves were often obliged to take up: '*In full ships on their sides or on each other*'; '*Not unfrequently found dead in the morning*'; and '*The flesh rubbed off their shoulders, elbows, hips*'.

This technique extends beyond *Description* (the version of the *Brookes* broadside Alexander explicitly names) to *Stowage*, the one she does not (Fig. 3.2). In this contemporary etching, the amount of written text provided is drastically reduced from the estimated 'twenty-four hundred words' (Rediker 317) included in *Description*, while at the same time being more freely interspersed among the visual materials (rather than fixed beneath them). One feature of this writing is that it is partly inscribed in the same 'calligraphic hand' as is used in places in *Description* and whose flowing elegance not only collapses the distinction between word and image but also clashes with the grotesque realities it records, as, for example, in the comments about the number of persons the *Brookes* transported prior to the Regulation Act. As this broadside discloses in the note squeezed into its top-right corner, the slaver 'had at one time carried as many as 609 Slaves', reaching this capacity 'by taking some out of Irons & locking them spoonwise (to use the technical term) that is by stowing one within the distended legs of the other'.

Such a stark contrast between the beauty of the calligraphic medium and the ugliness of the message is consistent with the analogical yoking together of profane and sacred spaces that occurs in the centre of the page in bold upper-case letters: **'PLAN SHEWING (sic) THE STOWAGE OF 130 ADDITIONAL SLAVES ROUND THE WINGS OR SIDES OF THE LOWER DECK BY MEANS OF PLATFORMS OR SHELVES (IN THE MANNER OF GALLERIES IN A CHURCH)'**. These two textual snippets are subtly reworked in Alexander's poem, as she revises 'spoonwise' into 'spoon-fashion' and alters the visual aspect of the parenthetical phrase just quoted, so that it reappears in her poem in the standard italic font which, as previously indicated, she uses at other points: '*In the manner of galleries in a church*'.

In reclaiming such fragments from the archive of representations to which the *Brookes* has given rise, Alexander contests the primacy of the visual mode, placing an imaginative counter-faith in the ability of the written word to act as an effective conduit of historical memory. Yet she is not content with simply letting that word speak for itself, as it were, but augments its powers, doing so by means of the arresting figuration of the *Brookes* as a 'sarcophagus', an entity defined by the *OED* as a 'kind of stone reputed among the Greeks to have the property of consuming the flesh of dead bodies deposited in it, and consequently used for coffins'. In Alexander, that is, the flesh of Clarkson's 'injured Africans' is not just flayed by its frictional movement against the 'chains' and 'bare boards' to which *Description* refers but actively eaten away from the bodies of those who do not survive such trials.

Ultimately, however, the written word can no more do justice to the truth of the slave trade than the visual image, as Alexander's poem would seem perhaps to recognise on reaching its conclusion.

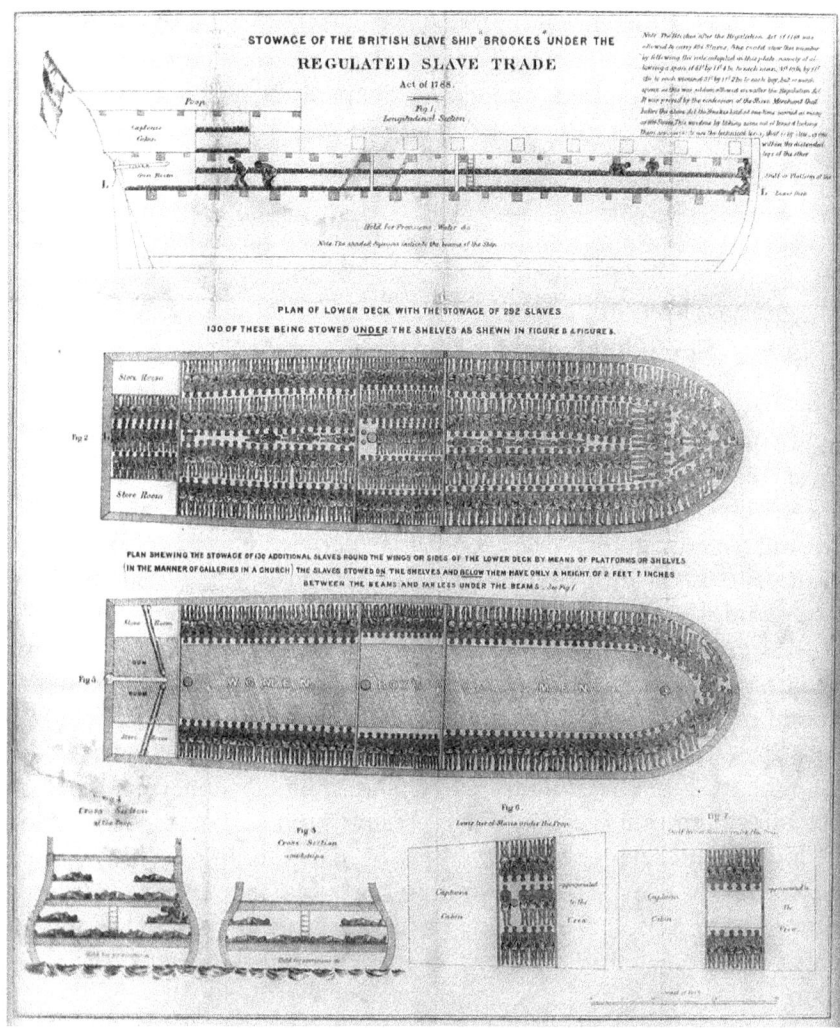

Figure 3.2 *Stowage of the British Slave Ship 'Brookes' under the Regulated Slave Trade Act of 1788,* c. 1788. Library of Congress Rare Book and Special Collections Division, Washington, DC.

At this point, the 'slave-ship' is 'empty, its cargo landed / And sold for twelve ounces of gold a-piece' (a sum which incidentally looks back or across to the dozen silvery ovals featured in Martin's painting), even as other slaves are said, in the poem's last line to have 'gone overboard'. In deploying so nondescript a phrase, Alexander's text not only nods towards the *Zong* episode, but also hints, ironically, at the imperfections of the linguistic medium it elsewhere affirms, leaving itself no option but to come to a sudden halt with two one-word sentences: 'Islands. Aftermath.' These respectively return the text to its beginning (and the painting that was its original impetus), restarting the processes of re-vision with which Alexander is preoccupied.

2. 'A Body is *Some* Body': Honorée Fanonne Jeffers's 'Illustration: "Stowage of the British Slave Ship 'Brookes' under the Regulated Slave Trade Act of 1788"'

The two *Brookes* schemata to which Alexander alludes in 'Islands' confirm her deliberately awkward description in 'Hayden in the Archive' of the Middle Passage as 'protagonist-less', presenting the spectacle of slaves reduced *en masse* to interchangeable and ill-distinguished figures. Even so, some of these figures were able to transcend such anonymising conditions, an especially salient literary example being Phillis Wheatley, who was brought from Africa to Boston aged just seven or eight in 1761 and went on to become the first black woman to publish a book in the United States, in the shape of *Poems on Various Subjects, Religious and Moral* (1773), just three years before the Declaration of Independence.

Wheatley's extraordinary life has stimulated numerous African-American responses, the most recent and accomplished being Honorée Fanonne Jeffers's *The Age of Phillis* (2020).[3] In 'Illustration: "Stowage of the British Slave Ship 'Brookes' under the Regulated Slave Trade Act of 1788"', one of the poems in the second 'Book' of this collection, Jeffers transfers Wheatley from the *Phillis* (the slave ship from which her first name was taken) to the *Brookes*, using the switch as a vehicle to Wheatley's interior world and specifically, the warping psychological pressures to which the Atlantic crossing exposes her:

>There is no air.

>Closer. The stinky aria.
>   The bodies' relentless outlines

>on either side.
>   Above, below –

>at some distance, the appearance
>   of Kente's intricate bands, or,

a longed-for version of what
        a village potter might throw.

I dream of breath,
        the stealing from

pretty faces, the smoothness
        of the best chocolate.

A tweakable, selfish nose.
        A body is *some* body. (I know that.)

And theft?
        The hoping for the death

of somebody else.
        Not of my family.

Not of my tribe.

        My Maker up there,
please, make the one

        next to me die. There is no air.
Give me a teaspoon of life.

I don't care how.

        I don't. (italics in original)

According to Clarkson, as noted in the discussion of Alexander's 'Islands', the image of the *Brookes*, in whatever version, precipitates a feeling of 'instantaneous . . . horror', and this claim would seem to be borne out by this poem's first phase (lines 1–9). Here the horror in question is experienced not only visually, however, but also through the combined senses of smell and hearing – 'The stinky aria' that usurps the air. Yet no sooner are these feelings of revulsion introduced than they are blocked, as the third-person speaker steps back from the image whose closeness simultaneously and synaesthetically oppresses to a safer vantage, from which the stifling conditions aboard the slave ship can be masked, thus changing the relationship between viewer and viewed in a way reminiscent of the spatial and ocular shifts in Alexander. With this retreat, the image of the *Brookes* is no longer associated with diaspora and despair but transformed into a symbol of Africa and, particularly, African artistry. Looked at from an apotropaic distance, it assumes the homespun and inviting 'appearance / of Kente's intricate bands' and perhaps even recalls 'what / a village potter might throw'.

Yet as the poem moves into its longer second phase (lines 10–26), the comforts and attractions tentatively achieved at the end of the first evaporate, replaced by a more unsettling mood. This change is accompanied by the entrance into the poem of a first-person speaker, who displaces the third-person narrator of the opening nine lines and is implicitly the young Wheatley herself, recounting her experience of being inside the slave ship, rather than beholding its representation from a point either too close to or reassuringly removed from it. In addition to this, there is a sense in which, from this moment onwards, the reader also enters the psychic territory of the poem's newly emergent 'I' and in doing so is brought into the presence of a mind whose thoughts and emotions are perhaps not organised quite as might be expected. While the *Brookes* can be likened to a mass prison, the conventional assumption is that there is at least a solidarity among the Africans condemned to it, united as they are in opposition to their white masters. But in Jeffers's poem, this assumption is challenged, as tensions and conflicts appear between the incarcerated slaves themselves. As Phillis dreams about the 'pretty faces' of the African villagers from whom she has been separated, she covets not only the 'breath' that 'steal[s]' from them but also that which emanates from the mouths of her rather more proximate shipmates. In contrast to how they are depicted in the *Brookes* diagram, these fellow slaves are endowed with hints of individual identity – 'A body is *some* body', after all – and yet at the same time eyed with murderous intent, as Phillis secretly hopes for the 'death // of somebody else' that will grant her more 'air', however noisome it might be. In this way, Jeffers also overturns the racial and racist stereotype, as the child-slave she portrays is no passive victim to be pitied and liberated by the merciful interventions of white abolitionists but someone determined to survive the Middle Passage at any cost, including the deadly 'theft' of others' breath. From this perspective, the irony of the poem becomes evident, since it is not the 'tweakable ... nose' belonging to one of the other slaves aboard the slave ship that is 'selfish' but that of Phillis herself. That said, as the poem closes, it is as if even Jeffers wants to retreat from the new image of enslavement she has crafted. While Phillis can be found wishing for the demise of one of her companions, responsibility for the act of suffocation she envisages is quickly displaced onto God: 'My Maker up there, / please, make the one // next to me die.'

3. Art and Abolition: Matthew Plampin's *Will & Tom*

Matthew Plampin's *Will & Tom* is divided into three sections, the first and much the longest of which is set mainly at Harewood House in Yorkshire during a single week in August 1797, with each of its seven chapters keyed to a single day in a linear series from Tuesday to Monday. The second and third sections (which do not have chapter-divisions) respectively unfold three months later in Covent Garden (Turner's birthplace) and in Charing Cross in 1803. In its central concern with Turner's fledgling career, the novel looks back to and complements the two long poems discussed in Chapters 1 and 2, which engage with a major painting from the artist's mature period.

As Plampin observes in his 'Author's Note', *Will & Tom* 'combine[s] the historical facts' of Turner's visit to Harewood with 'a number of elements' that are 'either invented or unverifiable'. In this sense, the work both manifests a similar approach to the past as characterises Jeffers's 'Illustration' and allows the reader to construe it as an imaginative speculation about some of the interpersonal and visual experiences that would eventually find their way into *The Slave Ship*. Plampin's 'Note' at the same time offers an insight into the genesis of his own work, particularly by calling attention to the 'two figures' in the left foreground of Turner's 1798 'eastern view of Harewood Castle', who, Plampin suggests, may represent the painter himself and his friend, fellow-artist and professional rival, Thomas Girtin – the one sitting upright and busily sketching while the other lies lazily by his side.[4] As Plampin cautions, it cannot be definitively established that Girtin was present at Harewood during Turner's time there, even as it nonetheless 'remains a clear possibility' (317) and one by which, equally clearly, Plampin is intrigued, using it as the inspiration for his text. Although *Will & Tom* could hardly be more different from David Dabydeen's 'Turner' (at first glance at least), the two works thus adopt a broadly similar approach in the manner of their engagement with the different phases of Turner's art: Dabydeen's poem gives voice to the drowned slave in the right-foreground of *The Slave Ship*, while Plampin's novel gravitates towards the pair of young painters tucked away amid the earthy hues of an early watercolour, naming and reframing them as its eponymous protagonists, both just twenty-two years old when the story begins.

Perhaps such resonances between 'Turner' and *Will & Tom* are ultimately less unexpected than they might appear, since, as the fictional world of the latter abundantly demonstrates, things should not be taken at face value. Either way, the texts' connections extend beyond their shared status as ekphrastic responses to dramatically different paintings by the same artist. This becomes evident from a more detailed reflection on the history of Harewood House itself: this 'vast mansion' (Plampin 3) was inherited from his cousin in 1795 by Edward Lascelles, the head of 'an ascendant gentry family' which, by that time, had risen from being 'super-merchant[s]' to a position of 'aristocratic eminence' (Smith 73) and whose enormous wealth was principally derived from euphemistic 'Atlantic interests'. These chiefly took the form of the slave-worked sugar plantations of Barbados, but other Caribbean theatres of cruelty were absorbed into the Lascelles' financial empire, including Antigua, Grenada, Jamaica and Tobago, as well as the South American territories of Demerara and Essequibo (Smith 7). The novel's primary location, in other words, is implicated in the same history of slavery as is addressed by Dabydeen in his text.

In 'Turner' the presence of that history is exhibited on the poem's surface from first to last, but emerges in *Will & Tom* more gradually and surreptitiously, only becoming explicit towards the end of 'Tuesday', the novel's opening chapter, in which the difficulties, class tensions and mysteries attending Turner's arrival at Harewood are delicately dramatised. Early on in the chapter, for example, Turner is conducted to his room through a dark 'basement' that seems like 'the lower deck of a huge merchant ship' – if not quite a slave ship – and whose 'air reeks of tallow and boot polish' (5). The disquieting effect which this part of the house has on the painter continues into the evening when he leaves his 'dingy bedchamber' (12) for a dinner held by his patron and the heir to the estate, Edward Lascelles the younger, 'known to his intimates as Beau' (18). Issuing from his 'casket chamber' (13) and proceeding upstairs to join the other guests and members of Beau's family, Turner finds himself 'at the rear of [an] entrance hall' filled with aesthetic splendours seemingly designed both to pay homage to the Lascelles' 'transcendent wealth' (15) and remind the aspiring artist of his lowly origins as the son of a 'wig-maker and barber' (Moyle 24). One of these splendours is 'a moulded ceiling of such Attic intricacy – such divisions and subdivisions, such a profusion of loops and laurels and minute, interlocking patterns – that it makes the eyeballs ache to study it' and creates an 'effect' which is 'oppressive' (Plampin 15). The sense of oppression produced by such magnificent and refined artwork is compounded when, prior to the dinner itself, Turner meets with Beau directly in the library beneath 'another of those staggering ceilings' (17), eager to negotiate the terms of the commission that has brought him to Harewood in the first place. As the narrator puts it, despite the fact that Turner's patron is largely unappealing in appearance (as well as snobbish, manipulative and cruel), 'every single aspect of his person' is 'shot through with a sense of easy dominion . . . brought about and upheld by the all-conquering power of cash' and exerted not only over Turner himself but 'the rest of humankind' (19).

As well as being discreetly signalled in Harewood's décor and the lordly demeanour of the estate's all-but-charmless heir, the brutal regime on which this country house is built is further intimated in the novel's evocation of the commodity with which slavery in the Caribbean is most closely associated: sugar. While his contemplation of the entrance-hall ceiling causes Turner an ocular pain so intense that he is forced to 'look[ ] elsewhere' (15), sugar and the delicacies it helps to create contrastingly attract the painter's eye, as indicated in the scene that takes place once Beau's repast has ended. Here the 'ladies' (29) of the company retire from the dining room, leaving it to be suddenly transformed into a locus of exclusively male delight:

> Servants bring in crystal brandy decanters, large tumblers and trays of sweetmeats, folding back the tablecloth to set them upon the polished wood beneath. Intrigued, Will leans forward to scrutinise the jewel-bright confections – selecting one that is a rich raspberry red and moulded in the shape of a conical sea shell. He gives the point a cautious nibble; the soft, jellied flesh dissolves instantly, flooding his mouth with a taste of summer fruit so succulent and intense that he nearly blurts out an oath. (29)

These regressive 'sweetmeats' are evidently so expertly fashioned and appealing that they could be works of art in themselves – the one that Turner chooses is even 'moulded' like the ceiling – and clearly afford a pleasure that is as much of the palate as the eye. Yet even as they tempt and sate, the 'jewel-bright confections' on offer here are less alluring than they might appear: the 'rich raspberry red' of the item Turner samples is suggestive, for instance, of blood, a connotation complemented and strengthened by the metaphor of the 'soft, jellied flesh' that dissolves so ecstatically in his 'mouth'.

In couching the consumption of these sugary treats in such equivocal terms, *Will & Tom* echoes the abolitionist discourse of the time, which frequently positioned the British sugar-eater as a kind of cannibal. In most cases, the equation between consumer and cannibal is figurative, as, for instance, in William Fox's widely read pamphlet, 'An Address to the People of Great Britain, on the Propriety of Abstaining from West India Sugar and Rum' (1791), in which, Fox argues, the 'consumption of the commodity' is so tightly 'connected' to 'the misery resulting from it, that in every pound of sugar used, (the produce of slaves imported from Africa) we may be considered as consuming two ounces of human flesh' (156). In Andrew Burn's 1792 reply to Fox, however, the cannibalism in question develops into grotesquely literal form. In this first-hand account, based on 'knowledge' derived from Burn's residence 'on a . . . Plantation in Jamaica' (4), the production of sugar is a deeply distasteful business, as the sweltering bodies of the slaves involved in readying it for shipment generate 'torrents of Blood and Sweat' (5) while 'pack[ing]' it 'in the Hogshead', 'tread[ing] it down with their feet' beneath the 'scorching rays of a vertical Sun' (6). These 'nauceous (sic) effluvia' (7), particularly sweat, become subsequently mixed up, along with 'many other savory (sic) ingredients' (6), in the commodity on which the 'dancing Blacks' (7) are working and are eventually ingested by other bodies located in British homes, stately or otherwise.

Given the links between the 'sweetmeats' (or sweatmeats) set out on the Harewood dining table and the visceral realities of the labour that goes into their production, it is perhaps appropriate that Turner's comfit should take the form of a 'conical sea shell', since this image functions as a memento of the Middle Passage, and in doing so also anticipates the climactic incident which brings the 'Tuesday' chapter to a close. Having secured the terms of his contract, Turner is keen to begin the studies for the six views of Harewood House and the surrounding estate that Beau 'desires' (32) as quickly as possible, not least because of a growing dislike for his patron's supercilious attitude towards his 'cockney project' (20), as Turner is disparagingly called. This he hopes to do by using the 'packet' (37) of a dozen tallow candles procured from Mrs Lamb, the enigmatic 'still-room maid' (36), who has made them according to her own 'special recipe' (37). As he discovers on returning to his 'quarters' (12), however, the candles are of insufficient quality for him to execute his task, even as they provide just enough light to illuminate the 'diagram' 'printed on the inside of the paper' (38) in which they have been wrapped:

A cargo ship is shown from several different angles – profile, elevation, cross-section – each one packed with tiny forms, serried rows of supine human beings. The printing is rudimentary, yet care has been taken to render every individual body; there are so many, however, and laid so close together, that Will's eye struggles to separate them in the low light. He recognises it, of course. These sheets were ten a penny a few years ago, nailed up by the Abolitionists in certain coffee shops or taverns. For a time they were much discussed; then, gradually, they weren't, the attention of London shifting elsewhere. He didn't even register their eventual disappearance from view.

Will sits slowly on his bed, staring at the image. This is trouble. The wellspring of the Lascelles' fortune is no secret: their West Indian holdings pay for it all, from the seats in Parliament to the gold buckles on the footmen's boots. Any material pertaining to Abolition will be contraband under their roof. If he's discovered with such a thing in his possession, it will surely be taken as a grave affront. He'll be dismissed. Word will get about – a reputation swiftly acquired. This crude print could well harm his standing with an entire stratum of London society. He has to rid himself of it at once.

Yet he does not move. His mind, quite involuntarily, has started to generate a picture. Chained Negro captives, children and adults alike, wallowing in gloom and filth. The dead left among the living – mothers with daughters, husbands with wives, sisters with brothers – their naked limbs entwined in lamentation. White lines of sunlight slanting in hard through cracks in the deck, tormenting the multitudes entombed below. Parched mouths gaping open in hoarse, hopeless cries.

He recoils sharply; the paper crumples in his hands. It can't be done. The misery is too great. Too vivid. As he looks away, he notices the diagram's heading – concise, descriptive only, yet loaded with outrage.

Stowage of the British Slave Ship 'Brookes' Under the Regulated Slave Trade. (38–9; italics in original)

Although this crepuscular 'image' portrays the sufferings of others – those 'supine human beings' drawn with ironic 'care' – and is itself a 'grave affront', Turner's initial response does not follow the Clarksonian assumption that the print will horrify all those who view it and thus elicit empathy. Rather Turner sees the broadside as the direct harbinger of an *ad hominem* 'trouble', since it is the manifestation of political and moral convictions antithetical to those espoused by his patron and consequently a material threat to the artistic, economic and social ambitions that the Harewood commission is designed to advance. While the 'wellspring of the Lascelles' fortune is no secret', the same cannot be said for the 'crude print''s circulation among the lower regions and ranks of the family abode, as it passes from 'still room' (13) to 'casket chamber' and servant to painter, requiring the latter to 'rid himself of it at once'.

Yet this illicit image of abolition, which Turner feels it is imperative for him precisely and immediately to abolish, proves to be surprisingly tenacious and in this sense not unlike the residues of 'the shell-shaped sweetmeat' that he had earlier 'carried ... from the table' and that start to 'liquefy against his skin' (31), remaining 'stuck to his palm' after the 'agreement' with Beau has been 'seal[ed]' (33). Indeed the print becomes a kind of Muse, prompting Turner to begin the composition of a mental 'picture' of the Middle Passage more personalised than the one he beholds, as the 'tiny forms' of the enslaved adopt familiar and familial identities as 'children and adults', 'mothers with daughters, husbands with wives, sisters with brothers'. It is as if the very image that seems at first to represent a danger or an obstacle to Turner's professional 'standing' and prospects has been changed into a resource for him to exploit creatively. Yet Turner's vision here is fleeting, collapsing under the weight of a 'misery' that is 'too great' and 'Too vivid' and that forces him (like the 'oppressive' ceiling earlier) to 'look[ ] away'. It is only in the sublime horror of *The Slave Ship*, painted more than forty years later, that Turner is able at last to bear witness to the spectacle of suffering that overwhelms him at this youthful stage of his artistic career and to give it permanent and concrete embodiment.

By the end of the novel's 'Wednesday' chapter, Turner has at least realised one of his ambitions, finally managing to destroy the troublesome and troubling print of the *Brookes* by 'feeding' it 'into the flame' from one of Mrs Lamb's 'tallow candle[s]' (60). Even so, this act of fiery destruction does not liberate the artist from the problems with which the print is associated, since the burning of this particular abolitionist image is only the prelude to the appearance of another, this time at the end of the novel's 'Thursday' chapter. In a scene which parallels the encounter with the *Brookes*, Turner once again enters his 'casket chamber' to find that Mrs Lamb has left him a second parcel of candles, ostensibly as a 'reward' for carrying a set of 'three slim silver trays' (51) to her still room – a somewhat humbler and less taxing commission than the one he is undertaking for Beau. On this occasion, however, the candles are not made of tallow but beeswax and 'identical to those burning upstairs [but] forbidden on the service floor' (92), the implication being that Mrs Lamb has not created but stolen them.

In contrast to their 'dirty grey' and 'sputtering' counterparts, whose light is 'barely adequate for reading, let alone making a sketch' (37), these superior 'white sticks seem to glow' and 'hold a trace of the radiance they will cast' (92). Yet the brightness they promise must be viewed as a mixed blessing, since it brings to light an image perhaps better left unseen:

> Again, there is print on the inside of the paper – an illustration this time, set in a rectangle in the top half of the page, with two columns of dense text beneath. The candles clack together as Will sets them on the bed; on impulse, he picks one up and touches it to the tallow stub. It flares immediately, smothering the tallow, filling the casket chamber as a flame fills a lantern.
>
> Will flattens out the sheet. It is headed *The British Slave Ship Zong Throwing Overboard the Dead and Dying*. The drawing, although inexpert, is unsparing in its confrontation of this notorious incident. Negro bodies cover a ship's deck, clad only in loincloths and irons. A number are being heaved up by sailors, by British tars, and tipped into the ocean. Most, despite the title, plainly live still. Some pray; some try feebly to resist and are lashed; all are surely doomed.
>
> Will is dimly aware of this case. A decade or more old, it has long been employed by the Abolition movement as the ultimate symbol of the slave trade's turpitude. As with the *Brookes*, his mind begins to roam around the image before him, to search out its possibilities – and again, there is a shock of revulsion at what he envisages. This time, however, he forces himself to persist. He dwells on the moments after the throw; what it would be to plunge into the limitless ocean, your limbs weighted and your body weakened by hunger and disease; the drag of the waves and the black chasm yawning beneath; the sun overhead, a drop of blinding fire, awful in its unconcern; and the despised prison ship, so cruelly transformed into your last chance for life, rolling off towards the horizon, forever beyond reach. (92–3; italics in original)

Although Plampin advertises this 'drawing' as depicting the massacre aboard the *Zong* and even gives it a title strongly redolent of Turner's masterpiece, the picture does not actually portray that 'notorious incident', it being the illustration found in Tenac and linked to another if apparently similar episode that took place somewhat later (Fig. 3.3). This is not, however, to accuse Plampin of historical error or a self-serving attempt to hoodwink the reader, but rather to recognise the way in which he himself has ingeniously reemployed a particularly powerful image, which clearly has a

Figure 3.3 'Négrier Poursuivi, Jetant ses Nègres à la Mer' ('Slave Ship Being Pursued, Throwing its Blacks into the Sea'), undated. Charles van Tenac, *Histoire Générale de la Marine*, vol. 4, Paris, 1847–8.

striking resonance with the *Zong* atrocity, for his own sophisticated fictional purposes.

Whether it is approached from a strict historical perspective or in terms of the anachronistic fictional frame that Plampin has wrought around it, the image is just as disturbing as that of the *Brookes*, even as the mechanism of its disturbance is different, not focusing on 'Negro bodies' crushed into the slave ship's hold but the murderous moment in which they are jettisoned. It draws attention, in particular, to the female slave who is in the process of being 'tipped into the ocean' by two French 'sailors', reimagined in Plampin as 'British tars'.

Turner's response to this scene resembles his reaction to the schema of the *Brookes*, insofar as he is once again moved to look beyond the immediacy of what he sees: his 'mind begins to roam around the image' and 'search out its possibilities', thus indulging in a freedom diametrically opposed to the conditions which beset the entrammelled slaves at whom he gazes. Yet his response is also different because he does not abandon but this time 'persist[s]' with his imaginative explorations, despite the 'shock of revulsion' that they cause. In one sense, those explorations both take him back to and transmute the material circumstances in which they occur, as the flaring beeswax candle reappears in the heightened form of an unpitying 'sun overhead', figured, as in *The Slave Ship* itself, as 'a drop of blinding fire'. On the other hand, they cast him forward into the 'moments after the throw' and in doing so raise the question of the meaning of the word 'your', which features three times in the course of the description of that terrifying durée. Is this seemingly innocuous pronoun intended as a means by which Turner raises a defence against his own speculations by thinking of himself in the second person or is it addressed in fact to the female slave as she crashes into the 'limitless ocean'?

These two abolitionist images make their purveyor seem a contradictory figure, since her role as still-room maid with a particular talent for making 'confectionary' (56) – she is mockingly celebrated by Girtin as being 'Without equal . . . in the domain of preserves, pickles and such like' (74) – obliges her routinely to work with the very commodity against which the abolitionists campaigned. But the contradictions are only apparent, as Mrs Lamb turns out in the end to be no more what she seems than is the sugar she sprinkles across the 'hundreds' of fanciful 'sweetmeats' (53) set out on those silver trays and created to titillate the mouths of the '*bon ton*' (17; italics in original): 'ruby red sea shells, like the one Will sampled; stars of jade with trailing tails; azure fishes beside coral-pink piglets' (53).[5]

On first arriving at Harewood, Turner assumes that Mrs Lamb is a 'heath gypsy' or 'gypsy maid' (7), while Girtin adopts the common opinion of the estate's other employees that she is a free-born Irishwoman who 'came over' to England in 'childhood' as 'Travelling stock' and 'Started off' earning her living 'in the kitchens of Leeds' (74). According to Mrs Lamb's own account, however, neither such private nor public assumptions about her identity are valid, a point she impresses upon Turner in an exchange which takes place, in the novel's 'Sunday' chapter, in one of Harewood's greenhouses – a building appropriately designed, for a scene of revelation, 'to trap as much light as possible' (71).

Here, amid 'tropical leaves swimming in sunlight', Mrs Lamb invites her interlocutor to reflect upon the 'field' from which the Lascelles 'harvest' their 'gold': 'Where does it come from, d'ye reckon, this fortune of theirs?' she asks, in a tone at once 'calm and ... incensed' (229). Turner is of course already aware (albeit reluctantly) of what it is that facilitates the Lascelles' luxury, as is the much more politicised and radical Girtin, who excoriates 'the floggings' administered in 'Lord Harewood's name' 'on black backs and shackled black limbs, many hundreds of miles from Yorkshire' (132). What Turner does not know, however, is that, unlike Girtin's, Mrs Lamb's concern with this regime of violence and suffering has a painfully personal dimension. As Turner sits 'motionless' on the greenhouse's 'dirt floor' (229), her question not only brings back Girtin's words but also revives the unwanted images of the two slave ships she has gifted him – and prepares the ground for his (and the reader's) enlightenment:

> Will recalls Tom's talk at Plumpton, of floggings and shackles; the terrible diagram of the *Brookes* and that scene from the deck of the *Zong*. He gazes at the still-room maid's enlaced fingers – at the slightest tint of ochre that warms her skin, which he in his ignorance took for a sign of gypsy blood.
>   'I'm a slave,' Mrs Lamb says simply. The disclosure has a strange effect on her, a deadening effect, causing her fury to decline rapidly to weariness. 'There it is, sir. I was born a slave. The legal property of the Lascelles family. And I'm their slave still, I suppose, in the eyes of the law.' (229; italics in original)

As well as producing an ironically 'deadening effect' on the one who offers it, Mrs Lamb's 'disclosure' concerning the secret of her birth clarifies the motives underlying the acts of larceny which she commits throughout the novel and which do not simply target the 'family''s expensive candles but encompass far more precious things, including items from Beau's much-loved collection of post-Revolutionary French porcelain, as 'cast in the workshops of poor King Louis and several of his departed courtiers' (32). As she recalls, it is the transatlantic tales of these 'riches' that spur Mrs Lamb to abscond at the first opportunity from the Nightingale Grove plantation in Jamaica which is her birthplace and make her way, as a young girl 'light-skinned enough not to draw any special notice' (230), to Yorkshire, her intention being to use her 'skill' with the Lascelles' 'slave sugar' (232) – learned from her mother in the plantation's kitchens – to secure a position at Harewood, thence exploiting the latter as a cover for her criminal activities. This elaborate and resourceful project is not animated by a desire to accumulate 'wealth' (231) for herself, however, but rather to prise it away from her 'masters' (230), thus exacting a symbolic revenge for the theft of her freedom which they have perpetrated.

Yet this is only to tell half the story, as Mrs Lamb's plans undergo a sea change and take on a much wider significance when her time in England brings her into contact with her 'first *Brookes*'. The encounter with this 'terrible diagram' and subsequently the 'Abolitionists' (231; italics in original) results in a kind of political conversion experience not unlike that which she seeks to bring about in the causewary Turner and gives new purpose to her original vendetta, leading her to pledge the funds generated from the sale of the Lascelles' stolen property to the 'anti-slavers' (260), 'so that literature' directed against the slave trade 'could be printed and posted, notices placed in newspapers and speakers dispatched about the country' and the 'matter ... kept before the British people'. As she observes, her strategy has an aesthetically 'pleasing shape' (232), just like Madame de Pompadour's 'chocolate cup' (81) or the 'Endymion centrepiece' (83), two of his artworks that Beau particularly cherishes: her prowess with sugar is the ruse by which, she hopes, she will be able to 'help halt ... sugar's flow' (232), as if dismantling the master's 'palace' (230) with the tools used to build it.

In addition to making Turner her confidant, Mrs Lamb enlists him as a partner in crime, a role to which he assents both on the grounds of his desire for her (she has already outlandishly seduced him in Lord Harewood's bedchamber) and because she promises to reunite him with his sketchbooks, which Beau confiscates shortly before this incident, when his always uneasy relationship with the painter reaches its nadir. As noted above, Girtin believes Mrs Lamb to be Irish and does not alter his opinion either when Turner relays her story to him or when he learns that his artist-friend has become her accomplice, accusing Turner of a libido-driven gullibility that has allowed him to be manipulated by a 'sharper' (261). The irony here, however, is that Girtin is himself a victim of manipulation and deceit (as well as his own cupidity), as evidenced in the 'affair' he carries on 'so brazenly' (143) with Beau's younger sister, the 'reckless' (258) Mary Ann. While Girtin himself considers this cross-class liaison to be transgressive and secret, it is in fact being deviously choreographed by Beau and his elder sister, Frances. This is so that they can repair the links that they had begun to establish with the Royal Family by dint of Mary Ann's recent (if brief and unfruitful) involvement with King George III's fifth son, 'the scarred Prince – Ernest Augustus'. As Turner tells Girtin, 'The Lascelles need your girl in the family way so they can marry her into royalty' (258), passing off her pregnancy as the work of the 'lover' who has 'jilted' (202) her, rather than their 'stud' (220).

The conundrum of Mrs Lamb's identity – is she a victim of slavery whose thievery is both morally justifiable and politically expedient or an impostor and a criminal? – is one that *Will & Tom* never formally resolves, as the accounts given by Turner and Girtin are left to vie with one another for credibility, just as Beau initially contrives the simultaneous presence of the two painters at Harewood as a 'contest' (45) staged for his 'entertainment' (47). The mystery is compounded by the abrupt nature of her departure from Harewood on the night that she and Turner steal a number of Beau's *objets d'art*, including the 'Endymion centrepiece', for which Mrs Lamb anticipates getting 'two hundred guineas' (240) alone. That departure is encapsulated in a single blunt sentence set off from the text to either side of it – 'Mrs Lamb is gone' (248) – which also marks the moment when she vanishes from *Will & Tom* itself, leaving Turner to wait in vain for her return in the penultimate section of the novel set in Covent Garden. Here he looks out for weeks 'for tall, well-made females and curly black hair; and gypsies too, and people in the plain attire he associates with Abolition' (278–9), confronting an absence which prefigures the deaths of his mentally unstable mother and of Girtin, both of which take place between this section and the novel's final part in Charing Cross.

Despite its refusal to pin down the truth about Mrs Lamb, *Will & Tom* provides several clues to suggest that it is Turner rather than Girtin whom the reader should believe, doing so by subtly connecting her to the abolitionist literature she promotes and ultimately to *The Slave Ship* itself. Two of these clues are built into Mrs Lamb's name, which operates, in the first instance, as a bridge between Plampin's novel and the brilliant abolitionist satire of William Cowper's 'Epigram':

> To purify their wine, some people bleed
> A lamb into the barrel, and succeed;
> No nostrum, planters say, is half so good
> To make fine sugar as a negro's blood.
> Now lambs and negroes both are harmless things,
> And thence perhaps this wondrous virtue springs,
> 'Tis in the blood of innocence alone –
> Good cause why planters never try their own.

First published in the *Northampton Mercury* in 1792, Cowper's succinct verse explores similar issues (albeit on a far more compressed scale) to those broached by Burn in 'A Second Address', especially in the lurid image of 'a negro's blood' used 'to make fine sugar'. At the same time, the poem establishes parallels between 'lambs' and 'negroes' supportive of the claims that Plampin's still-room maid makes about her identity, even as she herself is emphatically not the kind of 'harmless' victim Cowper postulates. Merely in physical terms, Mrs Lamb is a powerful figure who 'dwarfs and bewilders' Turner with her 'height and bearing' (36), just as she is the dominant force both sexually and otherwise in their relationship. She is also either insubordinate to or unintimidated by the servants above her station in the Harewood pecking order (notably Beau's valet, Mr Cope), while brawling with those beneath, including Gem the scullery maid, who, during one reported contretemps, she 'sock[s]' 'Square in the eye' (115). This is to say nothing of her rebellious agency as an accomplished thief of the Lascelles' valuables.

The second clue relates to the way in which Mrs Lamb's name resonates not only with Cowper's 'Epigram' but also the novel's initial ekphrastic rendering of the *Brookes*, or rather, the personal vision Turner superimposes upon it: 'Chained Negro captives .... The dead left among the living – mothers with daughters, husbands with wives, sisters with brothers – their naked limbs entwined in lamentation.' Here, either by accident or design, Plampin's diction is telling, as the 'lam' in 'lamentation' silently puns on and echoes the designation of his novel's central female character, thus implying that the sorrows of these 'captives' belong also to her. This is a bond strengthened later in the text, when, to use another homonym, Turner speculates not about Mrs Lamb's roots but her routes: 'And the voyage to England, Christ alive; had it been on a slave ship, like the abominable *Brookes*?' (238; italics in original).⁶

The third and final clue is bound up with the manner in which Mrs Lamb suddenly absents herself from the novel – a textual event touched on earlier. This unheralded narrative exit can perhaps be read as a repetition of her flight from the Lascelles' Jamaican sugar plantation as a 'runaway' (259), while also recalling the 'disappearance from view' of the abolitionist material she so urgently wants to keep to the fore of British public debate – another departure (albeit a more gradual one) which Turner, like much of the rest of London, it seems, 'didn't even register'. Or, in another possibility, her vanishing act can be connected to the fate of the female slave in the *Zong* illustration, herself soon to be seen no more when she is thrown over the side of the slaver, the difference being that Mrs Lamb implicitly takes her leave by choice, slipping into the start of a new life rather than being forced against her will towards the end of an existing one.

Although Mrs Lamb ultimately escapes the novel and Turner alike, there is a sense in which the artist holds onto her even so, first of all by means of the erotic drawing which he composes when back in his room shortly after their impromptu love-making. Rejecting 'the monumental nudes of Italy' (206) as potential models, Turner instead seeks inspiration among the 'plump, disporting bodies . . . arched and splayed' (206–7), of Thomas Rowlandson, 'of which he has a small, clandestine collection in the bottom of his print box' (207). These, he hopes, will help him preserve the 'womanly presence' (36) of his paramour against the 'absences of memory' (206):

> Mrs Lamb's right thigh is dashed in, and her substantial, rounded hip, with the skirts hitched atop it; then the expanse of flank leading up to the daunting vastness of her bosom. . . .
> Her arm, the one she used to prop herself above him, is done in three lines only, and he's back to the upper leg, the groin, the points of their connection; to the wide, rough-skinned knee he felt rubbing against his ribs; the stockinged calf flexing along his shin; the ankle that locked around his own. (207)

This sketch is completed just as swiftly as the 'unlikely union' with Mrs Lamb 'on the baron's counterpane' (208) and secretly carried around by Turner until it is discovered by Beau and Mr Cope (who are lovers themselves) in the confrontation that leads to the temporary seizure of the artist's sketchbooks. As Beau puts it, the picture 'has the look of a very close association indeed' between artist and 'troublesome servant' (223), but is itself closely associated, quite literally, with the 'scene from the *Zong*' (222; italics in original) when the latter (which, it transpires, Turner has mislaid) is dramatically produced during this episode by the valet in order to incriminate him as an abolitionist.

What this collocation of images suggests is that, within the fictionalised historical frame of *Will & Tom*, the picture of Mrs Lamb is just as much part of the raw materials that Turner will eventually incorporate into *The Slave Ship* as the *Zong* illustration he so carelessly loses, as the painting further preserves his fugitive lover in the ill-proportioned shape of the drowned female slave about to be devoured and dismembered by the ravenous and rapacious sea creatures crowding around her. In sacrificing the still-room maid to the violence of his artistic imagination, Plampin's Turner thus remains faithful to his original vision – that frenzy of fetishes – in which Mrs Lamb's body already seems to have been 'dashed' to pieces by the rapid strokes of the artist's porte-crayon: 'right thigh . . . substantial, rounded hip . . . expanse of flank . . . daunting vastness of . . . bosom. . . . arm . . . upper leg . . . groin, the points of their connection . . . wide, rough-skinned knee . . . calf [and] ankle'.

Conclusion

Ekphrastic engagements with abolitionist iconography (as opposed to *The Slave Ship*) are few and far between, and it is hard to think of any other significant examples besides those examined above, either in the period covered by this book or prior to it. Such engagements are nonetheless important because, like the double vision of *The Slave Ship* articulated in the diptych of poems by Dabydeen and Patrick, they demonstrate that the visual memory of the Middle Passage is not just a thing of the past – an object of historical inquiry – but a pliant material that can be turned to a range of imaginative purposes, which are all driven by the same anti-slave trade spirit. In 'Islands', Alexander not only conventionally frames the *Brookes* images in their own terms as expressions of the slave trade's inhumanity but also suggests, more innovatively, that they are nascent ekphrastic entities in their own right, in which the written word comments upon and amplifies what the prints reveal to the eye – perhaps even doing so with a greater capacity to mobilise the viewer into political action. In Jeffers, on the other hand, the project is to personalise the Middle Passage, mixing up fact and fiction in a way that moves past the interior life of the slave ship itself to that of the African subjects whom the ship contains – or one of those subjects at least. For Plampin, finally, the approach is both different to Jeffers's and yet comparable. In *Will & Tom*, Mrs Lamb is able to tell her story to a small degree, though hers is a tale of the plantation rather than the Middle Passage and ultimately subsumed by the larger narrative of Turner's artistic development. Equally, however, the manner in which Plampin explores that development once again entails a provocative synthesis of history and imagination.

Notes

1. Hayden himself makes an early if fleeting contribution to this tradition in the closing verses of his 'Aunt Jemima of the Ocean Waves' (1970), from which the quotation in this chapter's title is taken. Here the poem's speaker calls to mind 'An antique etching' in the shape of William Grainger's well-known 1794 engraving of Thomas Stothard's now-lost painting, *Voyage of the Sable Venus, from Angola to the West Indies*. As he contemplates this picture, he describes the 'naked' female slave who occupies its centre and rides 'a baroque Cellini shell' as a 'voluptuous / imago floating in the wake / of slave-ships on fantastic seas' (75).
2. This is to be seen, for example, in the artwork for the books by Unsworth, Thomas and Basker, respectively. See also the cover designs for the books by Rediker and Hudson.
3. In addition to Jeffers's book-length collection, important contributions to this tradition include Hayden ('Letter'), Jordan, Young and Drea Brown.
4. In reading this painting along these lines, Plampin follows Hill, for whom 'It is extremely tempting' to interpret the two figures in the landscape as representing the two artists, with Turner 'assiduously engaged in effecting his purposes by industry, while his companion languishes idly by, effecting his, no doubt, by genius' (156).
5. Plampin's depiction of Mrs Lamb as a skilled confectioner who is not what she seems perhaps owes something to Eliot's portrayal of David Faux in *Brother Jacob* (1864), her own tale of sugar, slavery and imposture. Equally, the central female figure in Plampin's text has affinities with Bertha Mason of Brontë's *Jane Eyre* (1847). Both women are strongly built, Jamaican-born, candle-bearing 'Spectres' (Plampin 223), concerned to exact vengeance (albeit to different degrees) upon the owners of the morally corrupt English mansions where they reside.
6. The name perhaps is also an echo of Jane Austen's unfinished *Sanditon* (1817), the irony being that the Miss Lambe in Austen's novel, although of mixed race – she is oddly described as 'half-mulatto' (64) – is not a servant but a West Indian heiress who is 'sickly and rich' (65).

Chapter 4

The Secret Afterlives of Dido Elizabeth Belle

Introduction

The visual work that anchors this chapter is David Martin's *Portrait of Dido Elizabeth Belle and Lady Elizabeth Murray* (Fig. 4.1). This picture presents the touching image of the mixed-race Dido and her white cousin enclosed in the grounds of Kenwood House and, at first glance at least, in contrast to the other visual materials discussed so far in this book, appears to have nothing to do with the baleful realities of slavery or the Middle Passage. As it turns out, however, the opposite is the case: Dido was the illegitimate daughter of Captain John Lindsay and an African woman whom, it is thought, Lindsay took from a Spanish slave ship while serving as a naval officer in the Caribbean during the Seven Years' War. The painting's connection to the slave trade deepens and ramifies when it is recalled that Lindsay was the nephew of Lord Mansfield, who, as well as being Kenwood's owner when the painting was commissioned, had been long established as Lord Chief Justice of England, presiding over a number of important legal cases concerning slavery in the years prior to the abolitionist campaign. The first was that of the fugitive slave James Somerset, which was heard in 1772, and the second that of the *Zong*, some eleven years later. *Portrait of Dido* is thus circuitously linked by the latter case to *The Slave Ship* and has been thoroughly explored in relation to its highly charged historical and political context by a number of critics.[1] The painting has also surfaced amid the realms of popular culture, both providing the inspiration for and featuring in Amma Asante's *Belle* (2014), a cinematic reworking of Dido's story for a mainstream audience. But as well as giving rise

Figure 4.1 David Martin, *Portrait of Dido Elizabeth Belle and Lady Elizabeth Murray*, c. 1779 (oil on canvas). Courtesy of the Earl of Mansfield, Scone Palace, Perth.

to Asante's film, the picture has prompted a number of ekphrastic responses over the last twenty-five years or so, which have not attracted critical interest. This chapter is devoted to three of these: Leonora Brito's 'Dido Elizabeth Belle – A Narrative of Her Life (Extant)' (1995); Emma Donoghue's 'Dido' (2002); and, rather more recently, Honorée Fanonne Jeffers's 'Portrait of Dido Elizabeth Belle Lindsay, Free Mulatto, and her White Cousin, the Lady Elizabeth Murray, Great-Nieces of William Murray, First Earl of Mansfield and Lord Chief Justice of the King's Bench' (2020).[2]

1. Stepping Out: Leonora Brito's 'Dido Elizabeth Belle – A Narrative of Her Life (Extant)'

The mixed-race female in *Portrait of Dido* is so represented as to appear not only in motion but also in the process of escaping the frame of the painting that puts her on show as she leans slightly towards the painting's left-hand margin. This sense of imminent leave-taking is taken one step further, so to speak, at the dynamic outset of Brito's text. Here Dido rises up 'early from [her] bed' one 'blue misty morning' in September 1779 to make a sudden (and clandestine) departure from her great-'Uncle's house', which brings her, in 'a short space of time', to the 'outermost perimeters' of his 'estate' and thence, equally swiftly, into the uncharted regions of the countryside beyond. Such an emancipatory transition from culture to nature – the 'shady groves and pretty meandering walkways' belonging to the '"sweet-box" at Caenwood'[3] to 'an altogether wilder, more untutored landscape' (47) – does not just announce a dramatic shift in Dido's situation, however. It serves, also and more broadly, as a trope for the liberatory movement of Brito's text beyond the frame of the painting, transporting Dido into an entirely different set of narrative possibilities generated out of her involvement in what turns out to be an entirely different interpersonal relationship: in the alternative imaginative universe that Brito constructs, the historically real Lady Elizabeth features not at all, her place usurped by the fictional George Augustus Hercules Adams, a figure radically distinct from Dido's refined painterly companion in terms of class as well as sex.

Yet even as Brito's story thus deliberately distances itself from and exceeds the image that is its immediate intermedial catalyst, it does so only to engage in a series of intertextual dialogues, the first and most significant of which is with John Milton's *Paradise Lost* (1667), to which Brito alludes repeatedly. This work initially enters the narrative as Dido readies herself, at the edge of Mansfield's property, for flight towards her new domain:

> My clumsy wooden pattens rocked against the secondmost hurdle of the stile causing me to put out both my arms like a scarecrow, to save myself from falling. Balancing thus, I pondered whether Adam and Eve had gone forth from Paradise on such a morning as this? If so, then they had rather rushed toward their banishment, I reasoned, than approached it with intimations of dread. For the world before me was glorious. Glorious in the studied green and blueness of its promise. (47)

Perhaps the most striking aspect of the Miltonic allusion here is the ironic contrast it sets up between Dido's own 'banishment', which is self-chosen, and that of Eve, imposed upon her as the result of a divine disobedience. This discrepancy between the respective plights of the two women necessarily calls into question the paradisean allure of the domestic abode from which Dido has resolved to abscond – 'that pretty white mansion of many many rooms' (47): after all, why would anyone want to flee such an accommodating haven, unless it were not quite as heavenly as it seems?

The differences in the predicaments of Dido and Eve are articulated in other ways, one of which concerns the types of fall which each endures. For Eve, the Fall in question takes a definitive upper-case if metaphorical form and has repercussions for humanity as a whole. Dido's fall, on the other hand, is lower-case and literal – a physical event that is also somewhat bathetic rather than epic (though certainly not without major consequences for her own future existence): simultaneously experiencing a 'sudden vision' (47) of the place she is about to abandon while gazing with tear-brimmed eyes at the prospect before her, Dido loses her footing on the precarious stile and 'topple[s] over . . . roll[ing] down, down, down, the steep and narrow woodland track' (48).

One of the effects of the 'green world' into which the less Eve-than Alice-like Dido descends with such comic inelegance is that 'it act[s] upon [her] senses strangely', coming to seem curiously submarine: although 'dry', the 'leaves on the trees' that are 'High above' her recumbent 'head' make a 'constant rustling noise' as they are 'stirred' by the wind and, to Dido's 'shell-like ears', sound 'murmurous as the sea'. These leaves lead her indeed to 'feel as though [her] body had lodged itself' at the sea's 'very bottom', just as it is amid the 'liquid green' of the light that engulfs her that she even fancies a passing 'snail' to be 'swimming through its own slime' (48).

Dido at first seems to be calmly at one with the weirdly aquatic conditions into which she is plunged, even having time to admire the 'crystalline beauty' of the snail's 'shell' and the 'prismatic glow of each' of its 'coil[s]' as it journeys slowly on. But her equanimity is abruptly transformed into a 'terrifying . . . panic' when she takes a 'deep breath' and her 'nostrils' become 'filled, not with good air, but . . . the poisonous exhalations of the plants and rotting vegetation around [her]': 'rearing up', she recalls, 'I began to thrash and struggle through the undergrowth, tearing my skin and clothing; desperate for air, life-giving air – yet conscious all the while that I was drowning. And that I *must* drown' (48; italics in original).

In contrast to Dido's unfortunate tumble itself, the fluid terms in which Brito renders her protagonist's woodland environment are surely not accidental but resonate both with the Middle Passage and, specifically, the *Zong* atrocity. Dido's fall is quite distinct from Eve's, but, at the same time, reminds the reader of the drowned and unknown slaves with which, through Mansfield, her personal history is inevitably linked. The events aboard the *Zong* themselves perhaps cast a disturbing retrospective light upon the ostensibly halcyon image that *Portrait of Dido* projects, obliging the viewer to consider the scene afresh. As she feigns to run in her 'romantic garb of vague construction associated with masquerade dress' (King 33), Dido inclines, as already noted, towards the picture's left, but is it possible that she might be in danger of falling too?

A further difference between Dido and her Miltonic counterpart is that while the latter is ejected from Eden in the company of another, Dido enters her own apparent 'Paradise' alone. This sense of isolation is underscored, moments before she loses her balance on the rocky stile, by the way the details of the natural world are 'magnified perforce' by the 'vale of tears' through which she beholds them: 'And I saw every leaf and berry and tangled stem of grass, separately. And every drop of dew that was upon them, brightly shining, separately. And every cobweb thread strung with beads of crystal, each one cold and shining, separately' (48). Nature here multiply mirrors the heroine's solitude, just as the text itself insistently mirrors meaning in form, three times separating off 'separately' from the main body of the sentences in which the word appears.

As Dido disentangles herself from the 'undergrowth' (48) that had sought so inhospitably to drown her, it transpires, however, that she is not alone, since it is at this stage in the narrative that she encounters Adams (her own latter-day Adam, as it were), engaged in one of the activities by which he improvises his living:

> What I remember next is the sunlit clearing. Ho! what she remembers next is the sunlit clearing. Dazed I stumbled into it, the patch of sunlight, and saw the man. Crouching on the far side of a steep bank. He was –
> Fishin. I was. (49)

As this passage indicates, Dido and Adams do not just occupy the same landscape, but also share (or contest) the same textual space, their voices taking it in turns to develop the narrative from this point onwards right up until the story's dénouement. The shuttle-like movement between the voices of the two central characters is undoubtedly the text's most original and compelling technical feature, even as what it reveals is a relationship that, for much of the time, is fraught with conflict, particularly when it comes to the vexed question of who is to have power over whom.

This issue is opened up by the fishing episode itself. As Adams recalls the incident, he first refers to his watery prey (as does Dido) as 'it', but once he has secured the catch – and the fish is battling for life in a 'mesh of netting' that, in Dido's words, is 'black and cloudy' and 'voluminous as a mourning veil' – his language becomes less gender-neutral and the doomed creature feminised: 'you should have seen me struggle! Oh yes, as she flipped and twisted, this-er-way an that' (49), he exclaims, before describing the uncompromising manner in which the fish's futile efforts are brought to an end: 'Smack! I stunned her with a rock that was lying near by. Then I whips her up by the tail and brings her head down smartly' (49–50). The classically self-titled Adams is the main source of humour in what is an often subtly comic text, but the violence he performs here certainly makes him seem menacing and all the more so when it is recognised that it is not just fish and other wildlife that he is looking to capture – 'snakes 'n sparrers, badgers and hedge-hogs. Warmints, water-beetles an such like' – but Dido herself. Appropriately, indeed, when Adams first notices 'The negro-girl' standing in the 'woodland glade', he immediately translates her into a 'creature' that would not be out of place amid his collection. In a remarkable simile, he thinks of her as being 'sombre as a linnet' and tries, accordingly, to attract her with a mock bird-call: '*Chirrup-eek, eek eek eek gweek. Chirrup-eek!*' Similarly, imagining her a 'poor ... slave-girl' who has 'runned away' from her 'Master' or 'Mistress', more probably, he applauds the 'jackdaw cunning' she has used (he assumes), to acquire her 'silks and satins', even though these have been reduced to 'tatters' and 'Draggins' as a result of her fall (50).

Yet as Adams wades across the river in which he is fishing and moves towards this 'child o' nature', 'talkin all the time [he is] a-walkin up to her', it becomes clear that he is intent on Dido not as prospective kill but sexual conquest. It is equally clear, however, that this 'wild thing in the woods' is fully able to refuse the victim's role that Adams has ordained for her as he 'tries [his] luck': 'I do not move', she proudly asserts twice as he makes his approach, his 'feet' treading on scrolled-up 'leaves' whose 'bronze' colour ominously matches that of Dido's own skin; she parodies the blandishment of his 'Hey my honey, hey!' by returning it with her own rather bitterer 'My honey. My sugar. My sweet'; and in a second allusion to *Paradise Lost*, is scathing at the thought that 'This lowly man' could ever be the 'author and disposer of [her] fate' (50).[4] Dido further deflates Adams's would-be dreams of domination by likening him to the very fish he had caught and killed. This occurs after she has haughtily faulted him for his 'base-born ignorance [and] servile heart' (together with a 'low-down native cunning' similar to that which he imputes to her). 'Come' (51), she tells the reader, adopting a more conciliatory tone:

> let me tilt the mirror to fall more kindly upon this sylvan scene. Look, there he stands, naked at the top half, but for an old straw hat upon his head. Light falls through the brim of the hat, the holey brim and casts a net-like shadow over half his face. The cold pink of his mouth moves, and I think of the fish. Poor fish! And of the man as fish; and of myself as a fisher of men. (51)

Here combining allusions to *Paradise Lost* and the New Testament,[5] Dido's comparison exposes Adams not to violent death but the 'more kindly' possibility of redemption from his roguish ways.

Dido's playful self-figuration as a 'fisher of men' not only endows her with a 'blasphemous' capacity for Christ-like salvation but also carries a certain sexual charge. This is compounded by the semi-'naked' (51) condition of the body at which she gazes and whose colour – so different to her own – she had already registered when watching Adams earlier: 'The body of him was white. When he pulled his shirt off' (49). It might even be argued that Dido's stasis as Adams 'advances' in her direction and she sees 'the whole of his person' (50) is as much a mark of attraction as of personal courage. Either way, the suggestion of Dido's desire for Adams remains fleeting and fragmentary in the text – an abstract notion and no more – even as, by contrast, it is in no uncertain terms that Adams's desire for his 'bright-eyed beauty' is concretised. As Dido laughs out loud at her irreverent identification with Christ, Adams joins in the 'merriment' (51), only to switch the mood quite drastically:

> he grasped at my shoulders with his hands, his blood warm hands that were safe as death; and tried to make me dance the dance. The old dance of Eve and Adam in that woodland spot. I saw the leaves, blackly patterned against the blue sky looking upwards. The sky was a deep, a perfect blue, and the leaves showed blackly against it, like holes in a fabric torn – then the red light dancing – Lord!
>
> For the briefest of moments, I struggled against a feeling of helplessness – such complete and utter helplessness as threatened to overwhelm me entirely. But, the gods being with me in force, I all of a sudden took heart, and gathering my wits and strength about me (for he was a puny enough fellow all told) I wrenched myself

violently free of him – hissing, in as deadly a voice as I could muster: *Quam vis ille niger quam vis tu candidus essus* (sic), oaf! (51; italics in original)[6]

In Adams's contradictory 'hands' – 'blood warm' and 'safe as death' at once – Dido is in danger here of suffering a fall that is not literal, as at the narrative's beginning, but figurative, as, in still another gesture towards *Paradise Lost*, her assailant 'trie[s] to make [her] dance' 'The old dance of Eve and Adam'. Although Dido observes that her sense of sexual vulnerability is merely momentary, the text works against this claim by seeming fixated on her crisis, conveying such a sense by means of the repetition of key words and phrases: it uses 'dance' three times (and echoes it in 'dancing'); twice uses 'helplessness'; and twice deploys the image of black leaves set over 'against . . . blue sky'. As these leaves create the illusion of making that sky appear like a 'fabric torn', they themselves link back to the 'tearing' of Dido's 'skin and clothing' as she fights against the drowning 'undergrowth', complete, incidentally, with its 'dancing fern' (48).

At this juncture, the erstwhile and precocious 'fisher of men' is herself urgently in need of salvation, duly provided not by the Christian 'Lord' to whom Dido cries out but agencies that are decidedly eclectic in their origin and nature alike. These include 'gods' whose provenance is unspecified but who, like Dido's mysterious mother, may originate from Africa; and Dido's own voice, which, ironically, possesses the very qualities – it 'hiss[es]' and is 'deadly' – associated with the 'snakes' that Adams says he 'ketches' as a 'speciality' (50). Those qualities suggest that one of the deities who intervene to protect Dido at this point might be Damballah, represented in African and black diasporic culture as a serpent (Brathwaite 43), even as the voice itself does not speak in an African tongue or issue an African curse but unexpectedly delivers a Latin phrase instead.

Either way, Dido's classical ventriloquism is 'enough' (51) to deter Adams's physical assault, but she is still obliged to suffer a verbal attack consisting of the many 'wearisome endearments' with which he regales her, until he himself becomes finally wearied by her 'continued coldness' and leaves off 'as suddenly as he'd began'. Yet no sooner does Adams desist from openly pursuing Dido whether by deed or word, privately thinking all the while that 'she'll come round' (52), than he begins to see her as exploitable in a different sense. As he muses to himself:

> Yet who'd have thought it, eh? A learned negro-girl, fallen into your path, a scholar, no less, that's what you've stumbled on. A phee-nom-enon! Stap me if she ain't with all them words. All them latin words that came a-tumbling from her mouth! I shakes my head an' smiles at the wonderful workin's of providence. And in my mind's eye, straight ahead I can see the letterin' (red 'n' gold ornamented) bold spread across: P R O D I G Y O F N A T U R E ! (most recently discovered, lost and found a-wandering, in old England's woods) Proprietor: Geo. A. Adams, esq. (52)

The shift from sexual to monetary exploitation which these reflections inaugurate is foreshadowed both by the duplicitous language of affection Adams uses – he calls Dido his 'guinea gold' and 'little treasure' – and the 'rain' that, as he is speaking, starts 'steadily falling' in a 'golden shower' of 'bright drops' on her 'upturned face', 'cover[ing] it, like so many coins' (52). It also leaves her in a double bind: the Latin words she utters might serve to thwart Adams's sexual ambitions, but simply provide him, ironically, with the opportunity to abuse her anew.

Before capitalising on what he describes as 'the contrariness of the situation' – 'a black gal' who is 'refined an' delicate seeming withal' – Adams must first persuade the 'missish' (52) Dido to agree to participate in his scheme (even as he had earlier sought to take his pleasure from her without any consideration of consent at all). This he does by subjecting his potentially lucrative public exhibit to a private performance of his own, in which the star turn is one of those snakes he is so adroit at capturing. Although Dido exhorts 'the humble showman' (53) to 'Stand off' as he begins his routine by 'hoisting' 'an adder' 'above [his] head' (52) her entreaties do not succeed. Her voice still retains an air of 'commandment' that, as Adams notes, is unusual for a 'black girl' and even resounds, as Brito puts it (punning on one of Dido's names), with 'bell-like tones', but it can only delay the entertainments from getting underway rather than prevent them from taking place at all. After briefly 'fall[ing] back in his tracks' (53) at the force of her 'Keep your distance, simpleton – hold!' (52), Adams presses forward with his pantomime in all its grotesque comedy even so:

> I'm makin' like a statue, can't you see? he cried. A living breathin' statue. Putting on the old heroic.
> The snake, a deep, blackish green in colouring, slid across the fellow's neck and shoulders as he stood there grinning. He held up one arm. The arm was deathly white, and the snake entwined itself

around it, like a beautifully jewelled arm-bracelet of jade and ebony. A look of simple pride came over the man's face as he witnessed my complete, albeit unwilling, fascination. Please to see! Please to see! he cried in his showman's voice. And for my next trick! Whereupon he ... took the snake by the tip of its tail and, opening wide his mouth, allowed the creature to inch its way down the column of his throat, until it all but disappeared. (53)

As it commences, this dumbshow may well seem to work a certain magic, as Dido's perception of the 'snake' changes and a formerly 'vile serpent' (52) is transmuted into 'a beautifully jewelled arm-bracelet of jade and ebony' that captivates her, however reluctantly. Yet the hue of Adams's upraised 'arm' – which connects whiteness with deathliness – strikes a more sinister note and returns the reader to the scene of the attempted rape, in which Adams lays hold of Dido with his death-safe hands. The links between the mesmeric theatre Adams enacts here and that earlier scene are most obviously articulated by the crude phallic symbolism of his 'next trick', as he 'open[s] wide his mouth' and 'allow[s]' the snake to enter it, in this way confronting Dido with the displaced and distorted image of the very penetration which she had resisted and forestalled. It is consequently no wonder that she should begin 'retchin'' as she 'witnesse[s]' this phase of the spectacle and an initial if 'unwilling' enchantment turn to disgust. As she is finally forced to sit down, 'with her two hands clapped across her mouth and her black eyes starin'', the suggestion, in other words, is that the posture she adopts is designed not so much to stop the contents of her 'heavin'' 'guts' (53) from escaping as to keep her bodily boundaries intact.

As Dido 'clap[s]' her hands – not in applause but in a gesture of revulsion – she brings Adams's performance to a dramatic end, as he 'curl[s] the snake tenderly' and returns it to its 'box', subsequently also 'stash[ing] ... away' the dead fish he had caught and being sure 'to cover its fat, silvery gleam with an abundance of moss and leaves'. Yet the showman continues in a slyly theatrical mode as he conducts these rituals: his 'face' occasionally adopts a 'mournful expression'; he issues a 'plaintive whistle' that elicits an 'eerie' 'feathered response in kind' from the 'dark surrounding woods'; and seems 'to have forgotten [Dido's] existence entirely' as he 'fasten[s] up the buttons on his coarse brown jacket' (54) in preparation for farewell. As might be expected of this 'conning man' (52), however, Adams is not engaged so much in valediction here as further enticement. Far from ignoring Dido, he has her firmly in mind, his demeanour a ruse designed to tempt the 'P R O D I G Y O F N A T U R E' to enter into his commercial schemes: 'Shall you come along with me then, shall you?' he croons. Earlier in the story, Dido had been unmoved and insulted by the chirruping bird call with which Adams had beckoned her, but answers the question he poses here in the affirmative and even echoes it, as she records this pivotal moment in her existence, with her own '*shall you? shall you? shall you?*' (54; italics in original). In so doing, she seems to assume avian qualities herself and is thus well-suited both to form an alliance with the similarly hybrid and Protean Adams – 'this snake-man, bird-man, adam-man and thief' (55) – and to make a success of 'drawing in the crowds at fair-time' at 'Womberwell's Menagerie of Beasts and Birds', where, as Adams promises, she (and he) will make 'a pretty penny' and be reputed a 'champion turn' (54).[7]

In her 'drifting state' (55), Dido sees the 'picture' of her future that Adams 'paint[s]' for her as 'rosy' (54) using terms that are dimly reminiscent, ironically, of her past and in particular, details in the portrait that inspires Brito's story, whether these be Elizabeth's pink-cheeked complexion or the rosebuds that festoon her hair. As Dido 'set[s] off' with her associate for 'the great city of London and its environs', she recognises that her 'new way of life' is riddled with dangers, especially for a 'female' who is 'black' and 'penniless', but nonetheless considers it preferable to her previous existence under the 'protection of [her] Great-Uncle's house'. As Dido explains, the reasons underlying her 'most precipitous of steps' (55) are rooted, specifically, in her encounter with a short passage from the diary of the exiled American loyalist, Thomas Hutchinson, which she comes across while at Kenwood. This records Hutchinson's impressions of a soirée he attended at Mansfield's home, just days before Brito's narrative begins:

What course of events, what ill wind had driven me thus far, my reader will perhaps be asking? . . . Ah, therein lies the tale! . . . My objective in setting down this history, has been in the way of an attempt to possess, rather than be possessed by it.

Extract from a diary (as nearly as can be remembered):

Caenwood, August 29th 1779
A black came in after dinner and sat with the ladies and after coffee walked with the company in the gardens . . . . She is neither handsome nor genteel – pert enough. I knew her history before, but My Lord mentioned it again. His nephew, Sir John Lindsay,

> having taken her mother prisoner in a Spanish vessel, brought her to England where she was delivered of this girl, of which she was then with child, and which was taken care of by Lord Mansfield, and has been educated by his family. He calls her Dido, which I suppose is all the name she has.
>
> Liar! I remember thinking as I read the above . . . liar! Liar! For I knew well enough the facts of my own history and that what had been set down by this diarist was but a wicked fabrication, a tissue of lies and half truths! My mother was indeed a poor black slave, *'stolen from Afric's fancied happy seat'*. But as to my father – why my father was none other than the Englishman who had taken her captive: that same Sir John Lindsay who was Knight of the Bath, Rear Admiral of the Red – and nephew of Lord Mansfield, the Lord Chief Justice of England, the highest judge in the land.
>
> (55–6; italics and third ellipsis in original)

Although Dido vehemently accuses Hutchinson of being a 'Liar!' and dismisses his account of her birth and upbringing as fictionalised, her own response is itself not wholly reliable, since the casual 'diarist' does not exactly falsify her 'history' as censor it, omitting, crucially, to acknowledge Lindsay's identity as her father, rather than just the benevolent chaperon to her enslaved and pregnant 'mother'. Dido's ire in this regard is compounded by her discovery that the 'source' of Hutchinson's silence on this matter, as she goes on to explain, is 'none other than' (56) Mansfield, linked to Dido by the very familial ties he disavows and would like, it seems, to keep secret.[8]

In describing her mother as *'stolen from Afric's fancied happy seat'*, Dido establishes a parallel between this 'poor black slave' and Phillis Wheatley, who uses such a phrase to figure her own uprooting in 'To the Right Honourable WILLIAM, Earl of DARMOUTH, His Majesty's Principal Secretary of State for North-America, &c.':

> I, young in life, by seeming cruel fate
> Was snatch'd from *Afric's* fancy'd happy seat:
> What pangs excruciating must molest,
> What sorrows labour in my parent's breast?
> Steel'd was that soul and by no misery mov'd
> That from a father seiz'd his babe belov'd:
> Such, such was my case. (74; italics in original)

But if these lines suggest how Dido's mother and Wheatley share the same 'fate' as victims of the Middle Passage, they also reveal a crucial discrepancy between Dido herself and her deracinated but exceptional poetry-writing counterpart and contemporary. In some ways, Dido and Wheatley are much alike – the one 'A learned negro-girl' from whose 'mouth' 'latin words' come readily 'a-tumbling' and the other classically educated and with a penchant (like Dido again) for Miltonic allusion.[9] Yet the distinction between them arises in terms of how they come to be sundered from their respective fathers: Wheatley describes herself as a 'babe belov'd', who is 'seiz'd' from the ambit of paternal care, leaving 'excruciating' 'pangs' and 'sorrows' in her wake, while Dido, by contrast, is given away by a father who appears to act without compunction.

Throughout the course of Brito's text, evidence abounds to indicate that Adams is untrustworthy: he has, for example, a 'wheedling voice' that utters 'grand, foolish words' (54) in which, for a while at least, Dido is 'only too eager to believe', 'collud[ing] with' (55) the visions of fortune and renown that they convey. Given this dubious profile, it is not surprising to find that, at the end of the story, he has vanished, replaced as Dido's interlocutor by another if more benign male figure, in a scene not theatrical but artistic:

> Heigh-ho! I see you hiding there behind the screen, says Master Smith, come a-poking his head round. Why, says he, snatching up some of my papers: Dido? Elizabeth? Belle? What a lot of names you have given yourself!
> That's right, Sir, says I, taking care to grab the papers back, and hold them safely. Black Bet's been called a few things in her time, and so she has.
> Oh I should not call you *Black Bet*, says the boy very seriously (for he is a nice boy, very grave and studious in his ways), I should rather call you 'Bronze' given that your colouring has that tincture of olive in it – I b'lieve that is the classical appellation – 'Bronze'.
> (The classical appellation.)
> Why bless you Master Smith, then Bronze it is.
> And you shall not mind it?
> Mind it? Why not at all Sir, says I with a smile. Nay, not at all, for I am what I am. (56–7; italics in original)

These final paragraphs are closely modelled on and indeed contain verbatim echoes of John Thomas Smith's 1828 biography of the Royal Academy sculptor, Joseph Nollekens and, specifically, Smith's encounters with the sculptor's elderly free black servant, Elizabeth Rosina Clements. As Smith describes her, Clements 'was a woman possessing a considerable share of drollery', whose appearance exerted a direct influence over how she came to be known: 'and from her complexion being of a chestnut-brown colour, somewhat tinctured with olive', he writes, 'she acquired from the shopkeepers, particularly those of Oxford Market, the nickname of Black Bet, but from the artists the more classical appellation of Bronze, under which she will hereafter be mentioned' (58). As the biography makes plain, Clements's long tenure in the Nollekens household was not a happy affair, marked as it was by poor wages, dearth of material comforts and little respect, courtesy or affection, either from the sculptor himself or his wife, both of whom were notoriously miserly. Yet in Brito's text, where Clements is recast, rejuvenated and rehumanised as Dido, she appears quite at ease both with her lot and herself and, especially, her skin, blessing 'Master Smith' in turn for the 'classical appellation' with which he blesses her. One reason for this, perhaps, is that, in contrast to the term 'Black Bet', 'Bronze' makes Dido's mixed-race ancestry more conspicuous, as it were, thus continuing to preserve the blood ties to her white father that Hutchinson and Mansfield strive alike to cover up.

2. Slavery at Home: Emma Donoghue's 'Dido'

Like Brito's, Emma Donoghue's narrative is set in 1779, yet begins not with Dido making an abrupt exit from Kenwood, instead placing the eponymous heroine firmly *in situ*, 'picking plums and grapes' in the 'Orangery' of the Mansfield estate one 'June morning'. Yet this is not the only or even most significant difference between the respective openings of the two texts. When the reader first encounters Brito's Dido, she is incensed by the knowledge gathered from Hutchinson's diary as to her great-uncle's feelings towards their kinship, but, in Donoghue, Dido's initial condition, conversely, is one of ignorance: 'I knew nothing,' she announces in the story's second sentence, drawing the reader into this version of her tale with the suspenseful invitation to wonder what it is precisely that she might be unaware about. Secluded in the conservatory, amid 'orange trees', 'peach trees and myrtles and geraniums, sweet marjoram and lavender' (170), Dido thus partakes of a prelapsarian existence from which the narrative will cast her out. As the story unfolds, it encompasses and explores those anxieties about belonging that are so important in Brito, but the knowledge into which Donoghue's Dido falls has ultimately less to do with her liminal and ambiguous position in the Mansfield household – somewhere between 'family member and superior servant' (King 32) – than with the wider perils faced by slaves in late eighteenth-century England (as opposed to its colonies) and specifically, the predicament of the fugitive Somerset, mentioned in this chapter's introduction.

The latter was an enslaved African brought from Boston to London by his Scottish owner, Charles Stewart, in 1769 but who absconded some two years later, only to be recaptured and consigned to a ship destined for the Jamaican sugar plantations, where he was to be resold. Somerset was spared this fate by the intervention of sympathisers and his case brought to the attention of Mansfield by Granville Sharp. After several months of legal debate, Mansfield eventually ruled that Somerset should be freed on 22 June 1772, in a much-celebrated decision that was also much-misinterpreted as having brought about an end to slavery within England.[10]

Portrait of Dido is of course the main source of inspiration for Donoghue's text and even features in a scene in which the processes of its composition are deftly dramatised. But 'Dido' also includes a number of other pictures (and sculptures) in its own right. The first of these artworks (now lost) was painted by Antonio Zucchi and appears as Dido proceeds from orangery to vestibule, en route to her regular morning exchange with her great-uncle in his 'Library': 'In the Hall, Diana ran along beside her nymphs and hounds; I traced her foot with my fingers' (170), she remarks. Apart from providing a moment of humour, the unlikely spectacle of the Roman goddess and her entourage sweeping through the Kenwood residence has another effect. While it conjures up the mythological past, the image has an implicit bearing on Dido's present, since, by entering into Mansfield's grand domain, she simultaneously enters into a world in which the activity of hunting so closely associated with Diana is still current. The difference, though, is that the hunter in Dido's time is not a glamorous female deity of classical provenance but Somerset's earthly master, intent on repossessing his renegade property.

One reason for Dido's lack of knowledge concerning the plight of Somerset is Mansfield himself. When Dido 'tap[s]' on the library's 'open door' (170), she finds the elderly judge engaged in reading an urgent letter that the slave has sent him but which he does not share with her, declining the offer that she 'fetch [her] writing desk and take down' Mansfield's 'answer' (171) to his petitioner. Dido's exclusion from this correspondence is paralleled in this scene by how she experiences Mansfield's library more generally. For her, it is less a textual than a sensory and an aesthetic space and one, moreover, in imminent need of a clean:

> The Library was all blue and pink, sparkling with gold paint and red damask, and the air was still cool; the chill was delicious on my neck. I looked at the backs of the books, the orange and green and brown glow of their leathers; they would need another dusting soon. (171)

Yet even as Dido remains unenlightened as to the secrets of Somerset's letter at this point, there are hints in this apparently innocuous passage of the regime from which he is struggling for deliverance: the 'backs of the books' are made of the same material as the whips that would be used on the backs of slaves, while the dusty volumes themselves contain faint memories of John Newton's *Thoughts upon the African Slave Trade* (1788), a text in which the former slave-captain turned clergyman and abolitionist recollects the typical conditions aboard the slavers on which he once worked: 'the Slaves lie in two rows, one above the other, on each side of the ship, close to each other, like books upon a shelf' (33). Residual as they are, such associations and echoes perhaps give new meaning to the 'chill' that Dido senses on her 'neck', even as they attest to situations that are anything but 'delicious'.

As well as encountering Mansfield *in propria persona*, Dido meets him in the shape of images, as further artworks station themselves about the text. There is 'the overmantel portrait' of the Lord Chief Justice 'in his long tomato-red baronial robes with a bust of Homer' (170);[11] and, in a continuity with Brito, the 'bust by Nollekens', complete with its exacting Horatian 'motto', '*Uni Aequus Virtuti*', which Mansfield 'indulgently' translates for his great-niece, as he 'look[s] up at his plaster self', as 'Faithful to Virtue Alone'. Dido encounters other images too, as she stands 'quietly in one of the Library's recesses', waiting for Mansfield to 'finish reading' (171; italics in original) his missive. One of these takes the form of her own mirrored reflection:

> The recess was lined with one of the great pier-glasses: seven and a half feet high, three and a half feet wide, the largest mirrors in England, or so Mr Chippendale assured my great-uncle. They had been brought from France by road and sea and road again, and not one of them had broken. The glass was not tarnished yet. It gave me back to myself: my hair was dressed very high and frizzy today, and my pointed face was the colour of boiling coffee. (172)

Dido's mirror-image is both literally and metaphorically less elevated than either Mansfield's portrait and bust or the 'allegorical paintings' of 'Justice', 'Commerce' and 'Navigation' (171) that are placed above her (the latter associated with her seafaring father), but it has the advantage of endowing her with a sense of wholeness or self-collection: as Dido puts it, sounding oddly like a slave reclaiming a previous freedom, the pier-glass 'gave me back to myself'.

In this sequestered moment, the kindly mirror into which Dido looks enables her to become the object of her own gaze, returning a reflection with which she is pleasingly at one. At the same time, though, the text subtly disturbs this sense of restorative plenitude, as Dido's observations about her appearance explicitly recall the less than generous terms in which Hutchinson frames her in his diary, in a sentence from the same passage used by Brito: 'She had a very high cap, and her wool was much frizzled in her neck, but not enough to answer the large curls now in fashion' (276). As the racist transformation of Dido's 'hair' into 'wool' suggests, the manner in which she is beheld by the white company around her is at odds with how she beholds herself and in a way that is, moreover, derogatory rather than flattering and so has the potential to undermine her self-regard.

Donoghue's Hutchinsonian allusion has an intra- as well as intertextual function, guiding the narrative towards its next scene, in which, as 'Great-Uncle Mansfield' puts it, 'glanc[ing] up from his letter', Dido is 'wanted on the terrace', there to be included in what, in an ironically exclusionary phrase, he calls 'Lady Elizabeth's portrait' (172), as composed, in this narrative at least, by Johan Joseph Zoffany. Here, after Mansfield leaves Kenwood to carry out his legal duties at King's Bench, Dido comes under the scrutiny of the artist rather than the diarist, even as the consequence is largely the same, as Zoffany constructs an image of Dido that she finds unacceptable, in terms of sexuality and race alike.

The most striking element in *Portrait of Dido* is the index finger of Dido's right hand, which directs the viewing eye towards the dimple on the right side of her 'pointed face'. While this gesture might seem to be the spontaneous sign of a mischievous personality, the story makes it clear that, like the painting as a whole, it is merely a contrivance, albeit a memorable one. As Dido recalls: 'Mr Zoffany was staring at me now, with a little frown. "Miss Dido – if you would be so good as to touch your finger to your cheek just here – most becoming." I obeyed. "Exquisite," he murmured. "What contrasts!"' (173). For Dido, the concept of 'contrasts' that so delights

Zoffany is understood in aesthetic terms and immediately leads her into a brief account of how it informs Robert Adam's architectural designs for Mansfield's residence.[12] Yet in the context of a narrative so heavily implicated in the history of British slavery, the concept cannot but be linked to the ideology of race which supported the institution and which essentialises the difference between whiteness and blackness, seeing the one as superior to the other.

The presence of such an ideology in Zoffany's art is discernible, first of all, in the respective tasks he assigns his two models. Elizabeth is 'to be seated on a rustic bench' reading Frances Burney's *Evelina* (1778) and thus aligned with culture and literacy (as well as fashionability), while Dido 'rushe[s] by' her, 'or pretend[s] to' (172), at least, carrying a 'basket of fresh-picked plums and grapes' which associates her with nature and, as Zoffany puts it, invests her with 'a touch of the exotic' (173). But racial essentialism displays itself, also, with regard to how the two girls are clothed. Elizabeth, for her part, wears a 'new French pink *saque*, with her late mother's triple rope of pearls around her neck and rosebuds in her hair' (172; italics in original), with the flowers 'suggest[ing] virginity' (Byrne 6). Dido, on the other hand, is tricked out in the 'special costume' Zoffany produces for her from his 'trunk' – 'a fanciful thing in loose white satin, with a gauze shawl and an ostrich-feathered turban to match' (172). Such garments redouble Dido's aura of exoticism but, as Paula Byrne notes, at the same time combine it with eroticism, a quality conspicuously lacking in her more straitlaced white counterpart:

> The silk of [Dido's] dress clings to her lower body as she moves. The trace of her thigh seen under the fabric is highly erotic in an age when even the outline of women's legs was rarely seen in public . . . .
>
> By contrast, the white girl's stiff hoops and petticoats conceal her body. The tight bodice imprisons her. The extra layer of gauze over her full skirt gives a strange, cage-like effect. (Byrne 8)

The painting's sartorial differences are shaped, that is, by a stereotypical racialisation of female sexuality, with white women regarded as sexually pure and black women as sexually licentious.

Even as she indulges Zoffany's 'theatricals', Dido is taken aback by their cumulative effect when the artist temporarily stops painting and 'beckon[s]' her, with 'one finger' (173) of his own, to view his work in progress:

> I ran to look over his shoulder at the preliminary marks on the canvas, and suddenly I saw what he meant. It was indeed a study

in contrasts. Elizabeth was shown against a great dark bush – how her face and dress would glow like an angel when they were painted in – while my sketched figure stood up as black as the plums I was carrying, black against the pale sky in my white turban, with one black finger pointing to my black face as if to say, *look, look*.

I did not know what to say. But the painter, absorbed in his work again, was not asking my opinion, so I went back and stood in position. (173–4; italics in original)

What seems to dumbfound Dido as she views this 'study in contrasts' is not so much the excessive sexuality implied by her 'loose' garments as the excessive blackness of her 'sketched figure', which makes her indistinguishable from the 'plums' she carries (a link suggesting Zoffany's desire that she might become for him something more than just a luscious visual feast). At the end of Brito's narrative, Dido is untroubled by the 'classical appellation' of 'Bronze' that Master Smith wishes to confer on her. She seems indeed to welcome it, perhaps because the word functions – more so than 'Black Bet', for example – as the signifier of the mixed-race identity that Hutchinson and Mansfield both disavow. Here in Donoghue's rendition of Dido's story, however, that identity is obscured by the artist's 'marks' – 'preliminary' though they are – the corollary being also to obscure her connection both to the glowing and angelic Elizabeth and the Mansfield family as a whole.[13]

A further effect of Dido's heightened blackness is to intensify the bond with her mother, a tie also suggested by the 'big gold earrings' (173) that Zoffany 'clip[s]' (172) on to her to complete her outlandish attire and that induce in her a 'curious sensation'. Yet such maternal links bring their own discomfort, by reminding Dido that she too would have been a slave, were it not for the fortunate circumstance of being taken under Mansfield's guardianship at birth. The daughter herself seems to recognise this possibility, as suggested by her subsequent reaction to Zoffany's 'canvas' (173). On returning to her 'position' in front of the painting, she becomes 'Oddly restless' and 'look[ing] past the little lakes' of Mansfield's estate, as well as 'Greenwich Hospital and the famous cathedral of St Paul's', is just able to make out 'the Thames, speckled with traffic'. As befits its status as a major conduit for the slave trade, this river stimulates in Dido an ephemeral memory of maternal oppression: 'I thought of my mother, who had been part of the cargo of a Spanish ship when my father had boarded it.' Perhaps it is for this reason, as the histories of the two women briefly overlap, that the 'curious sensation' caused by Dido's earrings becomes a painful one: as she comments, 'My earlobes were beginning to ache under their weight of gold' (174).

Like the Thames itself, the possibility that the well-protected Dido could ever become a slave seems remote – for all the burdening distortions and degradations intrinsic to Zoffany's vision. Even so, the horror that such a fate entails is brought home to her in her fleeting encounter, directly after the painterly scene on the terrace, with another slave, in the shape of Somerset himself, calling on Mansfield to check that he has safely received his letter and been able to address its pressing concerns. Earlier in the narrative, Dido had been prevented from gaining access to this document, but, after reassuring Somerset that she will 'pass on [his] message on his Lordship's return' and the 'stranger' has 'gone', she 'drift[s]' back into the library to discover 'the letter . . . still open on the desk'. Having verified that the 'name on the bottom' of the page is Somerset's, Dido's 'eyes stray[ ] up to the top' (175), starting to scan his message *in medias res*:

> *shackles and whipped me like a dog till the skin of my back was in ribbons. When after many years in England I ran away from this devilish master he had me kidnapped and pressed on a ship in the Thames wh was bound for Jamaica. Kind friends secured my release but now my so-called master demands me back and I live every day in peril. The matter is in your hands Lord Mansfield sir. I hear that you have on sevl prior occasions ruled that blacks should be returned for resale in the Indies out of respect for the law of property. I ask you now your Lordship if I may be so bold to respect the law of humanity instead.* (175–6; italics in original)

Dido already has a limited awareness of slavery from the shadowy example of her mother, but what this textual fragment reveals to her is that this oppressive system is not just safely hidden 'far away', where it affects and afflicts 'unimaginable people who were used to such things' and 'for whom nothing could be done' (176). It is, on the contrary, far closer to home, involving both physical suffering (shackles and whips that excoriate the '*skin*' and reduce it to unsightly and unfashionable '*ribbons*') and enforced transportation to '*the Indies*' in a voyage that, for the African-born letter-writer, repeats the original trauma of the Middle Passage and to which even the ship that imprisons him is '*bound*'.

Dido's radically expanded knowledge of slavery's scope is registered in somatic terms, as Somerset's metaphorical statement that '*the matter*' of his case is in Mansfield's professional '*hands*' is both literalised and reversed when she 'drop[s] the page' she is reading 'as if it was on fire' and begins 'shaking all over' (176). Although not a slave herself, Dido is alarmed by Somerset's story because it discloses the possibility that she could very well become one, sharing his fate as she shares the colour of his skin: she too could be part of the 'traffic' on the Thames.

Like the diary entry in Brito, Somerset's letter constitutes a turning point in Dido's narrative, giving her not only a new knowledge but also a new identity. After folding the missive and secreting it in her dress, she hears her name being 'Faintly' called from the 'Ante-Room' – '"Dido! Dido!"' – but now recognises it only as a type of stolen property, an inauthentic and alienating classical soubriquet previously belonging to 'an African queen . . . who was once abandoned on a shore' by her lover and kills herself as a result.[14] Similarly, on resolving that she must travel to London, find Mansfield and personally advocate for Somerset, her behaviour breaks with her usual habits and routines. She brushes past her 'pink-cheeked cousin . . . in the Hall', her 'heart pounding as if [she were] running a race' (176) and darts 'upstairs to fetch [her] shawl' before Elizabeth can stop her, commenting: 'I had never behaved like this in my life. I was Dido Bell, known to the family and visitors as a sometimes pert but amiable girl. What was I doing?' (177).

In a sense, though, such conduct is not entirely unheralded, but prefigured in the make-believe of Zoffany's painting, in which Elizabeth is asked to 'catch[ ]' Dido's 'elbow' as the latter feigns to run past her and to 'Reach out and caress [her] cousin in passing . . . to convey the warmth of familial friendship' (172). Equally, such un-Didoesque activities are prefigured in the painting by Zucchi which is featured at the start of the narrative and represents the fleet-footed Diana with her corps of 'nymphs and hounds'. As she moves beyond the confines of Kenwood and heads towards Mansfield's legal chambers, Donoghue's Dido becomes, like Brito's, a kind of runagate (like Somerset too), but, at the same time, assumes the guise of the huntress, gone in pursuit of her great-uncle and the justice he claims to dispense.

Throughout the narrative, London is constructed as a space that Dido should best avoid. It is a 'wearisome place . . . not healthful for a girl' (174), and even Mansfield is obliged, on 'summer days', to carry a 'nosegay' – sometimes made up of 'rosebuds' like those Elizabeth favours for her hair – when he is driving into 'the stinking city' (171). Yet England's capital threatens Dido's health, if not

Mansfield's, in other ways, as is evidenced when she arrives at the metropolis:

> The journey was a short one; it all went by me in a blur of stink and noise. I did not even know we had reached the Inner Temple till John [the coachman] pointed at the gate with his whip. As he was helping me jump down, a passing girl squealed 'Look at that dirty blackamoor got up like a lady!'
>
> Shock stopped my breath. I had never been spoken to that way in my life. My heart was stuck in my throat like a piece of gristle. What was I, I asked myself now? Blackamoor or lady? A terrible mixture. Neither fish nor flesh nor fowl. (177)

Dido's plight here is ironic: she finds herself worlds away from Kenwood (despite the brevity of her 'journey') and yet in a situation which, for all its strangeness, is also familiar, recalling, specifically, the painting-scene on the terrace. In that scene, Zoffany augments Dido's blackness in a way that causes its own 'shock' by segregating her from the radiant Elizabeth as part of a 'study in contrasts' that is also a study in racial essentialism. Similarly, in this later scene, the 'passing girl' exposes Dido as passing in another sense, pretending to be a 'lady' when she is nothing but a 'dirty blackamoor'. The difference between the two scenes is that, in the first, Dido draws attention to her skin, pointing at her own face 'as if to say, *look, look*', whereas, in the second, such signals are redundant, since her skin draws attention to itself, advertising her inferiority and otherness at large.[15]

While Dido makes no pointed gestures here, her coachman 'point[s] at the gate with his whip'. In so doing, he carries out an action that is quite appropriate for this particular narrative moment, since what Dido's skin also advertises is her potential to be subjected to the slavery which the whip so overtly symbolises. Indeed, as she enters the gate and 'march[es]' towards her 'great-uncle's chambers on King's Bench Walk' (177), it would appear that she has already assumed slavehood in the eyes of those whom she encounters. For example, she asks the porter if she can see Mansfield, only to be asked, in turn, to identify her 'master' and is then designated a fugitive when, like Somerset, she declares she does not have one: '"Runaway rabbit, are you, then?" he said with a dirty grin. "Who's paying for those fine frills?" He pulled at my polonaise.' Or there is the instance of Dido's brief meeting with Mansfield's junior 'colleague' – once the 'runaway rabbit' has escaped the porter's molestations and finally located her great-uncle's 'office' amid the 'warren of chambers': 'The younger gentleman . . . looked me up and down in amusement. "I didn't know you'd any yourself, Mansfield"' (178).

The shift in phrase from 'runaway rabbit' to 'warren of chambers' acts as a reminder that, despite the verbal and physical assaults she endures, Donoghue's Dido, like Brito's, is no victim and at this juncture still more hunter (or huntress) than prey. Certainly, once the insouciant associate has 'sauntered' out of Mansfield's office, Dido has 'pulled Somerset's letter out of her bosom' (178) and the story's two principals are left alone to grapple with its implications, it is clear that she wields a good deal of power over her great-uncle, imagining herself, in this final scene, as 'the girl in the fairy-tale, who demanded three wishes' (179). Dido's empowerment is evident even in seemingly incidental details, as when Mansfield attempts to justify keeping her 'hidden away at Kenwood' by insisting that the 'country air is much more wholesome' than the atmosphere in the city and protectively puts one of his hands over hers, an action leading her to observe that his 'skin was as soft as chicken feathers' (180). Considered in itself, such a simile debunks Mansfield's status as a figure of either authority or moral courage, but the effect is compounded when it is recalled that one of Dido's occupations on the estate that shelters her from the world beyond is that of 'poultry-keeper' (179), as if Mansfield were under her charge rather than the other way around.

Yet there is a sense in which Dido needs to exert power less over Mansfield than over herself, or, more precisely – to return to the epidermal motif – over her own skin, which jeopardises her personal liberty by promoting the idea that she is something she is not: 'How are people to know I'm free, if my skin says otherwise?' she asks. It is this epidermal contra-diction that calls forth the first of Dido's wishes, which centres on securing a more reliable written statement that she is a 'free person' and that thus defends her, once Mansfield has signed it, albeit 'crossly' (179), from the same fate as had befallen Somerset.

Although Dido is repeatedly assured by Mansfield during these often fraught closing exchanges that she is not '*lost property*' to be randomly 'seized' but 'one of the family' (179; italics in original), her doubts remain, leading her to allege that he originally took her in merely 'as an unpaid companion for Lady Elizabeth' and to demand that she is paid a 'salary' (180) for the sundry duties she performs at Kenwood which include those of 'dairy-maid' (179) – as well as 'poultry-keeper'. This is her second wish, to which the 'heavily' sighing Mansfield duly assents, with the proviso that the 'cold ring' of 'salary' be melted away beneath the warmer-sounding euphemism of 'a quarterly allowance' (180).

Dido's third and final wish is not for herself but the fugitive whose story galvanises her into action in the first place and whose situation brings her into an even more intense conflict with Mansfield than does her own. Furious at Mansfield's accusation that she is 'meddl[ing] in what doesn't concern [her]' (180), Dido responds with a set of counter-accusations:

> Rage, like ink, spilled across my eyes. 'Whom does it concern more than me,' I shouted, 'whose mother was a slave, your nephew's slave and whore? I wonder, did he free her before she died? Did he take the shackles off when she was giving birth to me?' Now I did not care if I could be heard all through the Inner Temple. 'Whom should such matters *concern* more than me, your little dusky plaything?'
> Lord Mansfield bent across the desk and seized me, then, enclosed me in his arms. I could smell the dust and sourness of his old robes. 'Dido,' he sobbed, 'Dido Bell, my sweet girl, how can you say such things?'
> I rested in his embrace for a few seconds, then pulled away. 'Let James Somerset go free.' (180–1; italics in original)

Early on in the narrative, Lindsay is imagined in romantically heroic terms as having 'rescued [Dido's] mother from captivity on a Spanish ship the year before [Dido] was born' (171–2). Here, however, he emerges as just another '*devilish master*', just as the mother herself is unexpectedly seen anew, in Dido's rage-blind eyes, as 'whore' rather than sexual victim. Dido herself assumes the disconcerting role of Mansfield's 'little dusky plaything', before reminding us of her more familiar identification with the one for whom she campaigns. This she does by proleptically articulating Somerset's freedom in her own physical movement: she briefly 'rest[s]' in Mansfield's 'embrace' and then 'pull[s] away'.

The fulfilment of Dido's three wishes is a matter of historical record: Mansfield confirmed her liberty in his will of 1783; gave her a quarterly allowance of five pounds (increased by birthday and Christmas gifts of five guineas each to make an overall annuity of thirty pounds and ten shillings [Adams 12]); and, of course, emancipated Somerset. The part played by the historically real Dido in bringing about that latter outcome is uncertain, although it was rumoured that her influence in the case was significant, despite the fact that she would have been only ten years of age at the time it came to court. As Hutchinson puts it, citing the vested interests of the day:

> A few years ago there was a cause before his Lordship bro't by a Black for recovery of his liberty. A Jamaica planter being asked what judgment his Lordship would give? 'No doubt,' he answered, 'He will be set free, for Lord Mansfield keeps a Black in his house which governs him and the whole family.' (276)

Whether or not there is any truth in these claims, the thought of a 'Black' (and a female one who is also a child) exerting sway over Mansfield is clearly not one a planter would relish, even as, in Donoghue's fiction, it is something that is just as clearly celebrated.

At the end of Donoghue's narrative, Dido enjoys a triumph that is both personal and political: her ties to her great-uncle and his 'whole family' have been properly acknowledged and affirmed and she has gained 'justice for Somerset'. Even so, the political element of this victory is bittersweet, as suggested by the simile in which Dido likens the 'power' she feels at this moment to the taste of 'sugar in [her] mouth' (181). As the story closes, Somerset may be free, but many thousands of black subjects living in England remained enslaved, some of them still to be forcibly taken – despite the niceties of legal judgment – to the cane-fields that he himself escapes.

3. A Different Emphasis: Interracial Sisterhood in Honorée Fanonne Jeffers's 'Portrait of Dido Elizabeth Belle Lindsay, Free Mulatto, and her White Cousin, the Lady Elizabeth Murray, Great-Nieces of William Murray, First Earl of Mansfield and Lord Chief Justice of the King's Bench.'

One way to approach the third and final text for consideration in this chapter is by means of the opening couplet, which, as well as being typically brief, establishes a striking tension between content and form: 'Dido moves quickly – / as from the Latin *anima*' (66; italics in original). While the first line of the couplet emphasises Dido's vivacity, her movement no sooner commences than it is impeded by the end-stopped second line, particularly with the trisyllabic '*anima*', glossed in the even briefer third line as 'Breath or soul') and it is notable that by as early as line six Dido is not moving at all but 'positioned'. This tension between movement and restraint pervades the poem as a whole, which regularly breaks up its own syntactic flow with couplets (like this first one) that are complete sentences and individual lines that are similarly self-enclosed and made up, in one case, merely of a single word: 'Please' (67).

The poem's alternation between the impulse towards movement and the impulse towards containment is consistent with the image from which it takes its inspiration, in which the white girl detains her literally more dashing counterpart with her outstretched right hand and seems, as Byrne suggests, to be 'pulling her into the frame' (3). This gesture is ambiguous and ambivalent, as mixed in its messages as Dido in her race. One means of construing Elizabeth's action is as a sign of the white possession or coercion of the black body on which slavery and the slave trade are predicated, while an alternative and more cordial option is to read it as a visual expression of the emotional ties that have grown up between the two figures and complement their blood relationship as half-cousins. A third possibility defines the gesture in more historically specific terms as symbolic of the ideological conflicts characterising the late eighteenth-century era when the painting was produced, as forces committed to maintaining the status quo of the slave trade find themselves incipiently challenged by forces equally committed to its abolition: Dido strives towards a brighter future from which Elizabeth withholds her.

Such pro-slavery forces in turn presuppose the sort of everyday racism encapsulated in Hutchinson's diary. In the painting itself, conversely, there are hints that the racial order of things is being ruffled, with Dido appearing to be not just equal in height to Elizabeth but marginally to exceed her. That said, Dido's superior stature is something of a compositional trick, fabricated by dint of the fashionable ostrich feather she sports in her Indian turban and the simple fact that her companion is seated, just as there are other aspects of the painting which quietly dispute its aura of racial progressivism. That sitting posture, for example, grants Elizabeth the leisure which Dido is denied by her domestic obligations. Similarly, the open book Elizabeth holds in her left hand and rests upon her lap is the sign of a civilised identity markedly at odds with the primitive otherness suggested by the exotic fruits Dido carries in the basket suspended from the crook of her right arm.

In Jeffers's text, the painting's ambiguities are downplayed, though certainly not eradicated, with Dido apparently restored to her racially superior position. Just as her name precedes Elizabeth's in the poem's title, so it appears as the first word in three of the poem's thirty-five lines, with Elizabeth's so placed only once. Elizabeth herself is described, in line four, as being 'Beside' Dido, a word which evokes a certain sisterly rapport and yet at the same time carries the implication that the white girl is merely an accessory to the black, rather than the other way around. In addition to this, the poem both draws attention to Dido's slightly greater height and underscores its symbolic significance in lines six to seven: 'Dido positioned in irony – // the lowest are taller here.' The irony 'here', however, is at least twofold: Dido's ostensibly more elevated stance may well provocatively question the racial order that prevails in the Hutchinsonian world outside the painting's frame, but as already noted, is dependent upon the good grace of her cousin's sedentary pose.

As well as effacing Dido's individuality by referring to her simply as an after-dinner 'Black', Hutchinson's diary suggests that she falls short of his standards of beauty, with her 'much frizzled' hair and tendency to be 'neither handsome nor genteel', though 'pert enough'. As Byrne notes, however, Dido is regarded quite differently by the one who paints her: 'the viewer' of his picture, she states, is 'left with little doubt that it is the black girl who has captured the imagination of the artist' (5) – living up to the meaning of one of her assorted names ('Belle' as 'beautiful'). While the exact nature of the racial hierarchy between white and black in the painting may be ambiguous, the aesthetic hierarchy, in other words, is not, with Dido clearly placed above Elizabeth as the more pulchritudinous and charismatic figure. In this sense, the painting transgresses orthodox prejudices regarding female attractiveness as they are articulated not only in Hutchinson's localised *ad feminam* account but also, for example, in the broader contemporary context of Thomas Jefferson's *Notes on the State of Virginia* (1785), 'Query XIV':

> The first difference which strikes us is that of colour. Whether the black of the negro resides in the reticular membrane between the skin and scarf-skin, or in the scarf-skin itself; whether it proceeds from the colour of the blood, the colour of the bile, or from that of some other secretion, the difference is fixed in nature, and is as real as if its seat and cause were better known to us. And is this difference of no importance? Is it not the foundation of a greater or less share of beauty in the two races? Are not the fine mixtures of red and white, the expressions of every passion by greater or less suffusions of colour in the one, preferable to that eternal monotony, which reigns in the countenances, that immoveable veil of black which covers all the emotions of the other race? Add to these, flowing hair, a more elegant symmetry of form, their own judgment in favour of the whites, declared by their preference of them, as uniformly as is

the preference of the Oranootan for the black women over those of his own species. (145)

The transgressive sense of Dido's superior beauty which the painting communicates is replicated in Jeffers's poem, with its comic figuration of Elizabeth as 'a biscuit figurine in pink' (66). While the colour of her attire resonates with Jefferson's 'fine mixtures of red and white', Elizabeth herself does not benefit from the privileges which her similarly pigmented and seemingly edible skin should guarantee:

Elizabeth should provide

an unkind contrast: pretty, blonde,
pale in uncovered places –

but no.
The painter worships the quickened Other.

Dido, his coquette of deep-dish
dimples, his careless, bright love. (66)

Elizabeth's dress links her both by colour and shape to the dome of St Paul's, shimmering hazily in the picture's far background, though it is not she but Dido whom the painter 'worships', a term whose usage is an ironic reminder of how Dido's identity in the poem swiftly changes: at this juncture, she is associated less with the initial 'soul' of the poem's third line than the flesh that turns her into a visual delight and whose 'deep-dish / dimples' seem to promise a more profound and enduring satisfaction than the evanescent sweetness of her biscuit-like companion.

In representing Dido in this manner, the painting, in another irony, is anything but transgressive, since it simply reproduces the conventional fantasy of the black female as readily yielding to the sexual pleasure of the white man. Yet it is significant that, even as the poem implies Dido's status as the painter's possession, it also designates her as a 'coquette', a word whose meaning is defined by the *OED* as 'A woman (more or less young), who uses arts to gain the admiration and affection of men, merely for the gratification of vanity or from a desire of conquest, and without any intention of responding to the feelings aroused.'

In the eyes of the one who paints her, Dido may be coquettish, but in those of the poem's speaker, she is not so much in the position of control that this implies as vulnerable, the perils of her situation exacerbated by a youthful naïveté. As the speaker puts it, switching to an idiom that is suddenly strikingly more colloquial and modern than before:

> Forget History.
> She's a teenager.
>
> We know what that means:
> cocky, stupid about reality.
>
> No thought of babies –
> feathers in her arms.
>
> She might wave them, clearing
> dead mothers from the air –
>
> and she's special –
> her great-uncle dressed her with care,
>
> hid her from triangles and seas
> outside this walled garden. (66–7)

As the dissonant references to 'babies' and 'dead mothers' suggest, the 'History' in question here is specifically that of the sexual relations between men and women. As played out across the lines of racial difference which organise the slave trade (with its ironically decorous 'triangles and seas'), such relations are typically violent and provide the broad context in which Dido's own mother – 'dead' or alive when the daughter is painted? – is implicitly located. While this obscure figure may have enjoyed a relationship with Dido's father which, in Byrne's words, 'was probably – though by no means certainly – loving and consensual', she may, equally, as Byrne also notes, have 'endured the full horrors of capture in Africa and a transatlantic voyage [and] may well have been sexually assaulted – possibly more than once' (48) prior to Lindsay's advent. It is therefore unsurprising that 'We' should be urged to 'Forget' this history of female enslavement and abuse, whose presence is ironically reanimated by the very linguistic gestures that would dispel it and whose worrisome traces are evident in the equivocations of how Dido is 'dressed ... with care' by her 'great-uncle'. This phrase suggests Mansfield's mindful affection towards his great-niece, but hints also at Dido as a figure who, despite her outward appearance in the painting, is more fundamentally apparelled in suffering and grief that are unseen and unspoken.[16]

The danger Dido courts beyond the boundaries of her *hortus conclusus* – a space that is at once sheltering and stifling (like the poem's extravagantly foreshortened sentences) – is finally twofold. By moving beyond those boundaries, she runs the risk of repeating not just the history that may or may not have engulfed her enslaved mother but also the fate endured by her love-stricken and ultimately self-destructive classical namesake (to whom Donoghue similarly alludes). Whether or not such a fate is a coding of what happens to Dido's mother is purely speculative, but what is more certain is the way in which Jeffers ends her poem by rewriting her classical source. Here she both transforms the melodramas of heteronormative desire into an illicit homoerotic intimacy between white girl and black and attempts (as does the painting) to fix it before it disintegrates:

Let her be.
Please.

No Dying Mythical
Queen weaving a vivid, troubled skin –

but Dido, full of girlhood,
and Elizabeth reaching

a hand. *Behave, cousin,*
she begs.

Don't run away from me. (67; italics in original)

The speaker's generalised exhortation that Dido's growth remain arrested at the stage of 'girlhood' coincides in these lines with Elizabeth's plea that her '*cousin*' does not '*run away*' from her but '*Behave*[s]' herself by staying forever in place. The poem's final irony, however, resides in the formal alteration that befalls it at this juncture, as the couplets symbolising the girls' togetherness throughout the text are suddenly disrupted by the ominous solitude of its last line.

Conclusion

Although in many ways quite different from one another, the three texts analysed in this chapter also have much in common. As well as all addressing the questions of slavery and race posed by *Portrait*

Figure 4.2 After Scipio Moorhead? *Phillis Wheatley, Negro Servant to Mr. Wheatley, of Boston.* Frontispiece to *Phillis Wheatley, Poems on Various Subjects, Religious and Moral*, 1773. British Museum.

of *Dido*, they are each marked by a certain doubleness. In Brito, this doubleness is articulated in the constant interchange between Dido's narrative viewpoint and that of Adams, the 'Showman' and 'ketcher by trade' (50). In Donoghue, by contrast, the dyadic pattern is less conspicuous – the text switches neither narrative perspective nor social milieu – but present nonetheless, as Dido's story is interlaced (albeit with self-conscious anachronism) with that of Somerset. Such doubleness is also a feature of Jeffers's poem, with the difference being that, in this instance, Dido is not connected by the poem's speaker to figures either fictional or anachronistic, but considered instead, as indeed in the painting, in her relationship to Elizabeth.

That Jeffers should be minded to include a poem about Dido in a collection about Wheatley is perhaps appropriate, not just in terms of the coincidence that brings the latter to Boston as a child in the probable year of the former's birth, but also with regard to their images. As already observed, the most eye-catching aspect of *Portrait of Dido* is the way in which Dido points to her face with her finger, a flamboyant gesture which points in turn to the frontispiece to Wheatley's *Poems* (Fig. 4.2). In this oval portrait, possibly based on a 'drawing or painting' (Slauter 89) by the elusive slave-artist Scipio Moorhead, the 'Negro Servant to Mr. John Wheatley' is depicted seated at a writing table composing verses with her right hand while touching her cheek, *à la* Dido, with the index finger of her left. The digital connection between the two young women may be purely coincidental – the finger at the cheek is a common enough eighteenth-century pictorial motif, after all – but it is nonetheless a felicitous one from this book's perspective, guiding it, in the next two chapters, towards a more sustained and expansive analysis of African-American ekphrasis than has been undertaken so far.

Notes

1. See, for example, Byrne 3–11; Card; Walvin, *Slavery* 151–72; and Germann.
2. For another short story written in response to *Portrait of Dido* see Tisa Bryant's 'The Problem of Dido' (2007). This narrative alternates between Dido's tale and (drawing on Duras) the story of Ourika, a young black girl brought from Senegal to Paris a few years prior to the French Revolution and raised (like Dido) among the social elite. Levy

has stated that Dido's portrait provides the cue for the imaginary painting evoked in *The Long Song* (2010), which depicts the uneasy trinity of a Caribbean plantation-master (Robert Goodwin), his wife and their mixed-race slave, Miss July, with whom Robert is having an affair. For Levy's comments on this debt, see her interview with Fischer in Baxter and James, 134. For yet another response to the painting, see Lawrence Scott's *Dangerous Freedom: Elizabeth d'Aviniere's Story* (2020), which is set in 1802, some two years before Dido's death. In contrast to other treatments, this novel focuses on Dido as she looks back as wife and mother on her Kenwood time as Mansfield's ward and is also notable – in a further departure from the usual pattern – for the space it gives to the narrative of Dido's relationship to her mother, Maria.

3. This phrase is taken from Sancho's letter of 9 June 1780, in which he gives a vivid account of how Mansfield's Kenwood residence becomes caught up in the Gordon Riots, but, unlike his property in Bloomsbury Square, is lucky enough to avoid serious damage: Mansfield's 'house in town suffered martyrdom', he writes 'and his sweet box at Caen Wood escaped almost miraculously, for the mob had just arrived, and were beginning with it, when a strong detachment from the guards and light-horse came most critically to its rescue' (347–8). The idea of Caen Wood / Kenwood as a 'sweet box' is appropriate, since 'Caen' itself is an anagrammatic box containing 'cane', the tropical plant from which the sweet-tasting sugar that sustains the slave trade is extracted.

4. In Milton's epic, these are the designated offices that Adam ideally holds with respect to Eve. See *Paradise Lost*, IV.635.

5. These consist, respectively, in 'this sylvan scene', which echoes *Paradise Lost* IV.140 and 'fisher of men', echoing Mark 1.17.

6. The Latin phrase that ends this passage is a slight mistranscription of line sixteen of Virgil's second Eclogue, which reads, 'Quamuis ille niger quamuis tu candidus esses' (*Virgil's Eclogues*, p. 10). It is translated by Krisak as: 'though he is dark and you are fair' (p. 11).

7. Here the (anachronistic) allusion is to George Wombwell (1777–1850), creator in 1805 of Britain's 'first large-scale traveling menagerie' (Ritvo 207) and one of the most famous and successful menagerists of the Georgian and early Victorian eras.

8. Brito's rather unsympathetic treatment of Mansfield (which is also found in Donoghue but less so in Jeffers) diverges sharply from historical evidence of the affection in which his ward was held both by Mansfield himself and his family at large. On this point, see, for instance, Adams 12; Byrne 170–1; and Steedman 108. Such affection is recorded even by Hutchinson, albeit in terms which reveal how it cuts across the prejudices of the time: '[Mansfield] knows he has been reproached for shewing a fondness for her – I dare say not criminal' (276).

9. A useful and original analysis of the engagement of Wheatley's poetry with Milton is provided by Loscocco.
10. For a comprehensive account of the Somerset case, see Wise.
11. Although Donoghue's story is explicitly concerned with the Somerset case, it is obliquely linked to the *Zong* episode by means of the description of the 'robes' adorning the Lord Chief Justice as 'tomato-red'. This phrase recalls Twain's own recollection, in *A Tramp Abroad*, of the response that Turner's painterly rendering of the *Zong* incident generates in one of its viewers: 'A Boston newspaper reporter went and took a look at the Slave Ship floundering about in that fierce conflagration of reds and yellows, and said it reminded him of a tortoise-shell cat having a fit in a platter of tomatoes' (157–8).
12. As well as remodelling Kenwood along neoclassical lines from 1764 to 1779 (Julius Bryant 24, 26), Adam was around the same time involved (along with John Carr) in the design and construction of Harewood House, the principal setting for *Will & Tom*. On Adam's role in the shaping of the latter property, see Mauchline.
13. Donoghue's construction of this scene perhaps owes something to Larsen's *Quicksand* (1928), a novella in which another young mixed-race woman, Helga Crane, confronts and is similarly alienated by the image of her that is created by the self-absorbed white artist, Axel Olsen: 'The picture . . . . wasn't, she contended, herself at all, but some disgusting sensual creature with her features' (89).
14. The tale of the 'African Queen''s desertion by Aeneas and her subsequent suicide is most famously recounted by Virgil in Book 4 of *The Aeneid* (88–9).
15. The sense of breathless shock and disrupted identity that Dido experiences as she is interpellated by the squealing girl recalls Fanon's description of his traumatising encounter with the white gaze in *Black Skin, White Masks*, as discussed in Chapter 1 (note 8).
16. Like the 'tomato-red . . . robes' in Donoghue, this phrase functions as a gentle reminder of the implication of Dido's narrative in the story of the *Zong*, since the slaver's original name was *Zorg* (Dutch for 'care'), but carelessly altered (ironically) when it was 'repainted' (Philip 208). Jeffers herself addresses the events aboard the *Zong* at one point in *The Age of Phillis* in 'Catalog: Water' (29–36).

Chapter 5

African-American Ekphrasis and the 'Peculiar Institution'

Introduction

Although it has so far only been touched upon, the question of how African-American writers have used ekphrastic techniques to negotiate images of slavery is a large one that deserves to be addressed not only at greater length but also and more specifically with regard to the 'peculiar institution' of American slavery itself. The exploration of this issue begins in this chapter, which brings together and considers a suite of texts from four authors – John Edgar Wideman, Yusef Komunyakaa, Natasha Trethewey and Terrance Hayes. Even as these figures are all well-known and indeed preeminent within the field of African-American letters, the texts themselves (like much of the material covered earlier) have been almost entirely overlooked.

1. From Sights to Sounds: John Edgar Wideman's 'Listening'

The first text in this ekphrastic mini-gallery is Wideman's 'Listening', a two-page prose sketch described by Jeffrey Renard Allen as a 'brilliant riff' (93) on William Sidney Mount's *Bar-Room Scene* (1835) (Fig. 5.1). Wideman's text was originally published in 1994 in Edward Hirsch's *Transforming Vision: Writers on Art*, a multigeneric assemblage of writings based on the holdings of the Art Institute of Chicago, which include paintings, sculptures, prints, drawings and photographs. It takes its place within Hirsch's collection as one of just four African-American pieces out of forty-six

Figure 5.1 William Sidney Mount, *Bar-Room Scene*, 1835 (oil on canvas). The William Owen Goodman and Erna Sawyer Goodman Collection, Art Institute of Chicago. © 2021 The Art Institute of Chicago / Art Resource, New York / Photo SCALA, Florence.

contributions overall, with the others being from Robert Hayden, Rita Dove and Charles Johnson.

As Wideman explains, at the time of working on this commission he is in Maine rather than Chicago itself and so obliged to compose his text at one remove, simulating the experience of a museum visit by perusing a copy of *Master Paintings in the Art Institute of Chicago*, and it is in this glossy and expensively produced volume that he encounters Mount's painting, a work which, as he remarks, he had not seen previously. This sense of dislocation from and externality to the museum is as much symbolic as geographical, since, apart from in Mount's picture itself, the tome Wideman inspects contains, as he points out, virtually no other images of African-descended people with whom he can identify. This being so, it is no surprise that he should be attracted to *Bar-Room Scene*, as it provides an intriguing study in the seemingly intransigent realities of racial inclusion and exclusion.

As its title would suggest, *Bar-Room Scene* is a painting whose action is set inside a tavern and features a group of four white males of varying ages observing a fifth white male figure, adorned in a ragged jacket and holding an empty beer-mug above his head as he jigs along the line between two floorboards, his back turned to the painting's viewer. Yet even as the dancer at the centre of the picture is watched and encircled by a quartet of white gazes he is at the same time being seen by other eyes, belonging to a rather stout-looking working-class African-American man who stands unnoticed in the tavern's right-hand alcove, his feet perhaps lightly tapping in time with the rhythm of the dance.

Mount's scene confronts Wideman not simply with a countenance that is familiar to him but with a set of circumstances that he knows well too, leading him to posit a kinship between himself – invited to write about any of the artworks in an art-historical institution that seems largely oblivious to his existence – and Mount's free but marginalised (and isolated) African American. Like the latter presence, Wideman is on the edge of things as he flicks his way across the images and commentaries in *Master Paintings*, or indeed imagines himself walking through the distant galleries of the museum itself.[1]

Even as Wideman empathises with the African-American figure in Mount's scene on the basis of a mutual marginality, he draws that figure into relationship with other elements in the tableau. He notes, for example, how the tiny spots of white paint (betokening gleams of light) on the three glass decanters and the solitary glazed clay jug, located on the painting's left margin, are in turn reflected in the tiny flecks of white in the eyes of the African-American man on the opposite side of the picture, just as the jug's brown rotundity is answered in the man's own colour and shape. This compositional reciprocity between the various elements on either wing of Mount's triptych-like design underscores the sidelining of the African American while at the same time implicitly reducing him to the level of a serviceable but nondescript object.

As well as drawing attention to the link between the invisible world of everyday things and an excluded black man, Wideman suggests a more consequential connection, this time between the outcast who has slipped into the painting's obscure recess and the dancing white man stealing the limelight in the triptych's central section. One way he does this is by emphasising the similarity in the positioning of the two figures' feet, as the toes of the African American standing in the corner with his back against the wall replicate the dancer's own toes moving down the line of the floorboard with the precision and poise of a tightrope-walker. It is as if, despite the walking stick which perhaps connotes his infirmity, the black figure is nonetheless in step with his white counterpart.

Such a sense of affinity is strengthened when it is recognised, as Kevin Michael Scott argues, that Mount's dancer is an impoverished Irish immigrant, his identity carefully coded by 'a host of circumstantial details':

> First, his clothing marks him as poor, as does his ax and his willingness to perform for what must be a paltry sum (probably the cost of an ale). Each of these descriptions also strongly marks the figure as an immigrant given the typology of the era. With the gradual transition from independent labor to wage labor, especially in and near the cities, and the resultant worries about being labeled a 'wage slave,' as much menial labor as possible was left to immigrants willing to take any position. The Irish, especially, were already earning the reputation of being a servant 'race.' This was especially true in New York City – the first audience of nearly all of Mount's genre works. The dancer's itinerancy and drunkenness echo the theatrical type of the flighty Irishman much more than any other, and the ribbon on his hat was just becoming a common signifier of Irishness. (245)

Scott's reading both corrects Wideman's claim that the tavern in the painting is rural rather than urban and suggests that Mount's relatively youthful-looking African-American man and the faceless dancer are linked not just with regard to the disposition of their feet. They are also affiliated in terms of how they stand racially vis-à-vis the 'boy and the three seated men' in the painting, who 'serve as "the four ages of the Yankee," from initiate to emeritus' (Scott 242). For these normative white figures, African-American and Irish subjects are all but interchangeably inferior, sharing a set of stereotypical traits, which, according to the 'popular mind' (Lott 98), include, *inter alia*, 'lustiness . . . casual (if seldom deadly) violence, undependability and even occasional thievery' (Scott 245) – as well as the 'itinerancy and drunkenness' already adduced.

Such 'surely uncharitable equations of black and Irish' (Lott 98) might seem to provide a promising footing on which to forge an alliance against the Yankee, the common enemy at the centre of this racial triptych. In this regard, it is worth noting that, although the scene Mount portrays is marked by an apparently unalloyed gaiety, it also features two tools which have the capacity to produce a less convivial mood. The 'black man carries in an inside pocket of his coat a hatchet, the head of which protrudes just above his left knee' (Scott 247), while the Irishman possesses a 'long-handled axe' set aside, for the duration of his dance, on the floor in the painting's right foreground. As Scott suggests, these items signify the 'menial labor' to which both figures are restricted; but they can also be construed as having other purposes, not so much perpetuating inequalities of race and class as potentially avenging them by means of a violence that may not be quite as 'casual' as the stereotype presupposes. As Elaine Scarry argues:

> The weapon and the tool seem at moments indistinguishable, for they may each reside in a single physical object ... and may be quickly transformed back and forth, now into the one, now into the other. At the same time, however, a gulf of meaning, intention, connotation, and tone separates them. If one holds the two side by side in front of the mind – a hand (as weapon) and a hand (as tool), a knife (weapon) and a knife (tool), a hammer and a hammer, an ax and an ax – it is then clear that what differentiates them is not the object itself but the surface on which they fall. (173)

Yet while they can be read as being in possible partnership, the two outsider-figures in *Bar-Room Scene* are also fundamentally at variance, the tension between them springing from the choreographic activity in which the Irishman indulges. As Wideman observes the black man in turn observing the capering figure in the middle of Mount's painting, he is led to ask why the man's face bears a smile and what it is that he might be recollecting. Wideman resolves these questions by suggesting that Mount's dancer is explicitly intended to evoke memories of the theatre performer Thomas Dartmouth 'Daddy' Rice, who, as noted in Chapter 2, was the creator in the late 1820s of 'Jump Jim Crow', a blackface entertainment which inaugurated the tradition of American minstrelsy. As Sean Murray suggests, Rice's routine arose from his 'possibly apocryphal encounter' with an old and decrepit slave whose 'song and stilted dance' he witnessed and then 'appropriated' while the slave was 'work[ing] in a stable' (357). Far from being a sympathetic mimesis of black cultural expression, however, Rice's act was a mockery of the disabled slave's performance and demeaned and diminished African Americans in general, caricaturing them as happy-go-lucky and witless, all in the name of white delight and Rice's professional advancement alike, or, in Lott's laconic phrase, 'sport and profit' (3).

From this perspective, it might be wondered why the African-American man should seem amused by the spectacle he is witnessing, until, that is, the reader-viewer follows Wideman's injunction to ponder the painting more deeply and realises that the man's smile should not be taken at face value. Rather, it should be read against the grain, as an instance of the strategic 'mask' by which African Americans are able protectively to conceal from the 'world' their 'torn and bleeding hearts' (Dunbar). If Mount's black man is able to see himself in the scene of merriment the painting discloses, it is only to the extent that the reflection distorts and alienates, leaving him both within and without the scene at one and the same time.

Although the dancer in Mount's picture is patently a poor imitation of the hugely successful Rice, it is implied that he nonetheless similarly exploits and commoditises African-American culture to his own advantage, carrying out his performance in exchange for the beverage with which to fill the tin tankard he is holding aloft. As well as reinforcing the stereotype of Irishman as drunkard, the dancer's appetite for alcohol puts him humorously out of step with the largest of the three barely decipherable notices on the tavern's golden-hued rear wall, which advertises a temperance meeting (somewhat ironically given its location in a public house). More significantly, that appetite bolsters the argument that the dancing Irishman and the watching African-American figure in Mount's painting are implicitly in conflict, given 'the near universality of temperance sentiment among abolitionists' (Walters 81).

As noted earlier, the ambigram-like presence of the tool-weapons in *Bar-Room Scene* troubles the overriding impression of jollity that the painting creates, pointing to the potential for violence between the Yankees on the one hand and the Irish and black men on the other, even as the latter pair also might have reason to fight among themselves. As Wideman suggests in his text's peroration, however, all the figures in the picture seem more attuned to a far greater destruction, in the form of the American Civil War which began some twenty-six years after the painting's composition and lends several aspects of the image a premonitory and mournful edge: for Wideman, the few flecks of red that scatter about the canvas are, for instance, harbingers of the blood that will be spilled in the course of the conflict; the inaudible sound of the clapping hands that keep the dancer's time is amplified into the cacophonous discharge of artillery; the smoke curling upwards from the pipe held by the oldest Yankee becomes a portent of conflagration; the uplifted eyes of the white boy perhaps look beyond their immediate object (the dancer) to the boy's own death in combat or maybe even that of the imaginary drummer-lad who Wideman sees as the boy's future double; the vacant-eyed appearance of the three spectators who are sitting down foretells the look of soldiers returning from the fray, wounded both physically and psychically; and finally, the casual malice of 'Jump Jim Crow' is heard anew by the sequestered black man as the sound of military music.

2. Slavery and Sacrifice: Yusef Komunyakaa's 'Modern Medea' and 'The Price of Blood'

The two poems considered in the second section of this chapter are Yusef Komunyakaa's 'Modern Medea' (1998) and 'The Price of Blood' (2004), both of which engage with paintings by the white southern artist, Thomas Satterwhite Noble, that were produced in the immediate aftermath of the national apocalypse that *Bar-Room Scene* seems to anticipate. The first poem enters into dialogue with Noble's *Margaret Garner* (1867) – or, more precisely, the wood engraving (based on Mathew B. Brady's photograph of the picture) that was published in *Harper's Weekly* and other national journals and papers in the same year. The second writes back, for its part, to *The Price of Blood: A Planter Selling His Son* (1868).

As one who has drawn extensively upon his experiences during the Vietnam War in several collections and *Dien Cai Dau* (1988) most powerfully, Komunyakaa can be thought of, at least in these parts of his corpus, as a soldier-poet, and in this respect has something in common (rather surprisingly, given other obvious differences) with Noble, who himself invites classification as a kind of soldier-artist. Born in Kentucky in 1835 (coincidentally the year of *Bar-Room Scene*), Noble grew up in a state of privilege as the scion of a 'prosperous' if unglamorous-sounding 'hemp rope and cotton bagging . . . manufacturer who employed slaves and black wage labor on his hemp farm' (Boime 30), going on to study painting with Thomas Couture for approximately three years in 1850s Paris, before serving as a Captain in the Confederate Army. In the light of this background and the South's eventual defeat by the North, it is perhaps again surprising that Noble should want to take slavery as his subject matter, producing between 1865 and 1869 a series of some eight canvases that is 'considered his most significant body of work' (Furth 37) and includes the two paintings mentioned earlier. Noble's turn towards the subject of slavery becomes more curious still when it is observed that the works that he composed in this vein are largely critical of the regime he had fought to preserve. As critics have argued, however, Noble's allegiance to the pro-slavery cause in all probability had more to do with loyalty to his family (Furth 47) and to the 'conservative element of his native Kentucky' (Boime 35) than a genuine conviction as to slavery's legitimacy. It is as if the national conflicts that the war unleashed are replicated in the artist's shifting personal politics.

At first glance, *Margaret Garner* (Fig. 5.2) appears to be an unequivocal indictment of American slavery, designed to elicit sympathy for the infanticidal mother at its heart by forcing its audience to acknowledge the circumstances that have compelled her to act as she does. Perhaps the most obvious way in which it achieves these effects is by mirroring Margaret's posture in that of the young man who stands opposite her, as he points down towards the two fresh corpses occupying the picture's middle foreground and stares in open-mouthed disbelief and accusation at the man by his side: Margaret may have murdered the two sons sprawled out on the floor but, the painting suggests, the responsibility for the atrocity lies elsewhere, specifically with the regime of white power.

Yet if *Margaret Garner* is intended to evoke pathos for the slave-mother, it does so at the expense of historical fidelity, as becomes

Figure 5.2 Thomas Satterwhite Noble, *Margaret Garner*, 1867 (oil on canvas). Courtesy of the National Underground Railroad Freedom Center. Photograph Phil Armstrong.

clear when the painting is juxtaposed with the actual story on which it draws and which, as noted in Chapter 1, is also the catalyst for Toni Morrison's *Beloved*. That story begins on the evening of 27 January 1856, when Margaret and her husband, Robert (both in their early twenties), together with their four young children (Thomas, Samuel, Mary and Priscilla) and Robert's parents fled their enslavement in Kentucky and walked across the frozen Ohio River into the free state of Ohio itself, making their way to a safe house in Cincinnati. This icy passage echoes the set-piece river transit of Eliza Harris in Harriet Beecher Stowe's *Uncle Tom's Cabin* (1852) and was to have been the first step on a path leading the family, via the Underground Railroad, to the Canaan of Canada, the Promised Land for so many slaves seeking to escape the South. In contrast to Eliza's flight, however, the Garners' escape attempt was unsuccessful and ended in catastrophe, as their owners, Colonel Archibald Kinkead Gaines and James Marshall, quickly tracked them down and, together with several United States deputy marshals, broke into the house, demanding the Garners' capture and return under the Fugitive Slave Act of 1850. Faced with these invaders (and prospects), Margaret strove to make another icy crossing – this time from life to death – by attempting to kill her children and herself alike.

Although Margaret was able to murder only one child before being arrested and imprisoned for trial, her extraordinary actions immediately aroused huge national interest and excitement, which no doubt both fed off and fuelled coverage of the incident in the press. An excerpt from the *Cincinnati Enquirer* provides a brief flavour of how the episode was being reported:

> a deed of horror had been consummated, for weltering in its blood, the throat being cut from ear to ear and the head almost severed from the body, upon the floor lay one of the children of the younger couple, a girl three years old (sic), while in a back room, crouched beneath the bed, two more of the children, boys, of two and five years (sic), were moaning, the one having received two gashes in its throat, the other a cut upon the head. As the party entered the room the mother was wielding a heavy shovel, and before she could be secured she inflicted a heavy blow with it upon the face of the infant, which was lying upon the floor. (qtd. in Weisenburger 73)

This gruesome local account slightly decreases the ages of the two boys, since Thomas and Samuel were six and four, respectively – and also slightly increases the age of the 'girl', Mary, who was just two and a half. In 'all other details', however, the *Enquirer*'s 'description' is 'consistent with other news reports, themselves taken from statements of the posse members, and more importantly with statements offered during the coroner's inquest held Monday afternoon and Tuesday 28–29 January 1856, as reported in all the city papers' (Weisenburger 299n).

Apart from its historical value, the *Enquirer*'s account clearly demonstrates one of the most salient ways in which Noble has deviated from his source, showing how he customises the past for his own artistic and political purposes, as he revisits the scene of the crime and alters the identity of the murder victim, replacing the 'weltering' daughter whose 'throat' is 'cut from ear to ear' with the bodies of two male children, both of whom are evidently much older than Margaret's actual sons. As Leslie Furth has argued, in making this change, Noble simultaneously does two things: first, he makes Margaret's actions seem all the more 'subversive' by increasing their financial impact upon her owner, since 'a pair of young boys would have represented a much more precious commodity in terms of labor and sale value than a girl'; and secondly, he avoids offering his audience the image of 'a slain infant' that would have been deemed 'too macabre' and hence detracted from the sympathy for the mother's predicament that he seeks to cultivate (40).

Together with this particular revision, Noble makes a second change which once more compromises the historical record, while also this time working in fact to diminish the viewer's sympathy for Margaret and reinforcing the racial prejudice of the day. In the 1850 census for the area of Kentucky where Margaret was then living, her racial identity is recorded with a hastily scrawled 'm' (Weisenburger 39), standing for 'mulatto', a categorisation which brands her as the product not only of miscegenation but (tacitly) also quite probably rape, or at the very least some form of sexual coercion. As Weisenburger argues, it is not unreasonable to suppose, in addition, that 'one or more' (48) of Margaret's children had a white father too, the most plausible candidate for that office being none other than her owner, Gaines himself. Whatever the truth of the matter, the idea that Margaret's offspring were the result of sexual violence is certainly implicit in the court address made during Margaret's trial by the suffragist, abolitionist and orator, Lucy Stone, when she comments on how 'The faded faces of the negro children tell too plainly to what degradation female slaves must submit' (qtd. in Coffin 565).

Yet no such faces inhabit Noble's painting, as the artist provides the viewer with a quite different tableau and colour scheme to those appearing in the historical archive: not only does he remove from sight the light-skinned child whom Margaret murders, but also endows both the mother and the four boys he attributes to her with dark complexions, using 'generous dabs of burnt sienna and raw umber' (Morgan 100) in order to do so. By changing the palette of history in this way and effectively turning Margaret into 'an animalistic woman of African descent' (Morgan 105), Noble disavows white male sexual violence towards the female slave and transforms the murderous mother into an object of disgust rather than compassion. At the same time, the animalising and Africanising of Margaret aligns the painting with the stigmatising of blackness that characterises Noble's age and that Frederick Douglass so incisively captures and critiques in 'The Color Line' (1881). As Douglass puts it, using a lexicon strangely apposite for this painterly context:

> Few evils are less accessible to the force of reason, or more tenacious of life and power, than a long-standing prejudice. It is a moral disorder, which creates the conditions necessary to its own existence, and fortifies itself by refusing all contradiction. It paints a hateful picture according to its own diseased imagination, and distorts the features of the fancied original to suit the portrait. As those who believe in the visibility of ghosts can easily see them, so it is always easy to see repulsive qualities in those we despise and hate. (501)

As Noble reconstructs Margaret's story in his painting, so Komunyakaa reworks Noble in 'Modern Medea', or at least the engraved version of the painting that appears in *Harper's* (Fig. 5.3). This is Komunyakaa's poem:

> Apex, triangle ... a dead child
> on the floor between his mother
> & four slavecatchers in a Cincinnati hideout.
> Blood colors her hands
>
> & the shadow on the wall
> a lover from the grave.
> She sacrificed her favorite
> first. He must've understood,
>
> stopped like a stone figure.
> Where's the merciful weapon, sharp
> as an icepick or hook knife?
> We know it was quick,
>
> a stab of light. Treed
> as if by dogs around an oak –

Figure 5.3 Mathew B. Brady, *The Modern Medea – The Story of Margaret Garner, Harper's Weekly*, 1867. Photographs and Prints Division, Schomburg Center for Research in Black Culture, The New York Public Library.

she stands listening to a river
sing, begging salt for her wounds. (ellipsis in original)

The first point to note about this typically condensed and allusive poem is its classical title, which comes not from the original artwork but *Harper's*. This new title (*The Modern Medea – The Story of Margaret Garner*) elevates Margaret from history to myth, placing her on a par with the eponymous protagonist of Euripides' *Medea* (431 BCE), even as the parallel is profoundly inappropriate. In Euripides' tragedy, Medea murders her two sons in order to avenge herself upon their father and ex-husband, Jason, when he abandons her for another woman: she is an 'artist in obscenity' (36), driven by a towering sense of sexual betrayal and sexual jealousy. In Margaret's case, conversely, infanticide occurs for very different reasons and is above all an act of black maternal resistance against white power.[2] The change in title that occurs between the painting and its 'print reproduction' (Morgan 113) thus provides another example of how the historical truth is rendered awry even by those who claim to represent it, and Komunyakaa would no doubt be aware of these complications and ironies.

Beyond the poem's title, the next significant detail is the geometric terminology of its opening words – 'Apex, triangle' – which picks up on how Noble's image organises the spatial relationships between its various figures. That image in fact contains two triangles, one of which is on the right-hand side of the picture and consists of Margaret herself and her two surviving sons, who seem to want to scale her tree-like form (Komunyakaa likens her to an 'oak'). The other occupies the middle of the scene and is in an inverted position, its lines stretching down from Margaret's headscarf and the 'Blood' that 'colors her hands' to the 'dead child / on the floor' and then back up to the man with beard and hat (presumably intended as Gaines), before crossing back to the headscarf, with the lines linked by items that, in the painting at least, are all coloured bright red: the headscarf, the child's blood and the man's shirt and collar. As Morgan observes, by so arranging his composition, Noble upends the 'European painting convention' for investing figures with heroic stature, not 'expressing higher ideals, lifting viewer eyes and sending spirits soaring' but plunging eyes and spirits down towards slavery's nadir: in thus disrupting the 'grand Greco-Roman tradition', it is, she writes, 'as if Noble had hung an African mask over a face in a classical frieze' (112).

As the poem develops, it represents Margaret's murder of her 'favorite' in terms of sacrifice, using an idiom that invests the act of infanticide with a Christian aura, as if the mother is yielding up her child as God the Father gave up His Son in order to save humanity from sin and grant it Eternal Life. Once again, however, the parallel seems dubious and ironic, despite the cruciform disposition of the 'favorite''s body, since there is little in the way of redemption to be had amid the shambles of the 'Cincinnati hideout' that Noble depicts and Komunyakaa describes.

Together with being represented in the language of sacrifice, the dead child is portrayed as having been 'stopped like a stone figure'. This is an intriguing simile, not least because it seems equally to appertain to the 'four slavecatchers' who have swiftly pursued Margaret and her family across state lines, but whose onrushing movement now appears to have ground to a sudden halt. These figures appear paralysed by the child's corpse, which lies at their feet as if it were a threshold they cannot cross. Margaret is no Medea, but perhaps she is depicted in painting and engraving alike with a touch of the Medusa, the classical Gorgon whose stare has the power to petrify – to turn to stone and to terrify – all those who behold it directly?

Like *Margaret Garner*, Noble's *The Price of Blood: A Planter Selling His Son* (Fig. 5.4) is concerned with child sacrifice, albeit of a kind quite different to that explored in the earlier painting. The rudiments of the scene it presents are glossed by Albert Boime:

> The theme of the picture is the sale of a mulatto male by his father-master, who has just completed the negotiations with the slave agent. A glimpse of a picture on the wall reveals it to represent The Sacrifice of Isaac, thus underscoring the curious expressions and gestures of the seated father and standing son. The youth has been sold into slavery for the pile of gold shown on the table. (52–3)

Although none of the figures involved in this triangular transaction is looking at any of the others, they are all connected by the 'pile of gold' that is appropriately and conspicuously displayed at the centre of the scene – bound, in other words, by impersonal mechanisms of economic exchange that benefit the planter and the trader alike, but merely commoditise the mixed-race 'male'. While the depiction of such dehumanising arrangements is shocking in itself, it becomes yet more so by dint of the fact that the planter exists in what Douglass calls 'the double relation of master and father' (*Narrative* 94) to the 'youth' stationed on the painting's left, the signs of his paternity etched in the young man's physiognomy, particularly his raised left eyebrow. The unholy nature of the entire business is compounded by the

Figure 5.4 Thomas Satterwhite Noble, *The Price of Blood*, 1868 (oil on canvas). Morris Museum of Art, Augusta, Georgia.

Biblical picture Noble ironically incorporates into his own painting. In the Old Testament narrative to which Noble alludes, Abraham's willingness to offer Isaac up to God is the mark of an unwavering religious faith that is duly rewarded when his beloved only son is saved from death by the heavenly intervention of 'the angel of the LORD' (Gen. 22.11). In Noble's painting, by contrast, the father's heartless sacrifice of his progeny is dictated by monetary rather than spiritual considerations and certainly unlikely to be averted by the providential intercession of any latter-day *deus ex machina*.

The base alchemy by which slavery turns flesh into gold clearly positions the planter's son as a victim and is reflected in the colour of his hands and unshod feet, which is similar to that of the neat towers of coins atop the decorative floral tablecloth. Yet Noble's painting also contains elements that allow for a different and more positive reading. Not the least of these is the graceful dignity of the son's stance, which is suggestive of a certain resilience of character and sense of superiority over the system represented by the two figures who collude against him – the father-master and

Figure 5.5 Thomas Gainsborough, *The Blue Boy*, 1770 (oil on canvas). Courtesy of the Huntington Art Museum, San Marino, California.

the slave agent. As Boime has noted (55), the son's poised pose is at the same time a direct visual echo of Thomas Gainsborough's *The Blue Boy* (1770) (Fig. 5.5), establishing a painterly kinship that further elevates Noble's figure: it implicitly places him on an equal footing with his aristocratically costumed white counterpart, thus disrupting the racial hierarchies by which slavery validates itself.[3]

Komunyakaa's response to Noble's painting takes the form of an eclectically not to say ecstatically allusive and sometimes cryptic poem included in *Taboo*:

> The planter's son now hates
>   the part of himself he loved
>   more than anything.

> You can see the faded image
>   of the Sacrifice of Isaac
>   bleeding through.
>
> A mockingbird mimics betrayal,
>   & now there's money for gifts.
>   Maybe the son's thinking
>
> of what Aesop said to Xanthus
>   about the caged bird. Aloof,
>   with one hand on his hip,
>
> he's cocky as his mother.
>   Pyramids of gold on the table
>   balance out the scene.
>
> Holding the bill of sale
>   in his hand, the slave trader
>   could be a circuit judge,
>
> a preacher, an undertaker.
>   The planter's averted eyes
>   take us to Colonel Tom
>
> dead on the floor in Langston's
>   *Mulatto*. Cora argues with God
>   beneath a chinaberry tree,
>
> with her head bowed, gazing
>   at a sign in the dust: Aurora's
>   grasshopper on an anthill.
>
> Where's the wife,
>   in the parlor listening
>   to their daughter play
>
> Schumann's 'Auf einer Burg'
>   so lightly it seethes through
>   the walls? The son flinches
>
> & puffs his chest like a banty
>   rooster, trying not to cry
>   as he holds back the sun. (42–3; italics in original)

Here the idea of the 'planter's son' as victim is again variously mooted. He is figured, for instance, as the subject of 'betrayal' and passed into the hands of a 'slave trader' who seems like an 'undertaker' (as if the father's callous actions will culminate in the death of his own child). At the end of the poem the son is to be found 'trying not to cry'.

As in Noble's picture, however, the son's victim-status sits alongside other potential identities, the first of which, that of runaway, can be glimpsed in the lines, 'Maybe the son's thinking // of what Aesop said to Xanthus / about the caged bird.' Here the allusion is to an exchange reputed to have taken place between Aesop and the philosopher, Xanthus, in an Athenian slave-market. As he ponders the merits and demerits of buying Aesop, Xanthus asks this slave of 'black and ungainly form' if, once purchased, he would ever attempt to abscond, to which the witty fabulist retorts: 'Did you ever hear a bird in a cage tell his master that he intended making his escape?' (Rogers 75). Indeed, it could be said that the son has already initiated the process of escape to which this allusion points or has at least encoded it in his posture by standing 'Aloof' from his surroundings.

As well as being a prospective fugitive, the son is associated with an arrogance and a danger that are also written into the language of the body: he has 'one hand on his hip', is described as 'cocky' and in the final stanza, in another avian image, assumes the guise of a 'banty / rooster', a small but feisty bird used in cockfights. In the poem's opening stanza, it appears that such aggression is to be self-directed, though it is unclear which 'part of himself' the son 'now hates'. Is his animus towards the white element of his identity associated with paternal treachery? Or is the loathing reserved for the blackness that condemns him to slavehood on the basis of *partus sequitur ventrem*, the legal principle by which children follow the condition of the slave-women to whom they are born? Whichever way this two-faced stanza is read, the most striking implication of the poem is that the son's hostile feelings will in fact be channelled outwards rather than inwards, fastening themselves upon the father-planter, a possibility which the latter himself seems to sense, as his 'averted eyes' direct the reader 'to Colonel Tom // dead on the floor in Langston's / *Mulatto*'. The allusion on this occasion is to Langston Hughes's *Mulatto: A Play of the Deep South* (1930), in which the title character, Robert Norwood, confronts his abusive white father and throttles him to death, thus escaping his oppressor in a rather more decisive manner than by just running away from him.

The allusive connection between Komunyakaa's mixed-race youth and the rebellious protagonist of Hughes's Harlem Renaissance melodrama is not without some bleak ironies, however, since the counter-violence of Robert's patricide has calamitous repercussions. It results, first of all, in the madness of his black mother, Cora, who is also the Colonel's mistress (and still to be seen 'argu[ing] with God / beneath a chinaberry tree' in Komunyakaa's text); and secondly, in Robert's frenzied pursuit by a vengeful white mob bent upon his destruction. Although the distraught and deranged Cora is not subjected to the spectacle of witnessing her child 'roasted' and 'swinging full of bullet holes' (44) from a tree, Robert's lynching is only forestalled by his suicide when he puts himself to 'sleep' (50) with a single shot from the Colonel's pistol.

As it closes, Komunyakaa's poem abruptly veers away from African-American literary to European musical traditions, the 'mixtries' (46) of Hughes's *Mulatto* to Robert Schumann's 'Auf Einer Burg' ('In a Castle') (1840). In effecting this unexpected if cosmopolitan allusive shift, 'The Price of Blood' evokes at its margin a parent–child relationship between the planter's 'wife' and her piano-playing 'daughter' implicitly marked by the kind of emotional harmony so thoroughly lacking in the father-son duet with which the poem is primarily concerned. At the same time, the lyrics by Joseph von Eichendorff that accompany Schumann's composition hint at a regretful discord between planter and spouse, particularly in their last verse:

> A wedding party is traveling down there
> along the Rhine, in sunshine.
> Musicians are playing gaily,
> and the beautiful bride – she is weeping. (qtd. in and trans. by Lewin 169)

3. Mixed-Race Subjects: Natasha Trethewey's 'Blood' and 'Enlightenment'

The two poems considered in this chapter's third section are Natasha Trethewey's 'Blood' and 'Enlightenment', both taken from *Thrall* (2012) and both marking a return to and development of the questions of miscegenation and mixed-race identity raised in the reading of Komunyakaa. Prior to analysing these texts, it is worth noting that their thematic concerns pervade Trethewey's *oeuvre* and are intimately connected to her identity as the child of a white father (who was also a poet) and a black mother and who was born, moreover, in a time and place (1966 Mississippi) when, as she notes, 'miscegenation was still illegal, as it was in about twenty states in the rest of the nation' (*Conversations* 183). If Trethewey's poetry is historical, it is thus also personal, just as her personal circumstances are a medium through which history is articulated. It might even be argued that ekphrasis is the ideal genre for her (or any writer) to address miscegenation and its consequences, since the ekphrastic poem, to adapt a term that Trethewey uses of her own *Beyond Katrina* (2010), is itself a 'literary hybrid' (*Conversations* 203), compounded from verbal and visual elements alike.

Like the two Komunyakaa poems, Trethewey's 'Blood' involves a response to a postbellum image of slavery in the umbrous shape of George Fuller's *The Quadroon* (1880) (Fig. 5.6). As it begins, however, it is apparent that 'Blood' is not simply interested in the

Figure 5.6 George Fuller, *The Quadroon*, 1880 (oil on canvas). Gift of George A. Hearn, 1910. © 2021. The Metropolitan Museum of Art / Art Resource, New York / Photo SCALA, Florence.

black genre scene that inspires it but also in what the painting reveals about the artist's disposition towards the mixed-race female slave who is his subject:

> It must be the gaze of a benevolent viewer
> upon her, framed as she is in the painting's
> romantic glow, her melancholic beauty
> meant to show the pathos of her condition:
> *black blood* – that she cannot transcend it. (italics in original)

Fuller's status as 'benevolent viewer' of the young woman he so romantically 'frame[s]' becomes clearer when placed in the context of the personal experience to which, as Sarah Burns argues, his painting looks back. In contrast to Noble, Fuller was a Northerner (born in Massachusetts in 1822), but made three visits to the antebellum South in the 1850s in search of new material – in the form of everyday scenes from slave life – with which to expand and invigorate his artistic repertoire. During the first of these trips, he attended a slave auction, where he witnessed the sale of a person not unlike the one who appears in his painting thirty years later, recording his indignation at and sorrowful fascination with the spectacle in a letter home of 26 January 1850:

> Who is this girl with eyes large and black? The blood of the white and dark races is at enmity in her veins – the former predominated. About 3/4 white says one dealer. Three fourths blessed, a fraction accursed. She is under thy feet, white man. . . . Is she not your sister? . . . She impresses me with sadness! The pensive expression of her finely formed mouth and her drooping eyes seemed to ask for sympathy . . . . Now she looks up, now her eyes fall before the rude gaze of those who are but calculating her charms or serviceable qualities . . . . Oh, is beauty so cheap! (qtd. in Burns, 'Images' 36)

Here the manner in which Fuller regards this light-skinned slave differs markedly from the 'rude gaze' of the 'dealer[s]' around him, who 'but calculate her charms and serviceable qualities' in monetary and implicitly sexual terms. For him she is instead both the living embodiment of the racial 'enmity' that divides the nation and will propel it into Civil War and a bittersweet object of aesthetic pleasure and affective pain in roughly equal measure. No doubt he would wish this impressive figure well just as sincerely as he does her painterly avatar.

Yet if *The Quadroon* bears witness to Fuller's benignity towards the downtrodden figure who looms so large at the centre of his canvas, the picture simultaneously and more importantly constitutes a commentary on the culture in which the artist and his mixed-race muse come face to face and particularly on how the psychological life of the latter is externally regulated by a Manichean 'calculus of color' (Sollors 112), in which whiteness is 'blessed' and blackness 'accursed'. As Eloisa Valenzeula-Mendoza puts it: 'The sorrow' Fuller feels 'for this mixed-race woman is born of the fact that her light skin and beauty, the latter being perceived as a product of the former, does not make up for the "black blood" that courses [or curses] through her veins' (347).

Even as the quadroon 'cannot transcend' the *'black blood'* that the poem's language quietly pathologises, she is able briefly to escape the toil to which that blood consigns her:

> In the foreground she is shown at rest, seated,
> her basket empty and overturned beside her
> as though she would cast down the drudgery
> to which she was born.

This moment of respite at the same time contains a hint of something more radical, since, by not performing her tasks, the quadroon interrupts the capitalist logic of the plantation that converts black labour into white profit, as the image of the 'overturned' 'basket' becomes a symbol for the overturning or casting down of the very system that makes her downcast. Equally, though, Trethewey's use of the conditional phrase, 'as though she would', is a salutary reminder that such a symbol is only that and ultimately just as 'empty' as the basket itself.

At this halfway stage in the poem (it is only seventeen lines overall), the specific nature of the quadroon's occupation within the plantation economy is made explicit: she is a 'gleaner', one whose role is to pick up produce from the field that has not been initially gathered in by other workers. Trethewey's diction here might seem a little incongruous, given that the activity of gleaning is more usually associated with cornfields, rather than the cotton fields that, as the poem puts it, are the quadroon's 'bucolic backdrop' and that invest her with a 'dim aura'. Either way, the quadroon is no sooner defined in these terms than she is dramatically redefined as a 'hopeless / undine', a phrase Trethewey herself gleans from a review of Fuller's painting when it was exhibited at the National Academy of Design in the year of its completion. 'The face' of Fuller's subject, the reviewer writes:

is like that of a hopeless Undine, whose tricksy graces and happy spirits have been clouded but not sanctioned by the love that has come to her. The woman is awakened and exalted, but the slave is lower than ever ... It is the history and burden of a race that this beautiful creature bears .... This is a true historical painting, and must survive the age in which it is painted. (qtd. in Burns, 'Black-Quadroon-Gypsy' 417)

The figuration of the quadroon along such lines might once again seem curious, since an 'undine' is a female supernatural creature which lives in water, rather than the type of natural being associated with the earthly (and earthy) labour that Fuller features in his painting. Conversely, the trope's aquatic connotations endow it with a subtle relevance, opening the poem out beyond the borders of the plantation (and the frame of Fuller's canvas) and towards the Middle Passage that would have ushered the quadroon's ancestors to America in the first place. If the quadroon-as-undine is an otherworldly figure, it is as much in a geographical as a paranormal respect.

While the poem begins with an observation on the apparent benevolence of Fuller's artistic gaze, it ends by suggesting the limits and blind spots that are intrinsic to his perspective:

> how different she's rendered
> from the dark kin working the fields behind her.
> If not for the ray of light appearing as if from beyond
> the canvas, we might miss them – three figures
> in the near distance, small as afterthought.

As Fuller notes in his account of the slave auction, white blood 'predominate[s]' in the makeup of the quadroon at a ratio of three to one, yet in his painting it is the quadroon who predominates within the quartet of slaves to which she belongs. She absorbs the artist's attention at the expense of the 'three figures' who are her 'dark kin' and who are depicted towards the painting's top-left corner, where they are engaged in harvesting the very cotton that she will later glean – her load much lighter than theirs. As if to mimic Fuller's relegation of these figures to the background of the landscape, Trethewey leaves their sex unspecified (they are in fact all female) and only comments on their size relative to the quadroon's imposing dimensions in the poem's last moment, as if the information she provides – 'small as afterthought' – were itself a trivial addendum. Trethewey even suggests that the visibility of the other slaves in the painting has less to do with Fuller's own artistic agency than the kindly intervention of the 'ray of light' that 'appear[s] as if from beyond / the canvas' and that, were it not for the secularising bathos of enjambment, seems to be of the same supernatural order as the despairing undine.

In contrast to 'Blood', which focuses on a painting produced towards the end of the nineteenth century, 'Enlightenment' takes its cue from one created at the century's birth, in the form of Gilbert Stuart's 'Edgehill' *Portrait of Thomas Jefferson* (1805) (Fig. 5.7). This image of one of the United States's Founding Fathers and chief architect of the Declaration of Independence of 1776 provides Trethewey with a starting point from which to examine the tension between 'historical memory and historical erasure' – one of her enduring 'obsessions' (*Conversations* 107) – as it is played out in the third President's much-debated involvement with one of his mixed-race slaves, Sally Hemings, by whom he is alleged to have had at least six children over a period of some fifteen years (Gordon-Reed 157). But as much as the poem has to do with a controversial episode in the infancy of the United States, its inquiry into the past is also a means of reflection upon the present. To what extent, the poem asks, do the ideas about race and racial mixing that Jefferson espoused and promoted, particularly in his *Notes on the State of Virginia* (1785), live on in the attitudes that the poem's father figure adopts towards his mixed-race daughter? Does the present entail a movement beyond the values of the past or a repetition of them?

If it is generally true that every picture tells a story, in the particular case of the portrait at the centre of 'Enlightenment', it could be claimed that at least two stories are in play, symbolically coded in the painting's curious – almost comic and certainly irreverent – chiaroscuro:

> In the portrait of Jefferson that hangs
>   at Monticello, he is rendered two-toned:
> his forehead white with illumination –
>
> a lit bulb – the rest of his face in shadow,
>   darkened as if the artist meant to contrast
> his bright knowledge, its dark subtext. (68)

The first story leads the reader back to the poem's title and the paradox of the Enlightenment project to which it alludes. That project places its faith in the benefits of scientific and rational

African-American Ekphrasis and the 'Peculiar Institution' 153

Figure 5.7 Gilbert Stuart, 'Edgehill' *Thomas Jefferson*, 1805 / 1821 (oil on mahogany panel). National Portrait Gallery, Smithsonian Institution; owned jointly with Monticello, Thomas Jefferson Foundation, Incorporated, Charlottesville, Virginia; purchase funds provided by the Regents of the Smithsonian Institution, the Trustees of the Thomas Jefferson Foundation, Incorporated, and the Enid and Crosby Kemper Foundation.

inquiry, even as the 'systems of classification and categorization' it helped to create, 'as embraced by early American ... thinkers' (Kinnahan) – including Jefferson – were often co-opted as a means of subjugating racial others and formed 'a precondition for the growth of modern racism based on physical typology' (Fredrickson qtd. in Valenzeula-Mendoza 338). Enlightenment, in other words, has its own devious chiaroscuro, pursuing a 'bright knowledge' which conceals a 'dark subtext'. The second story relates to what the poem softly calls Jefferson's 'affair' (68) with Hemings. Here the interracial blending which that liaison involves is once more inscribed in the shifting landscape of the portrait-sitter's strangely hybridised or 'two-toned' face. That face at the same time serves as the index or reminder of the hierarchy of power which structures the Jefferson-Hemings relationship and the larger world in which it occurs, with the upper area painted 'white' and the region below Jefferson's 'forehead' 'darkened' by 'shadow'.

While the poem focuses on a Founding Father in its first thirteen lines (perhaps one for each of the nation's original colonies?), it goes on to become more personalised, as the poem's 'I' introduces her ambivalent relationship to her own father into the historical scene. Recalling 'The first time [she] saw' Jefferson's painting in such patriarchal company, the daughter positions this new authority figure as an apologist for the one who 'gazes out' at her 'across the centuries'. As distinct from Jefferson himself, whose 'lips' appear in Stuart's portrait to be 'fixed as if // he's just uttered some final word', the persona's father speaks without restraint, carefully 'explain[ing]' to his young initiate the 'contradictions' (68) that define the life of his subject:

> how Jefferson hated slavery, though – *out*
>   *of necessity*, my father said – had to own
> slaves; that his moral philosophy meant
>
> he could not have fathered those children:
>   *would have been impossible*, my father said. (69; italics in original)

Yet while father and daughter are at protracted odds on these questions, 'debat[ing] the distance between // word and deed' 'For years' (69), the poem's verbal patterning makes it clear that the paternal voice is the one that dominates their exchange: 'I listened / as my father explained' (68); 'my father said'; 'my father said'; 'I'd . . . / . . . listen / as he named' (69). For all its loquacity (and self-assurance), however, that voice has its own silence, denying Jefferson's identity as father to Hemings's children but oddly neglecting to dispute the existence of the 'affair' itself.

As 'Enlightenment' progresses into its second half, the distinction between the persona's father and the historical figure he defends begins to dissolve, as if the one were the uncanny reembodiment of the other. This process of doubling is manifest in part in the lessons in natural history in which the father schools the daughter, as he escorts her from 'book / to book' and 'name[s]' 'each flower and tree and bird' that they encounter as they read, his copious 'knowledge' reminiscent of the taxonomies and tabulations set out in 'Query VI' of Jefferson's *Notes*, which Trethewey glosses as 'a field guide to Virginia' (69). As the daughter comes to realise, however, in her own instant of enlightenment, the resemblance between her father and Jefferson takes a more intimate and sinister form:

> I did not know then the subtext
>   of our story, that my father could imagine
> Jefferson's words made flesh in my flesh –
>
> *the improvement of the blacks in body*
>   *and mind, in the first instance of their mixture*
> *with the whites* – or that my father could believe
>
> he'd made me *better*. (69–70; italics in original)

As these lines suggest, the father not only sounds like Jefferson's Virginian 'field guide' as he takes his daughter on their library tour – becoming a kind of talking book himself, as it were – but also shares Jefferson's opinions on the issue of miscegenation, as articulated in the italicised 'words' included in the second of the two stanzas above. These words are taken verbatim from 'Query XIV' of Jefferson's *Notes* (148) and are perhaps among the 'citations' the daughter initially 'gather[s]' (69) or gleans from the paternal archive, before turning them back against their author and – more importantly – the one who so unthinkingly rehearses them. Jefferson's brutal dictum is not incarnated so much in the persona's 'flesh', in other words, as in the body of her text.[4]

Even as Jefferson regards the mixed-race subject as an '*improvement*' upon '*the blacks in body / and mind*', the irony is that the daughter sees little improvement beyond this mentality in her father. The latter, it seems, remains 'captive' to the 'past', whether at the time when he was 'young' and takes his daughter on the first trip to Monticello 'years ago' or when the two revisit Jefferson's abode at a point when the father has 'become' an 'old man' (70). The daughter herself, on the other hand, has advanced along a different path in the time that has elapsed between these two occasions, no longer passively 'follow[ing]' (69) her father-mentor from one book to another as the father follows Jefferson, but formulating a critical view of both figures. In doing so, ironically, she exemplifies the sort of enlightened autonomy celebrated by Immanuel Kant, one year before the publication of Jefferson's *Notes* and defined as the ability 'to use one's intelligence without being guided by another' (135).

As 'Enlightenment' arrives at its conclusion, it becomes evident that the past's enthralment of the present is not confined to the dynamics of the father-daughter plot, but detectable more widely amid the casual pulse of everyday exchange:

> Now, we take in how much has changed:
>   talk of Sally Hemings, someone asking,
>
> *How white was she?* – parsing the fractions
>   as if to name what made her worthy
> of Jefferson's attentions: a near-white,
>
> quadroon mistress, not a plain black slave.
>   *Imagine stepping back into the past,*
> our guide tells us then – and I can't resist
>
> whispering to my father: *This is where*
>   *we split up. I'll head around to the back.*
> When he laughs, I know he's grateful
>
> I've made a joke of it, this history
>   that links us – white father, black daughter –
> even as it renders us other to each other. (70–1; italics in original)

Although things may have 'changed' between the previous and current visits to Monticello that define the poem's temporal framework, the extent to which they have improved is debatable. Hemings's role as Jefferson's 'quadroon mistress' is now openly a topic of discussion among the Monticello sightseers, even as the questions that the faceless 'someone' asks about her are constrained by the same assumptions concerning the superiority of whiteness over blackness that the poem critiques, whether in relation to the persona's father or Jefferson.

At the same time, these lines look back to and echo 'Blood', in which Fuller's gaze operates according to a Jeffersonian logic that affirms the quadroon as a 'worthy' object of aesthetic attention because, like Hemings, she too is a 'near-white' rather than 'plain black slave'. The blend of linguistic and mathematical idioms that emerges at this moment in the text ('parsing the fractions') and immediately before it ('an equation // writ large at Monticello' [70]) itself rewards attention, not least because it evokes the elaborate 'algebra' Jefferson uses to explain and define the 'genetic origins' (Clark 2) and composition of Hemings's racial identity, as, for example, in a letter to Francis C. Gray of 4 March 1815:

Let the first crossing be of *a*, pure negro, with *A*, pure white. The unit of blood of the issue being composed of the half of that of each parent, will be *a*/2 + *A*/2. Call it, for abbreviation, *h* (half blood).

Let the second crossing be of *h* and *B*, the blood of the issue will be *h*/2 + *B*/2 or substituting for *h*/2 its equivalent, it will be *a*/4 + *A*/4 + *B*/2, call it *q* (quarteroon) being 1/4 negro blood. (qtd. in Clark 1; italics in original)

Thus reduced to a lower-case '*h*', it is not surprising that the persona should not be tempted by the prospect of '*stepping back into the past*' that the docent offers her. But as much as the 'black daughter''s decision to '*split up*' from her 'white father' at this juncture is a form of self-protection, it is also a means of protecting him, making light of the 'history' that has shaped his prejudices (and resulted in their mutual alienation) by turning the pain of the past into a harmless 'joke'.

4. Ways of Seeing – and Not Seeing: Terrance Hayes's 'Antebellum House Party'

While a literal return to the past may hold few charms for 'Enlightenment''s persona, it is, metaphorically speaking, what drives much of Trethewey's work, including 'Enlightenment' itself – she describes herself as a 'poet of history' (qtd. in McHaney 170), after all. Equally, such a backward step also provides the imaginative impetus for all the other texts discussed in this chapter, the last of which is Terrance Hayes's 'Antebellum House Party', a brilliantly satirical and sometimes surreal anatomy of racism in the slave-holding South.

This poem was first published in *The New Yorker* on 28 April 2014 and subsequently in Hayes's *How to be Drawn* (2015), as well as *Found Anew* (also 2015), an edited anthology of poetry and prose inspired by photographs in the South Caroliniana Library Digital Collections, for which writers variously connected to the Palmetto State were invited to 'take something old, perhaps forgotten, and make it new' (Jones and McManus xiv). Hayes's poem certainly fulfils this brief by choosing as his 'something old' a photograph which the library titles and dates as *Coffee after Dinner, Dean Hall Plantation, Berkeley County, South Carolina* (c. 1900) (Fig. 5.8); but at the same time he exceeds that brief by paradoxically making the photograph even older (in order to renew it).

Figure 5.8 *Coffee after Dinner, Dean Hall Plantation, Berkeley County, South Carolina* (c. 1900). Courtesy of the South Caroliniana Library, University of South Carolina, Columbia, S.C.

This he does by reimagining and rewriting the scene – as his poem's own title indicates – as if it were located prior to rather than after the Civil War. An uncharitable or impatient reader might dismiss such a temporal dislocation and relocation of the photograph as an example of careless research, but Hayes's idiosyncratic approach to the image is perhaps more positively viewed as a particular case of ekphrastic licence, whereby – like so many of the other writers considered in this book – he manipulates and reshapes the materials of history according to his own imaginative vision. As the poem puts it at one point, 'Imagination is often the boss of memory' (6), a formula which the text itself would appear to confirm and put into practice.

One way of beginning to think about Hayes's remaking of this disquieting post-prandial scene is by means of an (authentically antebellum) account of the plantation given by the Jamaican-born John B. Irving, in *A Day on Cooper River* (1842):

> It is recorded of a certain French Lady, that she exclaimed, on first visiting the city of Bonn, 'voilà Bonn! c'est une petite perle.' Now every one familiar with the character of our country, must know there is (sic) about Dean Hall no pictorial beauties, no scenery so magnificent, as to elicit so elegant an expression as this, from the lips of a stranger – but Dean Hall has a nobler and more enduring monument to boast of than the elegant compliment paid to Bonn. It is the place visited recently by a distinguished nobleman, who after scrutinizing, as was his wont, with an inquisitive eye, all things appertaining to the habits, food, clothing and treatment of the slaves, voluntarily tendered this honest conviction of his heart, 'It is impossible,' he said, 'for me an Englishman to say I am a convert to your institutions, but I candidly confess, from all I have seen, *my prejudices have been entirely eradicated.*' (9; italics in original)

Coming to Dean Hall in the recent wake of Britain's abolition of slavery in its Caribbean colonies in 1834, Irving's unnamed English 'nobleman' promotes a vision that itself invites scrutiny, since it is so markedly blind to 'the treatment of the slaves' Hayes wants to bring to light in his self-consciously anachronistic text. While that treatment does not include the kind of extreme physical violence stereotypically associated with slavery, it is nonetheless just as shocking for what it reveals about those other modes of violence to which slavery exposes black subjects, as manifested in the rhythms and routines of the everyday.

As Hayes's poem makes clear from the outset, the violence in question is the violence of dehumanisation:

> To make the servant in the corner unobjectionable
> Furniture, we must first make her a bundle of tree parts
> Axed and worked to confidence. Oak-jawed, birch-backed,
>
> Cedar-skinned, a pillowy bosom for the boss infants,
> A fine patterned cushion the boss can fall upon.
> Furniture does not pine for a future wherein the boss
>
> Plantation house will be ransacked by cavalries or Calvary. (5)

Here the poem's speaker adopts an instructional role, as if training a prospective guest in the mental etiquette expected within the 'Plantation house' in the antebellum era. At its root, that etiquette involves breaking down the cornered 'servant' into a 'bundle' of 'tree parts' attesting (ironically) to her physical strength – she is 'Oak-jawed, birch-backed' and 'Cedar-skinned' – and then reassembling them into a piece of 'unobjectionable / Furniture'. Such a way of seeing the slave is in effect a way of not seeing her, rendering her both as useful and as easily overlooked as the wooden armchair in which, in the photograph, her moustachioed 'boss' is seated. The process of making her invisible, it is worth noting, is in fact underway even before she is figured as furniture, as she is concealed beneath the euphemism that names her, less objectionably, as 'servant'.

It is not difficult to infer why the culture of the antebellum South should want to encourage such a frame of mind, since it has at least two advantages, the first of which is to absolve the plantation's white inhabitants of the guilt induced by the system from which they benefit. The master can, for example, 'fall upon' the slave – exploit her sexually, that is – without redress, as she is merely 'A fine patterned cushion', just as her breasts are nothing but a 'pillowy bosom' for his 'infants', a phrasing which both hints at and muffles another form of exploitation, in the shape of slave-mothers' enforced labour as wet nurses to the master's progeny.[5] The second advantage entailed in thingifying the slave is that it robs her of the kind of interiority mentioned in connection with David Dabydeen's 'Turner' in Chapter 1, or appears to do so at least. Ideally divested of thought, feeling and soul, the slave does not 'pine' (in a deliberately wooden pun) either for 'Calvary' (where the son of a carpenter was nailed to a tree) or the destruction of the regime that tortures her in less flagrant ways. Even so, the salvific 'future' in which the master's abode will be 'ransacked' by Union troops is preveniently ensconced in the word '*furniture*', as if the plantocractic order were secretly already at war with itself.

Following this momentary flash forwards to the redemptive sundering of the national house, the poem returns to the initial antebellum setting it has contrived for itself, detailing the various domestic objects into which the slave can be transmogrified by the master's all-unseeing gaze:

> A kitchen table can, in the throes of a yellow fever outbreak,
> Become a cooling board holding the boss wife's body.
>
> It can on ordinary days also be an ironing board holding
> Boss garments in need of ironing. Tonight it is simply a place
> For a white cup of coffee, a tin of white cream. Boss calls
>
> For sugar and the furniture bears it sweetly. (5)

For the most part, the forms and functions the slave respectively assumes and carries out in these lines seem innocuous enough, with the chilling exception of her role as 'cooling board', an object on which a dead 'body' – in this case, 'the boss wife's' – would be laid out in order to arrest the course of its corruption. The inclusion of this detail in the poem significantly disrupts the cosy status quo advertised in the photograph and – like the futuristic military allusion – is another sign of slavery's impermanence, just as the specification of 'yellow fever' as the cause of the mistress's death lends that passing event a retributive dimension, given the African provenance of the disease and its long-established association with the slave trade (McCandless 7).

As well as hinting at the poetic (or historic) justice of the mistress's demise, these lines suggest that the reduction of the slave to the condition of furniture is not wholly effective and that she retains vestiges of the interiority and humanity that slavery strives to eradicate. This is particularly evident when the 'Boss calls' for what is no doubt slave-grown 'sugar' and the 'furniture' responds by 'bear[ing] it sweetly'. In this ambiguous exchange, the 'it' is not just the commodity the slave carries – white like the 'cup of coffee' and the 'cream' to mix into it – but the master's voice, which she 'bears' in the alternative sense of 'endures'.

In possessing such resilience, the slave evinces a spirit which contravenes the duties expected of her, as outlined when the speaker stipulates that the purpose of 'Furniture's presence ... / In the den' is 'little more' than to impart a 'warm feeling' to its occupants (or denizens). One of these is the 'dog' already warming itself in front of the 'fireplace' and practising its own rituals of transformation, as it first 'imagines each log' at which it is 'staring' as a 'bone' that 'would taste like a spiritual wafer on [its] tongue' (5) and is then later to be discovered still 'Mourning' the loss of these 'succulent' if non-existent delicacies 'Long after they have burned to ash' (6).

With its remarkable if self-absorbed capacity to imagine and feel grief, the 'hound dog' (6), seems to have appropriated to itself two of the very characteristics of the human that the slave-as-furniture is denied. Equally, there is a moment in the poem when it appears that the slave has assumed the characteristics of the animal, even as such a complementary metamorphosis is rapidly dispelled by the enjambment that restores her more familiar status as household object: 'Let us imagine,' the speaker suggests, 'the servant ordered down on all fours / In the manner of an ottoman where upon the boss volume / Of John James Audubon's *Birds of America* can be placed' (6; italics in original).[6] But whether thought of as submissive quadruped or 'ottoman', the slave here is freighted with a load much greater than the sugar she had borne earlier, in the colossal shape of Audubon's ornithological *magnum opus*, on which he worked between 1827 and 1838. 'In its grandest and most complete form, the Double Elephant Folio edition', this book, as Gregory Nobles puts it, 'would be a huge, heavy, ungainly four-volume set of 435 plates, with each plate measuring 29 1/2 × 39 1/2 inches, each volume weighing more than forty pounds' (91). Yet the burden (pun intended) which this tome represents is not just physical but also crushingly moral, since the Haitian-born naturalist-painter and self-styled American woodsman who created it was also, at several points in his life, a slave-owner (Nobles 202–3), thus emulating his father, who, as 'merchant, planter, and dealer in slaves amassed a large fortune' (Herrick 36) in the Caribbean of the 1780s.

The metaphorical ottoman tasked with supporting Audubon's monumental book of birds is subsequently displaced by other items of furniture that are literal and sought after by wealthy 'Antebellum residents' eager to ensure that their 'dinner parties' are suitably 'photogenic'. These articles include 'encyclopedic / Bookcases' and 'luxurious armoires', as well as 'beds with ornate ... / Canopies' made out of 'cotton', a commodity produced, like sugar, from the rather less visually appealing activity of slave-labour. The demand for such artefacts has some ironic long-term consequences, however, as the poem shows in its closing phases, when it briefly makes a second departure from the antebellum era signalled in its title, moving the temporal frame beyond the liberatory vision of the ransacked plantation house to the early twentieth century, when the photograph was probably taken. What is apparent from this proleptic shift is that the acquisition of 'so much / Furniture' has resulted over time in 'far fewer woods', leading in turn to the offhand extinction of 'A few of the birds Audubon drew' so beautifully: 'The Carolina Parakeet, Passenger Pigeon, and Labrador Duck' (6).

Audubon himself would have contributed to this ecological disturbance by working methods that first required him to shoot the birds he wished to paint and then place them on wire armatures so that he could represent his subjects in ironically lifelike poses. In contrast to these murdered birds, the slave herself can look towards a brighter horizon: 'The best furniture / Can stand so quietly in a room that the room appears empty. / If it remains unbroken, it lives long enough to become antique' (6). In reverting to the use of furniture as metaphor here, the poem's final lines offer a reminder of how the white gaze looks upon the slave in such a way as to make her seem less a thing than a nothing. At the same time, they set a stronger and triumphant emphasis on the slave's ability to remain 'unbroken' by the dehumanising abuses that she suffers: she withstands them long enough to become 'antique' (both old but also precious) and as the anthropomorphising 'lives' suggests, ultimately has the power to transform herself back from inanimate to animate.

Conclusion

As they reflect on the commissions for *Found Anew* in the introduction to their volume, the editors express delight at how 'Some writers gauged unlikely depths in images other eyes might pass over without second glances' (xiv), a statement surely made with Hayes's poem in mind – in which, aptly enough, the act of overlooking is the principal concern – but equally applicable to all the texts this chapter has examined. What emerges from that examination is that ekphrasis works to provide African-American writers from the mid-1990s onwards with a particularly rich and sophisticated array of resources for excavating the 'depths' of the images which a white America has to offer them and for interrogating the ways in which the problematic of race has both changed and stayed the same over time. Yet ekphrasis has also been used to similarly powerful effect by African-American writers whose work arises in response to the call of images produced by artists who are black and located in a twentieth- rather than nineteenth-century context. One especially striking case in point is F. Douglas Brown, who writes back to and reimagines Jacob Lawrence's *Frederick Douglass* series (1938–9) in *Icon* (2018), and it is this text that is the subject of the book's sixth and final chapter.

Notes

1. Wideman's sense of alienation from the world of the white-created art museum is not new, having, for example, a striking mid nineteenth-century precedent in the work of William J. Wilson. Writing under the soubriquet of 'Ethiop' in a letter to the editor appearing in *Frederick Douglass' Paper* for 11 March 1853, Wilson records his visits to two art galleries in New York City, one containing 'daguerreotypes in oil' and the other 'some fine specimens of statuary'. While this latter gallery houses images of some of the luminaries of American history – 'Franklin and Adams, Lafayette and Jefferson, Clay and Webster' – it includes none of any 'distinguished *black*[s]' (italics in original), leading Wilson to make a plea for African-American self-representation, whether verbal or visual: 'we must begin to tell our own story, write our own lecture, paint our own picture, chisel our own bust', he urges, avoiding 'caricatures' in favour of 'correct emanations'. As it turns out, Wilson went on to meet this demand with his own 'Afric-American Picture Gallery', an ekphrastic text based entirely on imaginary paintings by imaginary black artists, published in *The Anglo-African Magazine* in seven instalments from February to October 1859.
2. The difference between these two acts of infanticide is recognised in 'Modern Medea', the brief gloss to Noble's image that appears in *Harper's* and that indeed echoes the artist's surname in making its distinction between the dramas of ancient and contemporary worlds: as Margaret resists relinquishing her children to their owners, she displays 'a far nobler jealousy than that which actuated the mythical Medea'.
3. The connections between *The Blue Boy* and American slavery extend beyond Noble's allusion, appearing also in the rather more recent and very different context of Quentin Tarantino's *Django Unchained* (2012). In this 'spaghetti-western inspired movie', the eponymous Django is 'a freed slave and bounty hunter' who 'wears a costume' that is overtly modelled on Gainsborough's famous painting and that becomes a 'major scene-stealer' (Hedquist 170) in the film as a whole.
4. The daughter's questioning citation of Jefferson in 'Enlightenment' has its analogue in 'Knowledge', another poem in *Thrall* based on

Johann Heinrich Hasselhorst's 1864 chalk drawing of the dissection of a beautiful eighteen-year-old female suicide, carried out in order to determine the ideal proportions of the female form. In Trethewey's text, the phrase she selects for inspection is taken directly from 'Her Swing', a poem published by her father in *Prairie Schooner* in 1980, in which he refers to her as a '*crossbreed child*' ('Knowledge' 30; italics in original). Although Trethewey describes this work as 'loving' and 'sweet' (*Conversations* 154) – she is nonetheless aggrieved by the 'language of zoology' ('Knowledge' 30) her father uses as he observes the playful activities of his three-year-old daughter, restoring order and balance to the world when her 'swingboard tilts in the wrangling chains' ('Her Swing' 48). That language, she argues, carries a disturbing 'edge' (*Conversations* 154) just as sharp and painful as the scalpel wielded above the dead girl by Hasselhorst's prosector.

5. For a thorough analysis of this complex issue, see West and Knight. See also Wood, *Black Milk*, for a provocative reading of the literal and symbolic dimensions of slave wet-nursing within the visual cultures of the United States and Brazil.
6. As it swerves away from the image of the slave-as-animal to slave-as-ottoman, 'Antebellum House Party' both invokes and revises the beginning of *Beloved*, when Beloved as poltergeist mobilises 124 Bluestone Road against Sethe. Here Beloved first causes the 'floorboards' of the house to 'shak[e]' so violently that Sethe loses her footing and slides 'down on all fours'; she then 'rushe[s]' a 'table' (18) towards Paul D, while at the same time displacing and overturning other items of furniture, including, respectively, a sideboard and a 'jelly cupboard' (19).

Chapter 6

Icon-versations: F. Douglas Brown, Jacob Lawrence and Frederick Douglass

Introduction

In *The Lives of Frederick Douglass* (2016), Robert S. Levine advocates a critical approach to Douglass's autobiographical writings that emphasises their dynamism and interconnectedness. The three autobiographies Douglass produced over a period of almost half a century – *Narrative of the Life of Frederick Douglass, an American Slave. Written by Himself* (1845), *My Bondage and My Freedom* (1855) and *Life and Times of Frederick Douglass* (1881; revised and expanded 1892) – 'can be read in isolation' from one another as 'artfully constructed' and 'finished work[s]' in their own right and yet are more accurately and fruitfully seen, Levine contends, as 'one large autobiographical project' that 'require[s]' the reader to move 'across and through the [texts] with a heightened attention to the ways in which Douglass revises his representations of key moments of his life' (2).

Such a process of revision is not something performed solely by Douglass himself but has been continued, in the wake of his death in 1895, by a number of other African-American figures. One of these is Jacob Lawrence, who offers an artistic reworking of those 'key moments' to which Levine refers in his *Frederick Douglass*, a series of thirty-two paintings created in 1938–9, one hundred years after Douglass, 'rigged out in sailor style' (*Life and Times* 644), finally 'left [his] chains' and made his way to freedom in New York on 'the third day of September, 1838' (*Narrative* 159). Yet if Lawrence revises Douglass – turning texts into images – so those images have themselves been turned into texts in F. Douglas Brown's *Icon* (2018), a kaleidoscopic collection of poems whose date of publication has its own significance, not so much commemorating Douglass's emancipation as his birth into slavery in Tuckahoe, Talbot County, Maryland, in February 1818.

Brown's profound imaginative investment in Douglass is perhaps at least partly explicable in terms of the biographical fact that the poet's given names bind him with such conspicuous intimacy to his iconic subject, with 'F.' standing for 'Frederick' (which is also the given name of Brown's father).[1] Either way, in gravitating towards Douglass so strongly, Brown makes what is to date the most sustained contribution to African-American poetry about this multidimensional historical figure, as *Icon* extends and enriches a tradition that runs from the early elegies of the 1890s to the present,[2] while adding something distinctive to this body of poetic reimaginings by mediating the construction of Douglass through Lawrence's art. In this latter respect, Brown's text simultaneously develops an important trend in African-American poetry, increasingly visible in the twenty-first century, in which black poets respond to and celebrate the work of black artists, as opposed to the white artists covered in the previous chapter.[3]

1. 'The Most Photographed American of the Nineteenth Century'

While Brown's revision of *Frederick Douglass* is *Icon*'s overriding concern, the text commences its ekphrastic work with two poems which engage with other visual materials, the first of these being 'Daguerreotype c. 1841'. Like several other pieces in the volume, this poem is spoken in Lawrence's voice and explores the painter's thoughts on seeing the first known photograph of Douglass (Fig. 6.1), taken anonymously in the year he makes his debut as public speaker at the Nantucket antislavery convention in Massachusetts.[4] Douglass's birth as a subject in the visual culture of the United States is in other words coeval with his birth as abolitionist, a coincidence curiously appropriate. After all, for 'the most photographed American of the nineteenth century' (Stauffer, Trodd and Bernier ix), the medium by which he was so fascinated (and that was so fascinated by him) had the potential to be readily harnessed to the antislavery cause and was indeed the abolitionists' 'greatest weapon': with his conviction regarding the 'truth value' or 'objectivity' of the

Figure 6.1 Sixth-plate daguerreotype of Frederick Douglass, c. 1841. Courtesy of Greg French.

photographic image, Douglass keenly embraced it as a means of both debunking slavery 'as a benevolent institution' and exposing it as 'a dehumanizing horror' (Stauffer, Trodd and Bernier xi). In the specific form of the portrait, which Douglass strongly favoured, photography could further overturn racist caricature and endow the African-American sitter with the same 'human weight and complexity' (Baldwin 176) to which his or her white counterpart seems automatically entitled – and which is so spectacularly withheld from the reified and cornered slave in the plantation photograph considered at the end of Chapter 5.

This sense of rehumanisation is confirmed in the opening two lines of 'Daguerreotype', most obviously from an economic perspective. Under the duress of slavery, Douglass's body must move in strict time to the capitalist rhythms of the plantation, its labour turned to profit by and for the master, yet here he has the luxury of being remunerated for doing nothing – other than posing for his picture: 'someone must have paid for you / to sit still', Lawrence conjectures.

The restoration of a briefly leisured humanity is reinforced by the poem's dress codes, as Douglass is not only rewarded for sitting still but 'handed ... hard cash' with which to purchase both a 'new haircut' and several items of clothing, including a 'vest', 'coat' and 'striped silk / stock which must be blue or purple' and is designed to 'stiffen / the collar' of its wearer's shirt. This ensemble of sartorial props at once exists in marked contrast to the coarse 'raiment' (*My Bondage* 76) Douglass recalls being allotted when a slave and lends him a quasi-monarchical bearing: the collar-stiffening stock is 'regal' in its colours and the 'dapper' vest and coat are seemingly pressed, similarly, to a 'royal' standard. Such fetching apparel is well-tailored to one who was consistently endowed with the grandeur of a sovereign, as, for instance, in Henrietta Cordelia Ray's 'In Memoriam (Frederick Douglass)' (1897), which exalts him as a 'majestic presence' on whom 'Nature' has 'most regally' bestowed 'her choicest gifts' (161), one of which is a 'regnant intellect' (162).

The language of regality with which Brown embroiders his description of Douglass's garments at the outset to 'Daguerreotype' is not accidental, but resonates with the antebellum construction of the cotton from which (apart from that prosthetic neckcloth) they would have been fashioned. Such a construction is evident, for instance, in an influential proslavery speech delivered by the South Carolinian senator, James Henry Hammond on 4 March 1858, in which cotton is crowned with the accolade of 'king' (12) in recognition of its economic might: it is as if Douglass has taken on the power and authority of the slave-worked commodity whose reign he wishes to end.

Yet if Douglass's clothing swathes him in such qualities, the effect is even more strongly produced by the phenotypes of hair and skin – his 'coif' and 'oiled face' (and the 'sheen' that comes from them) – and especially his 'handsome // ... eyes'. While these might be 'honeyed', they are also fiery. They seem to 'burn the edges' of the daguerreotype itself, compelling Lawrence, as self-admonishing 'gawker', to 'look // away' from the 'image', though not before he has absorbed the blunt but urgent message written into Douglass's incandescent gaze: '*work // to be done*'. The work in question here is no longer that of the plantation, however, but the abolitionist campaign. Equally, though, it is that of Lawrence's own art, which, he modestly hopes, will be able to 'capture a small glimpse' of the 'aura' emanating from the photograph – and the golden frame that surrounds it, in particular – and bring it 'back' to Harlem's equally '*small band*' of '*fresh-faced / dreamers*' (italics in original), to which, of course, he belongs.

2. Origin Stories

At the same time, Douglass's eyes speak not only to Lawrence the painter but also Brown the poet, who has much work of his own to accomplish at this initial point in *Icon* and sets about advancing it with 'Annunciation: Frederick Augustus Washington Bailey', the poem that immediately follows 'Daguerreotype'. This text shifts the focus from the question of Douglass's metaphorical birth out of slavery that is explored by its predecessor to the issue of his literal birth into it, drawing inspiration from two paintings of the Italian (as opposed to Harlem) Renaissance: Fra Angelico's *Cortona Altarpiece with the Annunciation* (c. 1432–3) (Fig. 6.2) and Sandro Botticelli's *Annunciation of Cestello* (1488–9) (Fig. 6.3). On the surface of things, the first of these devotional artworks could hardly seem more different from the image of Douglass in the daguerreotype, but is subtly linked to it by virtue of the golden halos that encircle the heads of the painting's two protagonists – the archangel Gabriel and the Virgin Mary – and that look back to the daguerreotype's aureole-like frame.

As Douglass indicates at the beginning of *Narrative*, his understanding of his own origins is radically fractured and uncertain, as much an enigma in its secular way as the event of the Incarnation to which the paintings look forward:

> My father was a white man. He was admitted to be such by all I ever heard speak of my parentage. The opinion was also whispered that my master was my father; but of the correctness of this opinion, I know nothing; the means of knowing was withheld from me. My mother and I were separated when I was but an infant – before I knew her as my mother. (93)

Such a dearth of genealogical knowledge becomes yet more pronounced in *My Bondage*, especially with regard to Douglass's

Figure 6.2 Fra Angelico, *Cortona Altarpiece with the Annunciation*, without predellas, c. 1432–3 (tempera and gold on wood panel). Cortona, Diocesan Museum. © 2021. Photo SCALA, Florence.

'*father*', who is 'shrouded in a mystery' his son has 'never been able to penetrate' (41; italics in original) and it also accords perfectly with the impoverished condition of Douglass's Tuckahoe birthplace, which *My Bondage* describes as a 'singularly unpromising and truly famine stricken district' (29) within Maryland. It is compounded, crucially, by a *sotto voce* haziness as to the precise nature of the sexual encounter between white father and black mother that brings the mixed-race slave-child into being and is more likely than not to have assumed the form of rape, a circumstance suggested by Douglass's cutting remarks about the general sexual economy of the plantation, which condemn 'slaveholders' for their 'lusts' and 'wicked desires' (*Narrative* 94).

The likelihood that Douglass's faceless father was also the rapist of his mother, Harriet Bailey, recalls the exploitative white male sexuality underpinning Thomas Satterwhite Noble's *The Price of Blood: A Planter Selling His Son* and is something which 'Annunciation' contrives to disavow. It does this, in the first section of the poem, based on the painting by Fra Angelico, by inviting (or instructing) the viewer of that image to contemplate it anew:

Figure 6.3 Sandro Botticelli, *Annunciation of Cestello*, 1488–9 (tempera and oil on wood panel). Florence, Galleria degli Uffizi. © 2021. Photo SCALA, Florence – courtesy of the Ministero Beni e Att. Culturali e del Turismo.

> Change the light and dove floating
>   upon daggered rays. Gaze a bit, take in
>
> the jungled lawn or gilded backgrounds. Hold space
>   elsewhere: altar, staircase, monastery plaster, chapel –
>
> to better orientate halos
>   or overflowing gowns, this space deep
>
> in southern heat, inescapable for generations
>   heat, a free life unthinkable heat. Reconsider
>
> distance, an angel addressing Harriot (sic) Bailey – not Mary. (19)[5]

In this bold and ingenious re-vision, the Biblical encounter between Gabriel and Mary (already transposed from Nazareth to Cortona) is further removed to the 'elsewhere' of the American South and emphatically recast, becoming one in which God's emissary directs his 'announcements' (19) towards a maternal presence who is very different from the Marian figure traditionally enshrined in Christian art – but just as blessed.

The extravagance of such a conceit – reincarnating Mary as Douglass's mother and by implication Christ Himself as Douglass – imbues the poem with an imaginative liberty that mocks the atmosphere of America's slave-holding states, where even the 'heat' oppresses and patrols, becoming 'inescapable for generations' and rendering a 'free life unthinkable'. More importantly, the conceit serves as a means of wishfully defending Douglass's mother from the sexual violence that in all probability would, as noted above, have led to her son's conception – and to which she would have been exposed as a matter of routine.[6] By identifying Harriet with Mary, that is, the poem circumvents the predations of the shadowy 'white man' to whom Douglass refers at the start of *Narrative*, since Mary's pregnancy occurs, after all, without the intercession of sexual intercourse.

In Fra Angelico's picture, Gabriel informs the Virgin of the mantle she will come to assume in the lines of scripture that he speaks and that are suspended in mid-air between him and her like golden threads – 'The Holy Ghost shall come upon thee, and the power of the Highest shall overshadow thee' – and she answers in kind: 'Behold the handmaid of the Lord; be it unto me according to thy word' (Luke 1.35, 38). In Brown's reworking of the scene, however, Harriet accepts her status as divine conduit less readily than does her Marian counterpart. Like the words that Mary utters in the painting, which are both upside-down and have to be read from right to left, Harriet is initially disorientated by the angel's message, experiencing feelings of 'fear' and 'shock', just as the 'daggered rays' supporting the 'dove' that symbolises the Holy Ghost seem to contribute their own sense of startling menace (and echo the title of 'Daguerreotype'). While Gabriel endeavours to 'dispel' Harriet's anxieties by solicitously 'wrapp[ing]' himself 'in the light of her likeness', it is evident from the poem's second section, which switches the visual ground to Botticelli, that such an expedient is not wholly effective and needs to be supplemented with other measures. Although Gabriel admits that his appearance before Harriet at this point in the text is an 'intrusion', it is not, he assures her, a 'violation' (19), even as he concedes that it might prompt some defensive manoeuvres on her part: 'I understand / shunning, / back-pedal – / evading eyes', he says. He combines this admission with care for Harriet's 'unformed or unframed' 'offspring', to whom he offers his 'cape' as 'protection', a gesture that at last elicits from Harriet the acquiescent '*yes*' (20; italics in original) that brings the poem to an end.

The next poem in *Icon* – 'Begotten: February, 1818' – extends the concern with the question of Douglass's birth, but does so, in contrast to 'Annunciation', by engaging with Lawrence rather than Fra Angelico or Botticelli and, specifically, panel 1 of the *Frederick Douglass* series (Fig. 6.4).[7] Such a shift immediately brings the 'space deep // in southern heat' more firmly into view, as in the poem's first stanza:

> Black runs wild in Talbot.
> Runs like the river runs
> Through water,
> Runs like a child
> Through childhood. (21)

Here the poem's opening line marks an acknowledgement of the colour that dominates Lawrence's painting and that is not only 'Ubiquitous' on the trinity of 'trees' in the scene, 'Grow[ing] in a buzz' on the 'elbows' of their arm-like (or river-like) branches, but also 'streaks / The reeds' and 'strides across / The plains' (21).

On the other hand, the 'Black' running wild at the start of the poem can be interpreted not as a reference to a rampaging pigment in an artist's palette but the energetic and undisciplined figure of the 'slave-boy' whom Douglass evokes in the first chapter of *My Bondage*, a reading that brings to light one of the ironies of slavery – namely, that such a boy in some ways possesses a greater freedom than 'the slaveholder's child' who is 'cared for and petted' (34), at least in the early phases of his existence. Douglass gives an extensive and largely satirical catalogue of these paradoxical advantages towards the end of *My Bondage*'s first chapter, a selection of which is listed in the following:

> The slaveholder, having nothing to fear from impotent childhood, easily affords to refrain from cruel inflictions; and if cold and hunger do not pierce the tender frame, the first seven or eight years of the slave-boy's life are about as full of sweet content as those of the most favored ... *white* children of the slaveholder. The slave-boy escapes many troubles which befall and vex his white brother. He seldom has to listen to lectures on propriety of behavior, or on anything else. He is never chided for handling his little knife and fork improperly or awkwardly, for he uses none. He is never reprimanded for soiling the

Figure 6.4 Jacob Lawrence, *Frederick Douglass* series, Panel 1, 1938–9 (casein tempera on gessoed hardboard). Collection of the Hampton University Museum, Hampton, Virginia. © The Jacob and Gwendolyn Knight Lawrence Foundation, Seattle / Artists Rights Society (ARS), New York and DACS, London 2021.

table-cloth, for he takes his meals on the clay floor. He never has the misfortune, in his games or sports, of soiling or tearing his clothes, for he has almost none to soil or tear. He is never expected to act like a nice little gentleman, for he is only a rude little slave. Thus, freed from all restraint, the slave-boy can be, in his life and conduct, a genuine boy, doing whatever his boyish nature suggests .... He literally runs wild. (34–5; italics in original)

While the first stanza of Brown's poem literally recalls the last two words of this extract, it also captures the sense of temporary freedom-within-slavery in its form, as repetition, assonance and enjambment combine to suggest a fluidity of movement that is checked and contained by the work of the end-stopped lines.

As 'Begotten' develops, the semantic indeterminacy characterising its first line reappears within the everyday details of the painterly scene to which the poem responds:

The women do chores
In the middle of this.
Do the bulk of black living.
They hold stars on their heads.
Call the gold, *grain*,
Or call the gold, *East*.
Call it, *ripe for the pluck*, or *safe
Passage*. Say, *make a move*,
And call it, *gone*. (21; italics in original)

The presence of such indeterminacy is most obvious in terms of the metaphorical 'stars' the enslaved 'women' carry as they go about their daily 'chores' and 'Do the bulk of black living.' These 'gold' objects are reminiscent of the 'halos' illuminating the heads of Gabriel and Mary and in turn the frame around the 1841 daguerreotype, but at the same time have an ambigrammatic quality, their meaning changing depending on who it is that looks at them. To '"OLD MASTER"' (*My Bondage* 33), these precious commodities, the poem's speaker suggests, are simply what they seem to be, innocuous bags of '*grain*' being brought in from the fields for storage, but to the slave they are secret signals, telling him or her that the conditions are now propitious for flight from the plantation, glossed in the text as the '*safe / Passage*' that will lead towards the '*East*' and eventually, of course, the North. The '*grain*' in question here needs, that is, to be read against the grain, as the joy of running wild in childhood is alchemised into the more mature delight of running away for good.

Although the emphasis up to this point in the poem is on how the slaves have the potential to guide themselves towards salvation, the speaker also petitions the divine as an alternative means of rescue, reading the tree growing out of the sand in the painting's centre-foreground as the 'Black hand of God' and imagining how the collective voice of the oppressed might appeal to Him for redemption: '*Save us.*' The possibility of such an intervention is at the same time compromised, however, by the description of the 'Hand out of the sand' as 'crooked', a term pointing as much to a sense of moral dubiety as physical form. It is also threatened by the three 'white men' who 'approach' the bent 'tree' and (in another equivocation) carry 'what could be shovels / Or rifles' on their shoulders, as if intent upon removing that stunted object from the scene (together with the hope it symbolises): '*Trying to dig // Or shoot God gone, / Right out of sight*' (21; italics in original).

Yet even if the marching assassins are able to effect God's death, they are no equal to higher forces mysteriously at play in this 'thinly populated worn-out district' (Lawrence qtd. in Wheat 49), as embodied in Douglass himself, whose nativity is celebrated in 'Begotten''s closing stanza:

> And still, here is this
> Baby, born unto this land
> In these matchstick
> Boxes, born unto the silt
> As bold as black lightning
> Or a tree. He's a quake,
> Cracking the earth
> From limb to limb. (22)

Here Brown uses a quasi-Biblical idiom that connects the poem (like the gold stars atop the heads of the labouring women) to 'Annunciation'. That idiom simultaneously and proleptically constructs the newborn as an apocalyptic and cleansing force, likening Douglass first to 'black lightning' and then a 'quake' with the capacity to rend the earth 'limb from limb'.[8]

3. Maternal Memories

As Douglass points out in the opening chapter of *My Bondage*, 'The practice of separating children from their mothers, and hiring the latter out at distances too great to admit of their meeting, except at long intervals, is a marked feature of the cruelty and barbarity of the slave system' (32) and a 'common custom' to which he was subjected 'when but an infant' (42). Yet even as the ties between Douglass and his mother are all but thus dissolved, the latter quite literally takes steps to restore them, secretly visiting her son, whenever possible, by walking some twenty-four miles there and back at night between the place where she has been 'hired out' as a 'field hand' (43) and the Wye River plantation owned by Colonel Edward Lloyd where Douglass is sent when around six years of age.

One of these meetings is dramatised in panel 2 of Lawrence's series (Fig. 6.5). Here the painting's visual codes themselves strive to counter the sense of severed familial bonds, as the golden colour of the night-shirt Douglass is wearing is mirrored in that of the mysterious object Harriet cradles in her hands (and the deliberately ill-proportioned candle positioned in front of mother and child on the cabin floor).

It is to this image that Brown turns in 'Darkness, My Mother', while at the same time deftly engaging with the source material on which Lawrence's painting also draws and which takes the form of Douglass's own rendition of these night-time rituals and in particular, his memory of their very last occurrence early in 1825, as described in Chapter III of *My Bondage*. As Douglass recalls, this farewell meeting takes place after he has committed an unspecified 'offense' (43) against Aunt Katy, the shrewish plantation-cook, who not only punishes him by 'making [him] go without food all day' but also threatens to '"*starve the life out of* [him]"' altogether. Douglass is relieved from his potentially fatal predicament, however, not by the 'very dry meal' he desperately improvises for himself when 'too hungry to sleep' (44; italics in original) but the timely advent of Harriet, who roundly castigates the 'sable virago' for the maltreatment to which she has subjected her boy and then treats him to a gingerbread '"sweet cake" . . . in the shape of a heart' (45).

In Brown's poetic rehearsal of Lawrence's scene, which is spoken in Douglass's voice, the nourishment Harriet brings her son is, in the first instance, less literal than metaphorical, manifesting itself in a 'gift to tell a tale into the wood & dirt' of his cabin that 'Feeds [him] for the rest of [his] life'. It could indeed be said that Douglass emulates his mother's tale-telling propensities in the here and now of this nocturnal rendezvous, excitedly weaving stories of his own around the tantalising item that Harriet's hands at once reveal and hide, restlessly flitting from one possible interpretation to the next:

Figure 6.5 Jacob Lawrence, *Frederick Douglass* series, Panel 2, 1938–9 (casein tempera on gessoed hardboard). Collection of the Hampton University Museum, Hampton, Virginia. © The Jacob and Gwendolyn Knight Lawrence Foundation, Seattle / Artists Rights Society (ARS), New York and DACS, London 2021.

> She cups gold for me, butter
> Or could be a cookie, a coin for a ferryman.
> Could be a canary or just a candle
>
> To guide her. Twelve miles
> Of danger, and back to danger. *Massa,*
> *I aint no fool, been here all along.* (italics in original)

Whatever the exact nature of the 'gold' Harriet bears, it is evident that the arduous journey she undertakes in order to present it to her son is the sign of 'a mother's care' and 'afford[s]' Douglass a 'bright gleam of a mother's love' (*My Bondage* 43). Perhaps the golden gift is itself the concrete expression of that affective gleam, in both painting and text alike?[9]

As much as they are sporadic, the clandestine encounters between mother and son are also painfully brief. In Lawrence's painting, the feeling of transience is articulated by the position of the door to Douglass's cabin, which Harriet has left ajar, as if not having time enough to shut it behind her (and hence create a fully enclosed space of intimacy); and in Brown's text by the recognition that the mother could take her leave with no more notice than she arrives, 'disappear[ing]', ghost-like, 'through / The seams, the boarded wall, and into // The nowhere of night'. While that night's 'blue diamond / Darkness' takes Douglass's mother away, it also brings her back, which is why he 'come[s] to love' it, even as she comes to love him in the different sense of the journeys she makes. Ultimately, though, it is not just Harriet's visits that are fleeting, but Harriet herself, since, as Douglass observes, it is not long after this final tryst that she dies, aged just thirty-three or thirty-four. Harriet's impending demise is intimated by Lawrence by means of colour, with the red of the upper part of her dress keyed to the red of the candleflame, while, in Brown, it casts an ominous new light on that 'coin for a ferryman' that Douglass thinks she might have brought him, raising the spectre of the mythical psychopomp, Charon. Yet even as the poem hints at the mother's death and laments that only a few 'glimmers' of her presence remain, it resists this sense of premature ending by concluding with a return to the vibrant flurry of speculations with which it begins. What the mother's hands contain could be 'Corn bread, coated with sugar // Or just the corn,' Douglass surmises, or possibly 'a shirt' on which she has 'stitched' her name and into which he will gradually 'grow' – as into the 'yoke' of slavery itself.

4. Violent Encounters

Along with subjecting Douglass to physical violence, slavery's dehumanising 'yoke' exposes him to the sufferings of others, particularly female slaves. The canonical site of such anguished empathy occurs in Chapter I of *Narrative*, where Douglass is obliged to behold the whipping of his Aunt Hester:

> I have often been awakened at the dawn of day by the most heart-rending shrieks of an own aunt of mine, whom [Mr Plummer] used to tie up to a joist, and whip upon her naked back till she was literally covered with blood. No words, no tears, no prayers, from his gory victim, seemed to move his iron heart from its bloody purpose. The louder she screamed, the harder he whipped; and where the blood ran fastest, there he whipped longest. He would whip her to make her scream, and whip her to make her hush; and not until overcome by fatigue, would he cease to swing the blood-clotted cowskin. I remember the first time I ever witnessed this horrible exhibition. I was quite a child, but I well remember it. I never shall forget it whilst I remember any thing. It was the first of a long series of such outrages, of which I was doomed to be a witness and a participant. It struck me with awful force. It was the blood-stained gate, the entrance to the hell of slavery, through which I was about to pass. It was a most terrible spectacle. I wish I could commit to paper the feelings with which I beheld it. (96)

In these lines, Douglass is 'awakened at the dawn of day' (a time ironically symbolic of hope and renewal) in a metaphorical as well as literal sense, as Hester's 'heart-rending shrieks' alert him, though still 'quite a child', to the true character of American slavery. Yet as much as he beholds this 'horrible exhibition' and 'terrible spectacle', he also seems to participate in it, as the distance collapses between Hester's identity and his own and he, like her, is 'struck . . . with awful force'.

This incident certainly qualifies as one of those 'key moments' in Douglass's life story mentioned at the start of this chapter. It not only entails a figurative birth into a new and traumatic knowledge of racial oppression, as Douglass 'pass[es]' through the 'blood-stained gate' leading to the 'hell of slavery', but also unsettles the customary eloquence for which he is famed, as language concertinas ('I well remember it. I never shall forget it whilst I remember any thing') and becomes exhausted ('I wish I could commit to paper the feelings with which I beheld it'). Despite its formative and momentous nature, however, this infernal episode is not one Lawrence himself chooses to remember, shifting his attention instead, in the third panel in his series, to a less well-known beating, not included in *Narrative*, but appearing in Chapter VI of *My Bondage*. The beating in question is performed upon another female slave, Nelly, renamed by Lawrence, in the panel's caption, as Millie. But while Lawrence turns towards this event as his painting's textual spark, he is interested less in visualising the whipping itself than the heroic struggle leading up to it, as Millie / Nelly 'sternly resist[s]' her overseer's attempts to 'drag her toward [the] tree' (*My Bondage* 70) at which, once she is fastened there, her punishment will be administered (Fig. 6.6).

Brown answers Lawrence's image in 'The Flogging', replacing the figure of Mr Sevier, the savage overseer featured in *My Bondage*, with that of Colonel Lloyd. As it opens, the poem reveals Millie's whipping to serve a double purpose: it is designed both as a brutal chastisement for whatever offence Millie has perpetrated (in *My Bondage*, the transgression is vaguely defined as a catch-all '"impudence"' [70]) and as an admonitory exercise, spelling out to all concerned the absolute nature of the master's power:

Colonel Lloyd make the babies watch

Colonel Lloyd try to break the babies,
  makes everyone watch

 Colonel Lloyd beat Millie until the sunset
  so everyone see how a woman spirit get broke.

As spectacular as it is sadistic, Colonel Lloyd's dominion is nonetheless subtly undermined by the terms in which it is couched. Even as he compels the 'babies' (the three children in Lawrence's panel) to 'watch' this violent scene, he can only 'try to break' them, rather than succeed in his mission. This being the case, he is surely even less likely to be able to negate the 'spirit' of a fully grown 'woman', even if he beats her until 'sunset', especially one based on Douglass's formidable Nelly, a figure who, despite being 'severely whipped' by the 'overseer', is not 'subdued', remaining 'invincible' and 'undaunted' (*My Bondage* 72) in her defiance.

The limitations of Colonel Lloyd's power are underscored by the subsequent and unflattering reference to his 'buck teeth'. In Lawrence's painting, these look as if they are about to bite, vampire-like, into Millie's neck in order that the master can drink her blood. In Brown's poem, by contrast, it is not the victim's but the

Figure 6.6 Jacob Lawrence, *Frederick Douglass* series, Panel 3, 1938–9 (casein tempera on gessoed hardboard). Collection of the Hampton University Museum, Hampton, Virginia. © The Jacob and Gwendolyn Knight Lawrence Foundation, Seattle / Artists Rights Society (ARS), New York and DACS, London 2021.

assailant's blood that is to the fore, as it 'drips to the ground and muddies his boots'. The unsettlement if not reversal of the master-slave relationship is similarly evident in the way Millie withstands her oppressor as she 'tug[s] at a tree' and 'hold[s] on' to it while Colonel Lloyd 'slip[s]'; and by the description of Colonel Lloyd's yellow whip, which hangs from the wooden post in the left foreground of Lawrence's painting. While this instrument of torture might appear, in Brown's word, to be 'glowin'' with a peculiar energy, it is outshone by the 'brilliance' of Millie's 'yellow headwrap', an article of clothing that both 'resonates' with the young Douglass's 'yellow shirt as he bears witness to the scene' (Bernier, '"Any"' 114) and extends the array of golden items populating *Icon* from the first: the frame around Douglass's first photograph; the matching halos sported by Gabriel and Mary; the stars carried by the women in 'Begotten'; and the indeterminate heart-shaped gift that Harriet procures for her son in 'Darkness'. As 'The Flogging' concludes, it is no surprise that Millie should prove to be such a stubborn adversary for her master to control and subjugate since the tree she grips is endued with the same divine strength that 'Begotten' has already identified as part of Douglass's landscape: 'Everyone see Millie hold the hand of God in that there tree, / And so do Colonel Lloyd / And so do Colonel Lloyd.' The latter might begin this poem by coercing 'everyone' to gaze upon the demonstration of his power but ends it recognising that it is he rather than Millie who will be beaten, not least because of the considerable support from a superior force on which she is able to draw.

In the much-vaunted chiasmus in Chapter X of *Narrative*, Douglass briefly suspends his 'humble history' (133) to address the reader directly with regard to the epochal self-recreation about to result from his almost-two-hour-long physical fight with Edward Covey, the so-called local '"nigger-breaker"' (128). 'You have seen,' he proclaims, sounding a little like a showman in the midst of a magic trick, 'how a man was made a slave; you shall see how a slave was made a man' (133). As Celeste-Marie Bernier notes, this epic confrontation is 'one of the most widely publicized moments in Douglass's life history', 'repeatedly restaged and reimagined' across the course of his writings and speeches and duly dramatised in panel 10 in what she aptly calls the 'iconic set piece' of Lawrence's series (Fig. 6.7). Yet as she also observes, Lawrence frames this Manichean encounter as a 'visual recreation of Millie's brave resistance' to white male violence, which he has 'depicted as victorious in panel 3' ('"Any"' 115). As rendered by Lawrence, in other words,

Figure 6.7 Jacob Lawrence, *Frederick Douglass* series, Panel 10, 1938–9 (casein tempera on gessoed hardboard). Collection of the Hampton University Museum, Hampton, Virginia. © The Jacob and Gwendolyn Knight Lawrence Foundation, Seattle / Artists Rights Society (ARS), New York and DACS, London 2021.

Douglass's 'bold defiance' (*Narrative* 138) of Covey constitutes 'a masculinized revisualization of Black female heroism' (Bernier, '"Any"' 115).

Although the scene represented in panel 3 is one in which Millie valiantly struggles against her torturer, the two figures at the same time appear to be locked together, in a grotesque irony, in a kind of dance. This sense of the choreography of interracial conflict is taken up by Brown and applied to Douglass's clash with his antagonist in 'Mr Covey, Shall We Dance?' This virtuosic poem responds to the tenth panel in Lawrence's series while at the same time taking a kind of supplementary inspiration (as the second part of its title suggests) from the 'Shall We Dance?' show tune featured in the film musical, *The King and I* (1956).

In *Narrative*, the protracted 'battle' with Covey is defined as transformative: it is 'the turning-point in [Douglass's] career as a slave', 'reviv[ing] within [him] a sense of [his] own manhood' (137) and propelling him towards a future in which he will 'never again' be 'whipped' (138). In the first stanza of Brown's poem, by contrast, Douglass undergoes other metamorphoses preparatory to this revival, paradoxically couching the physical and mental courage that will facilitate his renaissance in non-human terms:

> I am an ox, bare-chested,
>   no shoes, toes dug into
>   the dirt, pants hiked up
>   to my knees. (58)

This self-figuration is not accidental, but looks back to an episode occurring several months before the decisive conflict with Covey, when the latter puts Douglass in charge of a 'team of unbroken oxen' with which he is ordered to collect firewood on 'one of [the] coldest days in the month of January' (*Narrative* 129). The trope of Douglass as ox invests him with a 'proverbial type of strength, brawn, fortitude [and] obstinacy' (*OED*), but also foreshadows the outcome of the conflict: having no experience in the job he has been assigned, Douglass twice loses control of the unruly beasts, just as Covey will in turn lose his hold over Douglass, his refractory but sure-footed antagonist.[10]

Douglass's assumption of ox-like attributes initiates a self-mythologising strategy manifest elsewhere in the poem, as in stanza three, in which Covey is directly addressed – and perhaps intimidated:

> I am the nails holding
>   uneven boards upright.
>   I will not splinter or buckle
>   the soft wood nor will I yield
>   to treachery, your evil ways. (58)

The identification of Douglass with Christ in 'Annunciation' accords him divine power while also prophesying, less positively, the bodily pain that he will come to endure as a slave, especially under the 'breaking process' through which Covey 'carrie[s] [him]' (*My Bondage* 163). Here, however, Douglass does not endure a metaphorical crucifixion on the cross of American slavery but imagines himself, conversely, as the 'nails' supporting the 'boards' of the 'barn' where he and his oppressor grapple with one another. Like those boards, the contest between the adolescent slave (Douglass is sixteen years old at this juncture) and his adult foe might seem 'uneven', yet, in common with the 'soft wood', Douglass will neither 'splinter' nor 'buckle', countering Covey's physical strength and 'evil ways' with his own power and moral rectitude, respectively.

The prodigious bodily might advertised in the poem's first and third stanzas is also on display in its second, in which Douglass revels in the ability to 'bend iron with [his] / teeth and work the leather / that breaks a horse in two'. But this stanza additionally testifies to another type of prowess, drawing attention to Douglass's way with words as he nonchalantly informs the reader that he 'can spell *rhinoceros* backwards' (58; italics in original). The textual presence of this italicised noun contributes to the unexpected playfulness of tone that characterises much of the poem and might at first glance appear somewhat incongruous; but it becomes less so when it is recalled that Douglass himself invokes the term when describing how elated he feels at the ratification in 1870 of the Fifteenth Amendment, with its uplifting promise that 'The right of citizens of the United States to vote shall not be denied or abridged by the United States or by any State on account of race, color, or previous condition of servitude' (Gillette 71). As he puts it, this dramatic post-Civil War change to the Constitution 'seemed to shield' him 'as the hide of a rhinoceros' (qtd. in Biddle and Dubin 411). Not unlike the word that Douglass spells backwards with such aplomb, the Amendment was effectively reversed in the years after its adoption by the introduction of a range of discriminatory practices and laws deliberately aimed at the very 'citizens' – African Americans (or African-American men, at least) – whom it was intended to enfranchise (Gidlow 434).

Nonetheless, Douglass's oblique allusion to the protection afforded by suffrage (however fleeting) is a worrying sign for Covey, since it presupposes the contingency of the slave-holding South of which he is the unappealing embodiment.

The way in which Douglass mythologises himself in the opening three stanzas of 'Mr. Covey' provides him with an air of superiority that seems only to increase in stanza four, as the poem's dance-element takes its cue:

> Checkered devil, if you hold
>   a hammer, I'll hold your arms.
>   One cinched at your hips, the other,
>   high enough to twirl
>   you around this barn, and then
>   to Japan (yes, I know of that place, too). (58)

Even as Covey threatens to wield his 'hammer' against Douglass, he is prevented in forging this tool into a weapon by the controlling force of his hard-as-nails adversary-cum-dancing-partner. In thus holding his 'Checkered devil' in check, Douglass performs upon Covey the kind of animalisation and unmanning that slavery performs upon him. The first of these effects is discernible in the description of how Douglass 'cinche[s]' one of Covey's 'arms' to his 'hips', with the verb evoking the management of a horse or mule and specifically the action of tightly fixing a saddle to such beasts of burden by means of a girth (an association which in turn ties in with the equine violence in stanza two). The second is evident in the way in which Douglass takes the lead in this brutal barn dance, feminising the ironically titled 'Mr. Covey' as he powerfully 'twirl[s]' him beyond his local comfort zone and out towards the faraway spaces of Japan.

In her reading of panel 10, Bernier draws attention to 'Covey's yellow-and-red-checked shirt', arguing that it gives the painting a 'comic twist as the gaudy coloring evokes theatrical costumes' ('"Any"' 115). This sense of comedy also infuses stanza five of Brown's poem, where Douglass imagines the fight with Covey as a 'jig', in which enemies suddenly morph into lovers, as 'glances . . . mingle' and bodies are 'engulfed by sweat' before they fall 'kissing' and 'juicy' to the 'floor' (58). Such an eroticised recasting of roles is as brief as it is improbable, however, as the final three stanzas attest. Here the poem abandons its fanciful surmise in deference to the 'As it is' of a situation that is anything but comic, in which Douglass and Covey 'wrestle' in 'Combat's intimacy' rather than love's and the 'ax' at the 'feet' of the white man bespeaks his murderous intentions towards his black counterpart. In the down-to-earth reality of things, looks do not link in passionate alliance but instead provide a symbolic expression of the power shift that Douglass's 'feat // of resistance' brings about: he draws 'close enough' to Covey 'to see the red thread in [his] eyes' while Covey, for his part, turns away from such microscopic scrutiny and 'shame blurs / [his] vision' (59) as his reputation for breaking slaves is itself shattered. This relationship between Douglass's eyes and Covey's is doubly significant. First, it reverses the autobiographies' personification of slavery as a Medusa-like figure that is 'terrible to behold' as it 'glar[es] frightfully' (*My Bondage* 206) upon Douglass and his comrades in the episode when they nervously contemplate flight from the South. Secondly, it looks back to and again reverses the disposition of bodies in panel 3, as Douglass takes the place of the fiercely gazing Colonel Lloyd and forces Covey into that of Millie.

5. Reading, Writing, Speaking

As noted in the introduction to this book, part of *Icon*'s experimentalism involves its recourse, in two poems, to the presentational mode of PechaKucha, in which a presenter shows twenty PowerPoint slides to his or her audience, commenting on each of them for twenty seconds. Originating in the world of Japanese architecture and design in the early 2000s, PechaKucha is commonly translated as 'chit-chat' but is anything but that in this rather different context, where it is used by Brown to address two momentous events in Douglass's life: learning to read and the founding of his own newspaper, *The North Star* on 3 December 1847.[11]

The first of these poems is 'Why I Read: Partial Pecha' and takes its place in *Icon* immediately before 'Mr. Covey', just as it focuses on a period in Douglass's life that precedes the pivotal encounter with Covey himself. As befits its partial nature, the text is organised as a series of ten rather than twenty bite-sized stanzas (or slides), each deriving its square-bracketed heading from different elements featured in the eighth panel in *Frederick Douglass* (Fig. 6.8).

As the poem begins, with '[Empty Shelves]', a young Douglass is to be found 'idle on [a] forbidden height' (56), leaning at night on a tall (and gigantic) table and poring over Caleb Bingham's *The Columbian Orator* (1797), a popular primer he has 'purchased' with 'a few cents' 'earned . . . as a bootblack' (Lawrence qtd. in Wheat 56).

Figure 6.8 Jacob Lawrence, *Frederick Douglass* series, Panel 8, 1938–9 (casein tempera on gessoed hardboard). Collection of the Hampton University Museum, Hampton, Virginia. © The Jacob and Gwendolyn Knight Lawrence Foundation, Seattle / Artists Rights Society (ARS), New York and DACS, London 2021.

Although his ability to read is in its infancy at this stage in his life, Douglass has, conversely, a mature understanding of both the power of the written word and the radical implications of his efforts to comprehend and seize hold of it. Like the novice reader, the 'words' in Bingham's much-coveted schoolbook are 'Small' and 'black' but 'stronger than all [Douglass's] muscles combined' and thus capable of overpowering him, just as he will later overpower Covey – or destroy his reputation at least. This being so, it is no wonder that the shelves should be empty, the 'books' they contain safely swept beyond 'this slave's reach' by his vigilant 'capturers'. Yet if, as this implies, reading poses a threat to the white order, it is equally a danger to Douglass, who engages in an activity that both elevates him above his peers and has the capacity to lay him low: as he recognises, 'The mere mention of owning words, could kill [him].' Douglass's awareness of the potentially lethal risk that reading entails is restated in stanza four, '[Columbian Orator]', where his absorption in this book's 'tangled lines' allows him to hear not only the 'out loud truth they bear' but also the unspoken and less edifying possibility that they 'Might bring death', reducing him to 'a bloody mess before the day strikes the window' (56) with a vengeful if belated flourish of its own.

Considered in these terrifying terms, the act of reading requires as much courage as the future showdown with Covey. It additionally requires resourcefulness, as Douglass conscripts whatever is at hand into the urgent service of his self-education. One such instance of this improvisatory strategy occurs in the poem's second stanza, '[The Aloe in a Vase]', in which Douglass addresses the 'Little' plant in the bottom-right corner of Lawrence's painting and earmarks it for possible use as a 'paperweight'. As its depiction in the panel indicates (it is growing towards Douglass), this is a prospect that the 'aloe' is inclined to accept, embracing the new role for which it is volunteered with an unhesitating '"Yes."' That role is also one from which the aloe benefits, as Douglass 'water[s]' it with the 'spittle' produced when he 'attempt[s] pronunciation' of the words he struggles to read, using 'the best-made tongue in the land': nurtured by such tongue-in-cheek attentions, the young plant will 'Soon . . . rise high,' Douglass promises, 'to see what [he has] in store for these folks' (56), its rapid ascent answering his.

Douglass's desire to learn to read is aided not merely by his aloe-ally, but other quotidian things, including the mighty table at which he is stationed and which he apostrophises, in stanza three, '[Table with Wide Legs]', as a 'brother'. This accommodating fraternal object not only abets him in a literal sense as a surface on which to rest his elbows while studying but also serves as a kind of exemplar: it exhibits a firmness of construction and stance that Douglass strives to emulate in the progress that he is making in his reading and contentedly assesses as 'steady' (56). To consolidate and confirm his developing ability to 'gather words off a page', Douglass resorts, in stanza eight, the appropriately titled '[Steady Left]', to 'read[ing] upside down'. This difficult and unusual technique makes 'Inverted letters' seem 'like rain in reverse' (57) and is an eloquent symbol for the revolutionary significance of Douglass's ambition to marshal and master his recalcitrant ABCs: such an accomplishment, after all, would overturn the supposedly natural order of things which privileges white over black and against which he sets himself.

As much as reading is associated with death (as noted earlier), it is also seen as life-giving and indeed essential to Douglass's survival. This is suggested in the terms in which those gravity-defying and rainy letters are described, 'pouring up to quench and create a thirst' that he 'never knew existed'; and in the figure, in stanza six '[Three Books]', of Douglass as an insatiable consumer of texts, 'eat[ing] as much as any one page offers' and 'Then go[ing] back for more'. But whether it leads to death or life, Douglass's voracious reading-practice needs to be conducted in secret, as he 'Shine[s] shoes by day' and 'then sneak[s] to buy a book' (57) to be perused under cover of darkness. Just as the aloe and table help Douglass in his quest to grasp the written word, so he is assisted in the quest's concealment, in stanza five, by the collective efforts of the very materials from which his impromptu schoolroom is made:

> [Wooden Walls]
> We wade We witness We hold the hands of a boy greater than a thousand flocks put together We be his pulse, youthful sternness We his loyal beads dripping off our wooden faces before pooling on the floor We huddle tight so there's no peeking between the cracks No light to tattle (56)

In this humorous prosopopoeia, the boastful walls not only underline the consequence of the 'boy', they shelter but also seem to partake of it, proudly referring to themselves as an upper-case 'We' and descanting on the effectiveness with which they conspire to block the 'peeking' eye of the oppressor. Yet even as they 'huddle tight' against the threat of surveillance and the punishment to which it would inevitably lead, the walls, it seems, are ultimately limited in their powers. These are subtly ironised by the typographical 'cracks' in the stanza itself (the only one not punctuated in the poem), as visualised in the expanded white spaces that separate its phrases one from another.

As he reflects on his 'love of letters' in *My Bondage*, Douglass attributes it, emphatically, '*not*' to his 'admitted Anglo-Saxon paternity' but the 'native genius' of his '*mother*' (46; italics in original), Harriet. As he puts it, shortly after his account of their last meeting:

> I learned, after my mother's death, that she could read, and that she was the *only* one of all the slaves and colored people in Tuckahoe who enjoyed that advantage. How she acquired this knowledge, I know not, for Tuckahoe is the last place in the world where she would be apt to find facilities for learning. I can, therefore, fondly and proudly ascribe to her an earnest love of knowledge. That a 'field hand' should learn to read, in any slave state, is remarkable; but the achievement of my mother, considering the place, was very extraordinary. (45–6; italics in original)

This 'achievement' is indeed 'extraordinary', while at the same time turning the mother – 'sable, unprotected, and uncultivated' (46) – into a model for the son, as she sets and shapes the path that Douglass must follow in order to fulfil his own readerly aspirations.

Given such familial bonds, it is not surprising to find certain parallels between the scene of reading portrayed in panel 8 of Lawrence's series and the bittersweet scene of fleeting union and departure in panel 2. These parallels extend beyond the obvious general fact that each scene occurs at night and in secret and are facilitated by the artist's 'technique of repetition with variation across panels' (Bernier, '"Any"' 114). This technique is in turn adopted by Brown across poems and can be seen in 'Why I Read''s penultimate stanza, '[Candle Stick Prayers]'. Here the 'gold' that Harriet 'cups' in her hands in 'Darkness' reappears in the guise of the 'golden pages' of *The Columbian Orator*, the invaluable tome that, Douglass hopes, will 'lift [him]' (57) beyond his plight and that he exalts in *My Bondage* as a 'rich treasure' (116) and 'gem of a book', replete with 'spicy dialogues' (201).

The complement to 'Why I Read: Partial Pecha' is 'Why I Write: Partial Kucha.' Unfolding as a response to panel 21 of Lawrence's series (Fig. 6.9), this poem deals with the second of those epochal events mentioned earlier, in the shape of the establishment of *The North Star*. Although Douglass was manumitted one year prior to the creation of this newspaper, he begins the poem with echoes of the work songs he would have sung during his enslavement, intercutting these fragments with glimpses of his new orbit:

Figure 6.9 Jacob Lawrence, *Frederick Douglass* series, Panel 21, 1938–9 (casein tempera on gessoed hardboard). Collection of the Hampton University Museum, Hampton, Virginia. © The Jacob and Gwendolyn Knight Lawrence Foundation, Seattle / Artists Rights Society (ARS), New York and DACS, London 2021.

[Hair with a Right Side-Part]
O Lawd, find me in the field
I'm servant to these papers, servant to dark ink, a servant to my blood
O Lawd get me

O Lawd, find me in the field
I know how to work hard, how to bundle and haul, I fissure the soil
O Lawd stand me tall. (82; italics in original)

While Douglass must continue to 'work hard', his endeavours are no longer directed towards the goal of personal liberation but have a far broader collective scope. As the masthead to *The North Star*'s first issue grandly declares, the paper's 'object will be to attack SLAVERY in all its forms and aspects; advocate UNIVERSAL EMANCIPATION; exalt the standard of PUBLIC MORALITY; promote the moral and intellectual improvement of the COLORED PEOPLE' and above all, 'hasten the day of FREEDOM to the THREE MILLIONS of our ENSLAVED FELLOW COUNTRYMEN'.

Both 'Why I Read' and 'Why I Write' are themselves 'fissure[d]' or split apart from one another by a distance of some twenty-six pages in *Icon* yet remain united not only by the symmetry of their titles but also that play of 'repetition with variation' noted previously. Such a pattern is evident at three junctures, the first occurring in the second stanza of 'Why I Write', '[The Aloe in a Vase]'. As its parenthetical heading indicates, this stanza again features the plant that appears at the corresponding point in the former text (under the same rubric) and that has been Douglass's botanical sidekick 'since the beginning of words'. Yet while the steadfast aloe makes its return here, it does so with a difference: it has surreptitiously migrated from the left- to the right-hand side of Lawrence's painting and is no longer 'little' but, as the painting shows, has become big and tall, as Douglass had originally prophesied: in growing in this way, the aloe mirrors both Douglass's physical development from child to adult and the increased political influence that literacy affords him, as he raises himself out of the 'nothing' of slavehood, turns 'Inspiration' into 'testament' (82) and propagates the word of abolition.

Another instance of the pattern is discernible in stanza six, '[Book Shelf]', which harks back to both of the furniture-stanzas in the former poem – '[Empty Shelves]' and '[Table with Wide Legs]'. As the volumes gathered together on the shelf (and the writing desk) in panel 21 make clear, the 'times' in which Douglass is living 'are' indeed in the process of 'changing' as he builds his library and puts it on display. Equally, though, Douglass thinks of the openly stocked shelf as a 'Brother' whose 'paint matches [his] skin' (83), thus recollecting the manner in which he had addressed the wide-legged table that had supported his early reading efforts and experiments in the first place.

Perhaps the pattern's most significant and intricate manifestation is located in stanza three, '[Umbrella and a Cane]', in which the objects in the stanza's title assume the capacity for voice:

> We be the swan and the golden goose We be ready for storm or the southern sun We be feathered in black or skinned with clipped wings poised for a fight We be head turned and in tandem, swimming in the lake where justice was baptized (82)

While this moment of prosopopoeia recalls '[Wooden Walls]' (and like that stanza has the distinction of not being punctuated), the birds into which the umbrella and cane are humorously recast are equally reminiscent of those found in Chapter XIX of *My Bondage*, as the then-enslaved but geographically untutored Douglass begins to plot his escape: 'We had heard of Canada,' he writes, 'the real Canaan of the American bondmen, simply as a country to which the wild goose and the swan repaired at the end of winter, to escape the heat of summer, but not as the home of man' (206). That said, the avian creatures imagined into life in Brown's poem are quite different to those in Douglass. They are 'turned' not so much towards flight as 'fight', 'ready' and 'poised' to defend Douglass against what he calls the 'mobocratic spirit' (*Life and Times* 672). Such a spirit can alter and vex the political atmosphere just as suddenly in the North as beneath the 'southern sun' as, for example, in the episode recounted in *Life and Times* when Douglass and two other abolitionists are set upon during an antislavery convention held in Pendleton, Indiana, in 1843 (675).

In contrast to the one-on-one clash with Covey, Douglass's use of counter-violence as a defence against his Pendleton assailants does not work. As he picks up 'a stick . . . in the mêlée', he 'attract[s] the fury of the mob', which swiftly lays him 'prostrate on the ground under a torrent of blows', leaving his 'right hand broken' (675). Although that hand 'never recover[s] its natural strength and dexterity' (676), it is nonetheless sufficiently able to enlist other resources into the campaign against slavery, one of these being the text it produces for *The North Star* itself:

[Magic Curtain]
You make me a wizard with words, self-taught conjurer with eager sparks on dark. Golden polliwogs in shaded water. Commas or crescents, I write to that murk –: the vast troubles of slavery stretch to the floor (82)

Here Douglass transforms the 'crescents' on the 'Magic Curtain' hanging behind his right shoulder in Lawrence's painting into 'commas', just as the curtain 'make[s]' him 'a wizard with words'. Thus empowered, Douglass is able to take on the 'vast troubles of slavery' that 'stretch to the floor', his tireless labours evidenced in the stack of newspaper copy that can be seen in the bottom-left corner of the panel and to which he is in the process of adding. As it mounts, this mass of writing moves in the opposite direction to slavery's endlessly cascading troubles, following the aspirational line of the flourishing aloe that acts, once again, as a convenient paperweight.

In this painting, as in panel 8, Lawrence depicts Douglass alone, his solitude only amplified by the miscellaneous objects that surround him – aloe, books, umbrella, cane, curtain, *inter alia*. As Brown reimagines the scene, however, the 'Blood-lined articles' Douglass composes for his paper are set within a larger network of other African-American publications, as listed in the roll call of the poem's final stanza, '[Red Feather Pen & His Pointing Right Hand]': *Freedom's Journal, The Rights of All, The Colored American, Mirror of Liberty* and *Provincial Freeman*. *The North Star* might provide the 'guiding' light for the antislavery mission finally realised in the Emancipation Proclamation of 1 January 1863, but it does so, in other words, within the compass of a broad family of 'brother and sister presses'. Animated by the same 'spirit' and undertaking the same 'toil', these kindred publications 'share' the burden of 'undo[ing] what centuries have done' (83) to 'COLORED PEOPLE'.

As well as recognising the power of 'the written' to 'ward off ropes and chains' (83), Douglass fully understood that the spoken word could be at least as effective in prosecuting the abolitionist cause. He accordingly gave countless antislavery orations across the span of his career and it is this facet of his work with which Brown engages in 'Imagining Lawrence Imagine the 11th of August 1841'. This poem responds to panel 18 in the artist's series (Fig. 6.10), which shows Douglass delivering his maiden speech at the Nantucket convention briefly mentioned above in the discussion of 'Daguerreotype'.

Figure 6.10 Jacob Lawrence, *Frederick Douglass series*, Panel 18, 1938–9 (casein tempera on gessoed hardboard). Collection of the Hampton University Museum, Hampton, Virginia. © The Jacob and Gwendolyn Knight Lawrence Foundation, Seattle / Artists Rights Society (ARS), New York and DACS, London 2021.

At the outset of the poem, Lawrence ponders the task before him – how to represent Douglass as orator in paint – turning back for inspiration to the haunting photographic image featured at *Icon*'s beginning:

I want the gold of Douglass'
first daguerreotype, the frame

holding a frayed image –: pocked and near
crumbled if not for this gold rim

or gold in his skin, recently free
and glimmering. Can my brush strokes
match his spry 23-year-old tone? I think
not. (78)

Given the links between photography and abolition noted at the start of this chapter, it is only to be expected that Lawrence should 'want' to plunder 'the gold of Douglass' / first daguerreotype' as it colours both the 'frame' of the picture and the 'skin' of the picture's subject, 'glimmering' with a precious new freedom. Yet what Lawrence desires, as he speedily reminds himself, is also what he lacks (the other sense of 'want'), as Douglass – true to his status at the time as slave-on-the-run – escapes the 'strokes' of the 'brush' that seeks to 'match' his 'tone'.

Having arrived at an artistic impasse signalled in the adamantine self-deprecation of 'I think / not', Lawrence abandons his covetous contemplation of Douglass's photograph, shifting into speculations about how best to approach other areas of the planned composition, specifically the all-white audience of abolitionists at the Nantucket gathering:

Shall I paint a series of overcoats and top hats,

red and green hoods, blond hair galore? Should I capture
eyes and mouths, the expanse of blue

sky lyceum caught in their gaze and gasps
as they walk away: *such intellectual power – wisdom*

as well as wit? The astonished must be seen reveling
in a run-away slave's eloquence. (78; italics in original)[12]

In these lines, the audience Lawrence imagines portraying is of less importance in itself than for its status as a blank canvas on which to 'capture' the effects created by Douglass as he recounts his narrative and advances some 'blue // sky' thinking (about the possibility of abolition), fusing *'wisdom'* and *'wit'* into an 'eloquence' that leaves his listeners 'astonished'. Such 'eloquence' at the same time comes to be identified with and symbolised by the elusive gold of that 'first daguerreotype' which, despite the doubts voiced at the start of the poem, Lawrence is determined to pursue and record. As he vows, he will 'make [the] shine' emanating from Douglass's 'fine-tuned words // and ways' 'spill // to his shirt', both in this particular painting and 'in eight panels thereafter'. As Lawrence further anticipates, such 'luster' will in turn constitute the 'glory of summer' on the August (and august) day of Douglass's speech, as a charismatic 'leader' is 'birthed amongst a sea of pink' (78).

With its high-flown evocation of this glorious moment, Brown's poem partakes of the rhetorical elevation it ascribes to the Midas-tongued Douglass, who is pictured, in this panel, declaiming to the spellbound crowd while standing above them on the makeshift podium of a wooden chair turned back to front. As the poem moves past this moment and into its closing stanzas, however, a different mood takes hold. Here Lawrence balances out his celebration of Douglass's birth as mesmeric public speaker with the sober recognition of the seemingly perennial racism that African Americans endure from one epoch to another, as the vast aftermath of slavery spreads far into the future:

> Yet, I know hate is a brilliant color in and of itself
> even there in Nantucket. So paint a boy
>
> in a white tee, alone with his skepticism closest
> to Douglass' grandstand and grand
>
> gestures. This little boy: – hands on his hips, legs
> braced and firmly rooted in a white
>
> power stance. He is all hate planted
> in rich soil, blooming fledgling
>
> of things to come –: things the 20th century and beyond
> still bring to black folks. (79)

Here the poem's colour scheme is inflected anew as the gold associated with the coruscations of Douglass's speech is challenged by a hateful whiteness that is just as 'brilliant'. As if to underwrite the danger and hostility concentrated in the brutish 'boy', Lawrence stations him in the bottom-right corner of his painting, a position formerly occupied, in panel 8, by the friendly and supportive aloe, whose colour Douglass has borrowed for his 'cape' (79). This is a connection and displacement that Brown in turn picks up in the largely botanical language he uses to describe Douglass's pint-sized combatant, who is 'rooted in a white // power stance' and 'planted / in rich soil'. Given the threat which this 'blooming fledgling' poses (and which the violence at Pendleton confirms), it is not surprising that, as the poem closes, Lawrence should step outside the inner colloquy in which he has been so far absorbed to address Douglass directly, exhorting him that, whatever else he does – he might 'fuss, fight, / or flee' – he should 'keep an eye on that boy' (79).

6. Past, Present – and Future?

As one who lived between 1917 and 2000, Lawrence's unease regarding the hateful 'things' awaiting African Americans 'beyond' 'the 20th century' is imbued with a prescience ironically reminiscent of the 'Forethought' to W. E. B. Du Bois's *The Souls of Black Folk* (1903), with its ominous opening prediction that 'The problem of the Twentieth Century is the problem of the color-line' (3). It is also confirmed by the litany of post-millennial outrages against 'black folks' which *Icon* elegises in several poems dedicated to high-profile victims of police violence: Sandra Bland, Michael Brown, Eric Garner and Freddie Gray.

The last of these brutalised figures died in hospital aged twenty-five on 19 April 2015, his demise the result of spinal injuries incurred one week earlier after being arrested for carrying a pocket knife and subjected to a so-called 'rough ride' in a Baltimore police van.[13] Brown offers a vision of Gray's traumatic ordeal towards the end of his collection in 'Ghazal between Icons: An Imagined Conversation', and it is to this poem, written in response to panel 32 in the *Frederick Douglass* series (Fig. 6.11), that this chapter makes its final turn.

In contrast to Brown's experiments with the poetic possibilities afforded by the relatively recent and untried form of PechaKucha, this text draws upon the ancient Arabic genre advertised in its title, staging a dialogue between Douglass and Gray across nine

Figure 6.11 Jacob Lawrence, *Frederick Douglass* series, Panel 32, 1938–9 (casein tempera on gessoed hardboard). Collection of the Hampton University Museum, Hampton, Virginia. © The Jacob and Gwendolyn Knight Lawrence Foundation, Seattle / Artists Rights Society (ARS), New York and DACS, London 2021.

self-contained but interconnected two-line stanzas, with both interlocutors speaking from beyond the grave.[14] It begins with an epigraph from Chapter V of *Narrative*, in which Douglass recalls being sent from Colonel Lloyd's plantation to Baltimore in March 1826 and how this event 'laid the foundation, and opened the gateway, to all [his] subsequent prosperity' (111). Douglass remembers this first sojourn in Baltimore so fondly primarily because of the intellectual enrichment it facilitates, beginning when his 'new mistress', Sophia Auld, 'very kindly commence[s] to teach [him]' (112) the alphabet. Yet even as Baltimore is celebrated, it is simultaneously associated with negative experiences, not only when Douglass's elementary lessons in literacy are quickly vetoed by Mr Auld, his 'master' (113), but also when, some ten years later, he returns to the city to work in a shipyard and is set upon and 'horribly mangled' by a gang of four 'white apprentices' (151).

Douglass reprises this 'horrid fight' (151) in the words he speaks to Gray in stanza two of Brown's poem: 'Son of red brick and Westside, been with you in these blood-beaten Streets. / "Privileged men" nearly gouge the eyes out of me, a black Baltimore boy.'[15] As well as providing the basis for an empathetic solidarity with Gray, the memory of the fight serves as the catalyst for the anxious hopes Douglass expresses in stanza six, where he 'yearns to know things have changed' since his embattled day and that, moreover, his own lifelong struggle for racial equality has contributed to the process of transformation. As he puts it, beseeching Gray directly: 'Tell me our black shines gold. / Tell me I paved nothing but golden tulips for all blacks, dear Baltimore boy.'

In one sense, of course, there have been changes aplenty – and infinitely for the better – since Douglass's time, ranging from the abolition of slavery itself to the achievements of the Civil Rights Movement of the 1950s and 60s and the election of Barack Hussein Obama II to the United States Presidency from 2009 to 2017. Gray is clearly eager to reassure Douglass that his efforts have been worthwhile not only in terms of this broad national history but also in the more personal context of his own existence, addressing Douglass's concerns in stanza seven in lines that allude (like the earlier reference to the 'golden tulips') to Lawrence's painting: '*US flag, stem and post, higher than sea breeze, but not my goals. / Because of you, my dreams sky high – Imma proud black Baltimore boy.*' Yet even as Gray's bold assertions might sound heartening, their effects are ironised by the posthumous position from which they are spoken and above all the terrifying and ultimately lethal inhumanity of the treatment he endures while in police custody: '*I scream streaks, 33 minutes of cries and a lonely road. Unrelenting / Field swallowing the air of a black Baltimore boy*' (italics in original).

Even as the journey on that '*lonely road*' leads to Gray's death a few days afterwards, the death itself leads to no public acknowledgement on the part of the state, as the American flag, as the poem notes in its first stanza, is 'never' set at 'half-mast' on Gray's behalf. Acknowledgement comes, however, in the form of the poem itself, which ends on what for *Icon* is a characteristically positive and resourceful note: '*Mr. Douglass, none of us dies in vain, right? You – the lion who makes that truth. / Freddie, blue haze-heaven awaits. Beautiful as black and you, Baltimore boy*' (italics in original). Here it is this time Douglass who is asked to reassure and console, duly responding to the call with leonine strength. Transmuting Gray's words into 'truth', he prophesies a redemptive future which, despite its lack of definition (and the ugliness of the episode the poem commemorates) will be as 'beautiful' as Gray himself.

Conclusion

Panel 32 of the *Frederick Douglass* series ends Lawrence's meditation on his subject with a triumphant scene. As he writes in his gloss to the painting:

> Frederick Douglass revisited the eastern shore of Maryland – here he was born a slave, now he returned a free man. He left unknown to the outside world and returned well known. He left on a freight boat and returned on a United States revenue cutter. He was a citizen of the United States of America. (qtd. in Wheat 80)

Although 'Ghazal' culminates in its own kind of victory, the life and death of Freddie Gray that it remembers are marked by a withholding and denial of the very citizenship – defined as 'an internalized and socially recognized sense of generalized agency' (McIvor 163) – that Lawrence sees articulated in his own creation. In this sense, Lawrence's painting might seem something of an anti-Muse for Brown, yet it can also be viewed differently and more heuristically as a reminder of the power of ekphrastic texts to reframe the artistic visions on which they draw, renewing them according to their authors' own imaginative imperatives and the currents of the time.

The task of reframing and renewal is also one which this book has sought to perform by offering a fresh perspective on ekphrastic literature about slavery as it has developed from David Dabydeen's 'Turner' onwards, bringing to light a rich body of materials that (apart from 'Turner' itself) has to date received virtually no critical attention whatsoever. The importance of this corpus, it argues, is that it reveals the ways in which elements of slavery's visual archive (some well-known and others less so) live on powerfully in the realm of the literary. As it charts these complex voyages of image into word, the book at the same time looks towards a bigger picture: focusing mainly on black-authored work, it endeavours to bring a greater racial balance to a critical field in which the study of texts located in white literary traditions still predominates.

Notes

1. For an interesting discussion of the psychological, political and creative aspects of these onomastic connections see Brown's online interview with Santos; see also 'Un-Portrait of Frederick Douglass', where the letter 'F' provides Brown with the alliterative focus for further reflections on his relationship both to his father (and mother) and to Douglass, figured as 'lion-eyed icon' (Brown 74).
2. For a selection of the late nineteenth-century elegies see Helen Douglass 147–74. A snapshot of later contributions to the tradition might include Hughes, 'Frederick Douglass: 1817–1895'; Hayden, 'Frederick Douglass' (from which *Icon* draws its second epigraph); and Keita's *Brief Evidence of Heaven*, a book-length collection which shifts the commemorative emphasis in a different direction by retelling Douglass's story from the perspective of his first wife, Anna Murray.
3. Such a tendency is manifest in other responses to Lawrence's work besides Brown's, as, for example, 'The Migration Series Poetry Suite', ten poems by various hands on Lawrence's 1941 Migration Series included in Dickerman and Smithgall 172–87. See also Young's engagement with the work of Jean-Michel Basquiat in *To Repel Ghosts* and Harrington's response to the art of Horace H. Pippin in *Primitive*.
4. Even as the Nantucket convention marks the moment of Douglass's official emergence as orator, he appears unofficially in this role as far back as 1836, at a point when he is still a slave, albeit one engaged in plotting his first escape attempt. As he puts it in *My Bondage*, recalling his efforts to persuade five others to join him in this ill-fated scheme:

> The fact is, I here began my public speaking. I canvassed, with Henry and John, the subject of slavery, and dashed against it the condemning brand of God's eternal justice, which it every hour violates. My fellow servants were neither indifferent, dull, nor inapt. Our feelings were more alike than our opinions. All, however, were ready to act, when a feasible plan should be proposed. 'Show us *how* the thing is to be done,' said they, 'and all else is clear.' (201; italics in original)

5. The spelling of Harriet's name in this way does not occur in any of Douglass's autobiographies, but something close to it can be found in the plantation-ledger kept by Aaron Anthony, in which Douglass's master (and possible father) records the birth of one 'Frederick Augustus son of Harriott' in 'Feby 1818' (Bernier, 'Introduction' 16).
6. Brown evokes such everyday sexual hazards in 'A Slave Boy's Lullaby', where the master's lascivious observation of Harriet is observed in turn by her son: 'Massa keeps his eyes on her when she sneak / Eyes always on her bres, he cant even blink // Momma turn her cheek, massa thrust, whine and wail'.
7. The double colon in the title of this poem is one of several quirky 'punctuation gestures' that Brown uses throughout *Icon* and, as he explains in his 'Extended Author Notes', should be understood to mean '"as" or "as in"'.
8. Brown's use of the 'quake' trope is reminiscent of how Douglass himself employs it, perhaps most famously in 'What to the Slave is the Fourth of July?', an 1852 speech deliberately delivered on the day following Independence Day to signal African Americans' exclusion from the 'pale of this glorious anniversary' (*My Bondage* 340). Here Douglass invests his own oratory with the revolutionary potential to overthrow slavery and emancipate the United States from the 'fraud, deception . . . and hypocrisy' with which it blinds itself to its 'crimes':

   > At a time like this, scorching irony, not convincing argument, is needed. Oh! had I the ability, and could I reach the nation's ear, I would to-day pour out a fiery stream of biting ridicule, blasting reproach, withering sarcasm, and stern rebuke. For it is not light that is needed, but fire; it is not the gentle shower, but thunder. We need the storm, the whirlwind, and the earthquake. The feeling of the nation must be quickened; the conscience of the nation must be roused; the propriety of the nation must be startled; the hypocrisy of the nation must be exposed; and its crimes against God and man must be proclaimed and denounced. (*My Bondage* 344).

9. The nocturnal voyages that Harriet undertakes to visit her son and that involve bringing him a gift of gold suggest a parallel with the Biblical Journey of the Magi to Bethlehem (Matt. 2.11), thus maintaining the Douglass-Christ identification.
10. Although he turns out (luckily) to be wrong, Douglass himself interprets his relationship to the animals he is charged with handling in less

encouraging terms, sensing in their fate the image of his own: 'I now saw, in my situation, several points of similarity with that of the oxen. They were property, so was I; they were to be broken, so was I. Covey was to break me, I was to break them; break and be broken – such is life' (*My Bondage* 155).

11. The African-American adoption and adaption of PechaKucha as a poetic resource is most closely associated with Terrance Hayes. Brown pays homage to Hayes in each of the parentheses following the titles of the poems in which he deploys this particular technique.
12. The phrases italicised in these lines are from Samuel J. May 294.
13. The 'rough ride' is a 'practice in which officers deliberately drive erratically so as to throw unsecured detainees around the van and cause them injury' (Jaros 2211).
14. For a useful (corrective) overview of this poetic form see Ali 1–14.
15. The phrase in quotation marks in these lines is from *My Bondage* 225.

Bibliography

Abridgment of the Minutes of the Evidence, Taken before a Select Committee of the Whole House, to Whom it was Referred to Consider of the Slave-Trade, 1790. Number III. babel.hathitrust.org/cgi/pt?id=nyp.33433075911663&view=1up&seq=2&skin=2021.

Adams, Gene. 'Dido Elizabeth Belle: A Black Girl at Kenwood'. *Camden History Review*, 1984, pp. 10–14.

Alexander, Elizabeth. 'Hayden in the Archive'. *Crave Radiance: New and Selected Poems 1990–2010*. Graywolf, 2010, p. 240.

—. 'Islands Number Four'. *Words for Images: A Gallery of Poems*, edited by John Hollander and Joanna Weber, Yale U Art Gallery, 2001, p. 80.

Ali, Agha Shahid, editor. *Ravishing DisUnities: Real Ghazals in English*. Wesleyan UP, 2000.

Allen, Jeffrey Renard. 'Talking and Walking the Line: An Interview with John Edgar Wideman'. *Black Renaissance / Renaissance Noire*, vol. 6, no. 2, Spring 2005, pp. 92–113.

Asante, Amma, director. *Belle*. Fox Searchlight, 2014.

Austen, Jane. *Sanditon*. Edited by Kathryn Sutherland, Oxford UP, 2019.

Baldwin, James. *Notes of a Native Son*. Penguin, 2017.

Basker, James G., editor. *Amazing Grace: An Anthology of Poems about Slavery, 1660–1810*. Yale UP, 2002.

Baucom, Ian. *Specters of the Atlantic: Finance Capital, Slavery, and the Philosophy of History*. Duke UP, 2005.

Bernier, Celeste-Marie. '"Any Leadership Would Have to be the Type of Frederick Douglass": Black History, Black Heroism, and Black Resistance in Jacob Lawrence's *Frederick Douglass* Series (1938–39)'. *Kalfou*, vol. 7, no. 1, Spring 2020, pp. 109–18.

—. Introduction. *Narrative*, by Frederick Douglass, pp. 11–69.

—. '"THE SLAVE SHIP IMPRINT": Representing the Body, Memory, and History in Contemporary African American and Black British Painting, Photography, and Installation Art'. *Callaloo*, vol. 37, no. 4, 2014, pp. 990–1022.

— and Hannah Durkin, editors. *Visualising Slavery: Art across the African Diaspora*. Liverpool UP, 2016.

The Bible. Authorised King James Version. Edited by Robert Carroll and Stephen Prickett, Oxford UP, 2008.
Biddle, Daniel R. and Murray Dubin. *Tasting Freedom: Octavius Catto and the Battle for Equality in Civil War America*. Temple UP, 2010.
Bingham, Caleb. *The Columbian Orator: Containing a Variety of Original and Selected Pieces; together with Rules; Calculated to Improve Youth and Others in the Ornamental and Useful Art of Eloquence*, Boston, 1797.
Boeninger, Stephanie Pocock. '"I Have Become the Sea's Craft": Authorial Subjectivity in Derek Walcott's *Omeros* and David Dabydeen's "Turner"'. *Contemporary Literature*, vol. 52, no. 3, Fall 2011, pp. 462–92.
Boime, Albert. 'Burgoo and Bourgeois: Thomas Noble's Images of Black People'. *Thomas S. Noble: 1835–1907*, edited by James D. Birchfield et al., U of Kentucky Art Museum, 1988, pp. 29–60.
Brathwaite, Edward Kamau. 'Gods of the Middle Passage: A Tennament'. *Caribbean Review*, vol. 11, no. 4, 1982, pp. 18+.
Brito, Leonora. 'Dido Elizabeth Belle – A Narrative of Her Life (Extant)'. *Dat's Love*. Seren, 1995, pp. 47–57.
—. 'Staying Power'. *Cardiff Central: Ten Writers Return to the Welsh Capital*, edited by Francesca Rhydderch, Gomer, 2003, pp. 43–50.
Brontë, Charlotte. *Jane Eyre*. Edited by Margaret Smith, Oxford UP, 1998.
Brown, Drea. *Dear Girl: A Reckoning*. Goldline, 2015.
Brown, F. Douglas. 'Annunciation: Frederick Augustus Washington Bailey'. *Icon*, pp. 19–20.
—. 'Begotten: February, 1818'. *Icon*, pp. 21–2.
—. 'Daguerreotype c. 1841'. *Icon*, p. 15.
—. 'Darkness, My Mother'. *Icon*, p. 23.
—. 'Extended Author Notes'. fdouglasbrown.com/icon-extended-author-notes.
—. 'The Flogging'. *Icon*, p. 34.
—. 'Ghazal between Icons: An Imagined Conversation'. *Icon*, p. 115.
—. *Icon*, Writ Large Press, 2018.
—. 'Imagining Lawrence Imagine the 11th of August 1841'. *Icon*, pp. 78–9.
—. 'Mr. Covey, Shall We Dance?' *Icon*, pp. 58–9.
—. 'A Slave Boy's Lullaby'. *Icon*, p. 43.
—. 'Un-Portrait of Frederick Douglass'. *Icon*, pp. 74–5.
—. 'Why I Read: Partial Pecha'. *Icon*, pp. 56–7.
—. 'Why I Write: Partial Kucha'. *Icon*, pp. 82–3.
Bryant, Julius. *Kenwood: The Iveagh Bequest*. English Heritage, 2001.
Bryant, Tisa. 'The Problem of Dido'. *Unexplained Presence*. Leon Works, 2007, pp. 127–37.
Burn, Andrew. 'A Second Address to the People of Great Britain: Containing a New, and Most Powerful Argument to Abstain from the Use of West India Sugar. By an Eye Witness to the Facts Related', London, 1792.

Burney, Frances. *Evelina, Or the History of a Young Lady's Entrance into the World*. Edited by Edward A. Bloom with an Introduction by Vivien Jones, Oxford UP, 2008.

Burns, Sarah. 'Black-Quadroon-Gypsy Women in the Art of George Fuller'. *The Massachusetts Review*, vol. 26, no. 2, Summer-Autumn 1985, pp. 405–24.

—. 'Images of Slavery: George Fuller's Depictions of the Antebellum South'. *The American Art Journal*, vol. 15, no. 3, Summer 1983, pp. 35–60.

Byrne, Paula. *Belle: The True Story of Dido Belle*. HarperCollins, 2014.

Card, Jane. 'The Power of Context: The Portrait of Dido Elizabeth Lindsay and Lady Elizabeth Murray'. *Teaching History*, no. 160, Sept. 2015, pp. 8–15.

Cheeke, Stephen. *Writing for Art: The Aesthetics of Ekphrasis*. Manchester UP, 2008.

Clark, Emily. *The Strange History of the American Quadroon: Free Women of Color in the Atlantic World*. U of North Carolina P, 2013.

Clarkson, Thomas. *The History of the Rise, Progress, and Accomplishment of the Abolition of the African Slave-Trade by the British Parliament*. Vol. 2, London, 1808.

Cliff, Michelle. *Free Enterprise: A Novel of Mary Ellen Pleasant*. City Lights, 2004.

Coffin, Levi. *Reminiscences of Levi Coffin, the Reputed President of the Underground Railroad; Being a Brief History of the Labors of a Lifetime in Behalf of the Slave, with the Stories of Numerous Fugitives, Who Gained Their Freedom through His Instrumentality, and Many Other Incidents*. 2nd ed. with appendix, Cincinnati, 1880.

Costello, Leo. *J. M. W. Turner and the Subject of History*. Ashgate, 2012.

Cowper, William. 'Epigram'. *The Works of William Cowper: His Life, Letters, and Poems, Now First Completed by the Introduction of Cowper's Private Correspondence*, edited by T. S. Grimshawe, London, 1849, p. 630.

Craps, Stef. *Postcolonial Witnessing: Trauma out of Bounds*. Palgrave Macmillan, 2013.

Cutter, Martha J. *The Illustrated Slave: Empathy, Graphic Narrative, and the Visual Culture of the Transatlantic Abolition Movement, 1800–1852*. U of Georgia P, 2017.

Dabydeen, David. 'Dependence, or the Ballad of the Little Black Boy'. *Coolie Odyssey*. Hansib, 1988, pp. 48–9.

—. *A Harlot's Progress*. Cape, 1999.

—. 'Hogarth and the Canecutters'. Macedo 80–5.

—. Preface. Dabydeen, *Turner*, pp. 7–8.

—. *Slave Song*. Peepal Tree, 2005.

—. 'Turner'. Dabydeen, *Turner*, pp. 9–42.

—. *Turner: New and Selected Poems*. Peepal Tree, 2010.

D'Aguiar, Fred. *Feeding the Ghosts*. Vintage, 1998.

Dawes, Kwame. *Requiem: A Lament for the Dead*. Peepal Tree, 1996.
Dickerman, Leah and Elsa Smithgall; with contributions by Elizabeth Alexander (and Twelve Others). *Jacob Lawrence: The Migration Series*. Museum of Modern Art, 2015.
Donoghue, Emma. 'Dido'. *The Woman Who Gave Birth to Rabbits*. Virago, 2002, pp. 170–82.
Döring, Tobias. *Caribbean-English Passages: Intertextuality in a Postcolonial Tradition*. Routledge, 2002.
'A Double Whodunnit'. *Fake or Fortune?*, series 7, episode 4, BBC, 2018.
Douglass, Frederick. 'The Color Line'. *The Portable Frederick Douglass*, edited by John Stauffer and Henry Louis Gates, Jr., Penguin Books, 2016, pp. 501–12.
—. *Life and Times of Frederick Douglass*. *Autobiographies:* Narrative of the Life of Frederick Douglass, an American Slave, My Bondage and My Freedom, Life and Times of Frederick Douglass, edited by Henry Louis Gates, Jr, Library of America, 1994, pp. 453–1045.
—. *My Bondage and My Freedom*, edited by John David Smith, Penguin, 2003.
—. *Narrative of the Life of Frederick Douglass, an American Slave*, edited by Celeste-Marie Bernier, Broadview, 2018.
Douglass, Helen, editor. *In Memoriam: Frederick Douglass*, Philadelphia, 1897.
Drescher, Seymour. 'The Shocking Birth of British Abolitionism'. *Slavery & Abolition: A Journal of Slave and Post-Slave Studies*, vol. 33, no. 4, 2012, pp. 571–93.
Du Bois, W. E. B. *The Souls of Black Folk*, edited by Brent Hayes Edwards, Oxford UP, 2007.
Dunbar, Paul Laurence. 'We Wear the Mask'. *The Complete Poems of Paul Laurence Dunbar*. Dodd, Mead and Company, 1922, p. 71.
Duras, Claire de. *Ourika*. Translated and with a Foreword by John Fowles, Introduction by Joan DeJean and Margaret Waller, The Modern Language Association of America, 1994.
Eliot, George. *Brother Jacob*. The Lifted Veil; *and* Brother Jacob, edited by Helen Small, Oxford UP, 1999, pp. 45–87.
Eliot, T. S. *The Waste Land*. *The Complete Poems and Plays of T. S. Eliot*. Faber, 1969, pp. 59–80.
Emery, Mary Lou. *Modernism, the Visual, and Caribbean Literature*. Cambridge UP, 2009.
'Ethiop' (William J. Wilson). 'Afric-American Picture Gallery'. *The Anglo-African Magazine*, vol. 1, 1859, pp. 52+.
—. 'From Our Brooklyn Correspondent'. *Frederick Douglass' Paper*, no. 272, 11 March 1853.
Euripides. *Medea*. Medea *and Other Plays*, translated and edited by James Morwood, Oxford UP, 2008, pp. 1–38.

Fabre, Geneviève. 'The Slave Ship Dance'. *Black Imagination and the Middle Passage*, edited by Maria Diedrich, Henry Louis Gates, Jr and Carl Pedersen, Oxford UP, 1999, pp. 33–46.

Falconbridge, Alexander. *An Account of the Slave Trade on the Coast of Africa*, London, 1788.

Falk, Erik. 'How to Really Forget: David Dabydeen's "Creative Amnesia"'. *Readings of the Particular: The Postcolonial in the Postnational*, edited by Anne Holden Rønning and Lene Johannessen, Rodopi, 2007, pp. 187–204.

Fanon, Frantz. *Black Skin, White Masks*. Translated by Charles Lam Markmann, Pluto P, 1986.

Feelings, Tom. *The Middle Passage: White Ships / Black Cargo*. Dial, 1995.

Finley, Cheryl. *Committed to Memory: The Art of the Slave Ship Icon*. Princeton UP, 2018.

Fischer, Susan Alice. 'Interview: Andrea Levy in Conversation with Susan Alice Fischer (2005 and 2012)'. *Andrea Levy: Contemporary Critical Perspectives*, edited by Jeanette Baxter and David James, Bloomsbury, 2014, pp. 121–38.

Fox, William. 'An Address to the People of Great Britain, on the Propriety of Abstaining from West India Sugar and Rum'. *The Abolition Debate*, edited by Peter J. Kitson, Pickering & Chatto, 1999, pp. 153–65.

Fox-Amato, Matthew. *Exposing Slavery: Photography, Human Bondage, and the Birth of Modern Visual Politics in America*. Oxford UP, 2019.

Francis, Jacqueline. 'The *Brooks* Slave Ship Icon: A "Universal Symbol"?' *Slavery & Abolition*, vol. 30, no. 2, 2009, pp. 327–38.

Frost, Mark. '"The Guilty Ship": Ruskin, Turner and Dabydeen'. *Journal of Commonwealth Literature*, vol. 45, no. 3, Sept. 2010, pp. 371–88.

Furth, Leslie. '"The Modern Medea" and Race Matters: Thomas Satterwhite Noble's "Margaret Garner"'. *American Art*, vol. 12, no. 2, Summer 1998, pp. 36–57.

Germann, Jennifer. '"Other Women Were Present": Seeing Black Women in Georgian England'. *Eighteenth-Century Studies*, vol. 54, no. 3, Spring 2021, pp. 535–53.

Gerzina, Gretchen H., editor. *Britain's Black Past*. Liverpool UP, 2020.

Gidlow, Liette. 'The Sequel: The Fifteenth Amendment, the Nineteenth Amendment, and Southern Black Women's Right to Vote'. *The Journal of the Gilded Age and Progressive Era*, vol. 17, no. 3, 2018, pp. 433–49.

Gillette, William. *The Right to Vote: Politics and the Passage of the Fifteenth Amendment*. Johns Hopkins UP, 1965.

Gordon-Reed, Annette. *Thomas Jefferson and Sally Hemings: An American Controversy*. UP of Virginia, 1998.

Grant, Kevin, editor. *The Art of David Dabydeen*. Peepal Tree, 1997.

Gravendyk, Hillary. 'Intertextual Absences: "Turner" and Turner'. *Comparatist*, vol. 35, May 2011, pp. 161–9.

Green, Jonathon. *The Vulgar Tongue: Green's History of Slang*. Oxford UP, 2015.
Hall, Joan Wylie, editor. *Conversations with Natasha Trethewey*. UP of Mississippi, 2013.
Hammond, James Henry. *Speech of Hon. James H. Hammond, of South Carolina, on the Admission of Kansas, under the Lecompton Constitution. Delivered in the Senate of the United States, March 4, 1858*, Washington, DC, 1858.
Handler, Jerome S. and Annis Steiner. 'Identifying Pictorial Images of Atlantic Slavery: Three Case Studies'. *Slavery & Abolition*, vol. 27, no. 1, 2006, pp. 51–71.
Harrington, Janice N. *Primitive: The Art and Life of Horace H. Pippin*. BOA Editions, 2016.
Harris, Middleton A., Morris Levitt, Roger Furman and Ernest Smith, editors. *The Black Book: 35th Anniversary Edition*. Random House, 2009.
Härting, Heike H. 'Painting, Perversion, and the Politics of Cultural Transfiguration in David Dabydeen's *Turner*'. Karran and Macedo, pp. 48–85.
Hayden, Robert. 'Aunt Jemima of the Ocean Waves'. Hayden, pp. 74–5.
—. *The Collected Poems of Robert Hayden*, edited by Frederick Glaysher, Liveright, 1996.
Hayden, Robert. 'Frederick Douglass'. Hayden, p. 62.
—. 'A Letter from Phillis Wheatley'. Hayden, pp. 147–8.
—. 'Middle Passage'. Hayden, pp. 48–54.
Hayes, Terrance. 'Antebellum House Party'. Jones and McManus, pp. 5–6.
—. *How To Be Drawn*. Penguin, 2015.
Hedley, Jane. 'Black Ekphrasis? A Response to Carl Plasa'. *Connotations: A Journal for Critical Debate*, vol. 26, 2016–17, pp. 39–46.
Hedley, Jane, Nick Halpern and Willard Spiegelman, editors. *In the Frame: Women's Ekphrastic Poetry from Marianne Moore to Susan Wheeler*. U of Delaware P, 2009.
Hedquist, Valerie. *Class, Gender, and Sexuality in Thomas Gainsborough's Blue Boy*. Routledge, 2020.
Heffernan, James A. W. *Museum of Words: The Poetics of Ekphrasis from Homer to Ashbery*. U of Chicago P, 1993.
Herrick, Francis Hobart. *Audubon the Naturalist: A History of His Life and Time*. Vol. 1, Appleton and Company, 1917.
Hill, David. *Turner in the North*. Yale UP, 1996.
Hogarth, George. *The Songs of Charles Dibdin, Chronologically Arranged, with Notes, Historical, Biographical, and Critical; and the Music of the Best and Most Popular of the Melodies, with New Piano-Forte Accompaniments. To which is Prefixed a Memoir of the Author, by George Hogarth, Esq.*, London, 1842.

Hollander, John. *The Gazer's Spirit: Poems Speaking to Silent Works of Art*. U of Chicago P, 1995.
Howley, Ellen. 'The Sea and Memory: Poetic Reconsiderations of the *Zong* Massacre'. *Journal of Commonwealth Literature*, 2019, pp. 1–18.
Hudson, Martyn. *The Slave Ship, Memory and the Origin of Modernity*. Routledge, 2016.
Hughes, Langston. 'Frederick Douglass: 1817–1895'. *The Collected Poems of Langston Hughes*, edited by Arnold Rampersad, Vintage, 1995, p. 549.
—. *Mulatto: A Play of the Deep South*. *The Collected Works of Langston Hughes*. Vol. 5: *The Plays to 1942:* Mulatto *to* The Sun Do Move, edited by Leslie Catherine Sanders (with Nancy Johnston), U of Missouri P, 2002, pp. 17–50.
Hutchinson, Thomas. *The Diary and Letters of His Excellency Thomas Hutchinson*. Edited by Peter Orlando Hutchinson. Vol. 2, Boston, 1886.
Irving, John B. *A Day on Cooper River*, Charleston, 1842.
Jaros, David. 'Criminal Doctrines of Faith'. *Boston College Law Review*, vol. 59, no. 7, 2018, pp. 2203–58.
Jeffers, Honorée Fanonne. *The Age of Phillis*. Wesleyan UP, 2020.
—. 'Catalog: Water'. Jeffers, pp. 29–36.
—. 'Illustration: "Stowage of the British Slave Ship 'Brookes' under the Regulated Slave Trade Act of 1788"'. Jeffers, p. 26.
—. 'Portrait of Dido Elizabeth Belle Lindsay, Free Mulatto, and Her White Cousin, the Lady Elizabeth Murray, Great Niece of William Murray, First Earl of Mansfield and Lord Chief Justice of the King's Bench'. Jeffers, pp. 66–7.
Jefferson, Thomas. *Notes on the State of Virginia*. Edited by Frank Shuffleton, Penguin Books, 1999.
Jenkins, Lee M. 'On Not Being Tony Harrison: Tradition and the Individual Talent of David Dabydeen'. *ARIEL* vol. 32, no. 2, Apr. 2001, pp. 69–88.
Jones, R. Mac and Ray McManus, editors. *Found Anew: Poetry and Prose Inspired by the South Caroliniana Library Digital Collections*. U of South Carolina P, 2015.
—. Introduction. Jones and McManus, pp. xiii–xvi.
Jordan, June. 'The Difficult Miracle of Black Poetry in America or Something Like a Sonnet for Phillis Wheatley'. *The Massachusetts Review*, vol. 27, no. 2, Summer 1986, pp. 252–62.
Journal of Legal History, vol. 28, no. 3, 2007, pp. 283–370.
Kant, Immanuel. 'Answer to the Question: What Is Enlightenment?' Translated by Thomas K. Abbott. *Basic Writings of Kant*, edited by Allen W. Wood, Modern Library, 2001, pp. 133–41.
Karran, Kampta and Lynne Macedo, editors. *No Land, No Mother: Essays on the Work of David Dabydeen*, Peepal Tree, 2007.
Kearney, Douglas. 'MAST'. *Harriet: A Poetry Blog*, 24 January 2011, poetryfoundation.org/harriet-books/2011/01/mast.

—. 'SWIMCHANT FOR NIGGER MER-FOLK (AN AQUABOOGIE SET IN LAPIS)'. *The Black Automaton*. Fence Books, 2011, pp. 62–3.
Keita, M. Nzadi. *Brief Evidence of Heaven: Poems from the Life of Anna Murray Douglass*. Whirlwind, 2014.
Kennedy, David. *The Ekphrastic Encounter in Contemporary British Poetry and Elsewhere*. Ashgate, 2012.
— and Richard Meek, editors. *Ekphrastic Encounters: New Interdisciplinary Essays on Literature and the Visual Arts*. U of Manchester P, 2019.
King, Reyahn. 'Ignatius Sancho and Portraits of the Black Élite'. Reyahn King, et al. *Ignatius Sancho: An African Man of Letters*. National Portrait Gallery, 1997, pp. 15–44.
Kinnahan, Linda. 'Tourism and Taxonomy: Marianne Moore and Natasha Trethewey in Jefferson's Virginia'. *Humanities*, vol. 8, no. 4, 2019, 180. DOI: mdpi.com/2076-0787/8/4/180.
Komunyakaa, Yusef. *Dien Cai Dau*. Wesleyan UP, 1988.
—. 'Modern Medea'. *Pleasure Dome: New and Collected Poems*. Wesleyan UP, 2004, p. 354.
—. 'The Price of Blood'. *Taboo*. Farrar, Straus and Giroux, 2004, pp. 42–3.
Kriz, Kay Dian. *Slavery, Sugar, and the Culture of Refinement: Picturing the British West Indies, 1700–1840*. Yale UP, 2008.
Lang, Walter, director. *The King and I*. 20th Century-Fox, 1956.
Larsen, Nella. *Quicksand*. Quicksand *and* Passing, edited by Deborah E. McDowell, Rutgers UP, 1986, pp. 1–135.
Levine, Robert S. *The Lives of Frederick Douglass*. Harvard UP, 2016.
Levy, Andrea. *The Long Song*. Headline, 2010.
Lewin, David. *Studies in Music with Text*. Oxford UP, 2006.
Lhamon, Jr, W. T. *Jump Jim Crow: Lost Plays, Lyrics, and Street Prose of the First Atlantic Popular Culture*. Harvard UP, 2003.
Loizeaux, Elizabeth Bergmann. *Twentieth-Century Poetry and the Visual Arts*. Cambridge UP, 2008.
Loscocco, Paula. *Phillis Wheatley's Miltonic Poetics*. Palgrave Macmillan, 2014.
Lott, Eric. *Love and Theft: Blackface Minstrelsy and the American Working Class*. Oxford UP, 2013.
Lugo-Ortiz, Agnes and Angela Rosenthal, editors. *Slave Portraiture in the Atlantic World*. Cambridge UP, 2013.
Lyall, Andrew. *Granville Sharp's Cases on Slavery*. Hart, 2017.
Macaluso, Laura A. *Art of the* Amistad *and the Portrait of Cinque*. Rowman & Littlefield, 2016.
McCandless, Peter. *Slavery, Disease, and Suffering in the Southern Lowcountry*. Cambridge UP, 2011.
McCoubrey, John. 'Turner's *Slave Ship*: Abolition, Ruskin, and Reception'. *Word & Image: A Journal of Verbal / Visual Inquiry*, vol. 14, no. 4, 1998, pp. 319–53.

Macedo, Lynne, editor. *Pak's Britannica: Articles by and Interviews with David Dabydeen*. U of the West Indies P, 2011.

McHaney, Pearl Amelia. 'Natasha Trethewey's Triptych: The Bodies of History in *Bellocq's Ophelia, Native Guard*, and *Thrall*'. *Southern Quarterly*, vol. 50, no. 4, Summer 2013, pp. 153–72.

McInnis, Maurie D. *Slaves Waiting for Sale: Abolitionist Art and the American Slave Trade*. U of Chicago P, 2011.

McIvor, David Wallace. *Mourning in America: Race and the Politics of Loss*. Cornell UP, 2016.

Mackenthun, Gesa. *Fictions of the Black Atlantic in American Foundational Literature*. Routledge, 2004.

Major, Clarence. 'The Slave Trade: View from the Middle Passage'. *African American Review*, vol. 28, no. 1, Spring 1994, pp. 11–22.

Mannix, Daniel P. and Malcolm Cowley. *Black Cargoes: A History of the Atlantic Slave Trade, 1518–1865*. Longmans, 1963.

Matthews, Lieutenant John. *A Voyage to the River Sierra-Leone, on the Coast of Africa; Containing an Account of the Trade and Productions of the Country, and of the Civil and Religious Customs and Manners of the People; in a Series of Letters to a Friend in England*, London, 1788.

Mauchline, Mary. *Harewood House: One of the Treasure Houses of Britain*. Rev. ed., MPC, 1992.

May, Samuel J. *Some Recollections of Our Antislavery Conflict*, Cambridge, MA, 1869.

May, Stephen J. *Voyage of* The Slave Ship: *J. M. W. Turner's Masterpiece in Historical Context*. McFarland, 2014.

Milton, John. *Paradise Lost*. Edited by Stephen Orgel and Jonathan Goldberg, Oxford UP, 2008.

Mitchell, W. J. T. 'Ekphrasis and the Other'. *The South Atlantic Quarterly*, vol. 91, no. 4, 1992, pp. 695–719.

—. *Picture Theory: Essays on Verbal and Visual Representation*. U of Chicago P, 1994.

'Modern Medea'. *Harper's Weekly*, 18 May 1867, p. 318.

Molineux, Catherine. *Faces of Perfect Ebony: Encountering Atlantic Slavery in Imperial Britain*. Harvard UP, 2012.

Morgan, Jo-Ann. 'Thomas Satterwhite Noble's Mulattos: From Barefoot Madonna to Maggie the Ripper'. *Journal of American Studies*, vol. 41, no. 1, Apr. 2007, pp. 83–114.

Morrison, Toni. *Beloved*. Vintage, 1997.

Moyle, Franny. *The Extraordinary Life and Momentous Times of J. M. W. Turner*. Penguin Books, 2017.

Murray, Sean. 'That "Weird and Wonderful Posture": Jump "Jim Crow" and the Performance of Disability'. *The Oxford Handbook of Music and Disability Studies*, edited by Blake Howe et al., Oxford UP, 2016, pp. 357–70.

Nesbitt, Jennifer Poulos. *Rum Histories: Drinking in Atlantic Literature and Culture*. U of Virginia P, 2021.
Newton, John. *Thoughts upon the African Slave Trade*, London, 1788.
Nobles, Gregory. *John James Audubon: The Nature of the American Woodsman*. U of Pennsylvania P, 2017.
The North Star [New York], vol. 1, no. 1, 3 December 1847.
Olson, Ted. 'Jim Crow'. *Oxford Companion to African American Literature*, edited by William L. Andrews, Francis Smith Foster and Trudier Harris, Oxford UP, 1997, pp. 398–9.
Patrick, William B. 'In the New World'. Patrick, pp. 37–50.
—. 'The Island of Birds'. Patrick, pp. 64–71.
—. 'The Slave Ship'. Patrick, pp. 51–63.
—. *These Upraised Hands*. BOA Editions, 1995.
Philip, Marlene NourbeSe. *Zong!*. Wesleyan UP, 2008.
Piersen, William D. 'White Cannibals, Black Martyrs: Fear, Depression, and Religious Faith as Causes of Suicide among New Slaves'. *Journal of Negro History*, vol. 62, no. 2, Apr. 1977, pp. 147–59.
Plampin, Matthew. *Will & Tom*. HarperCollins, 2015.
Plasa, Carl. 'Ekphrastic Poetry and the Middle Passage: Recent Encounters in the Black Atlantic'. *Connotations: A Journal for Critical Debate*, vol. 24, no. 2, 2014–15, pp. 290–324.
Ray, Henrietta Cordelia. 'In Memoriam (Frederick Douglass)'. Helen Douglass, pp. 161–3.
Rediker, Marcus. *The Slave Ship: A Human History*. Murray, 2007.
Ritvo, Harriet. *The Animal Estate: The English and Other Creatures in the Victorian Age*. Harvard UP, 1987.
Rogers, J. A. *World's Great Men of Color*. Vol 1. Touchstone, 2011.
'Royal Academy Exhibition'. *Blackwood's Edinburgh Magazine*, Sept. 1840, pp. 374–86.
Ruskin, John. 'Of Water, as Painted by Turner'. *The Works of John Ruskin*, edited by Edward Tyas Cook and Alexander Wedderburn, vol. 3: *Modern Painters 1*, Cambridge UP, 2009, pp. 537–73.
Sancho, Ignatius. *Letters of the Late Ignatius Sancho, an African. To Which are Prefixed, Memoirs of his Life*, 3rd ed., London, 1784.
Santos, Nix. 'What's in a Name? F. Douglas Brown', 7500magazine.com/fdouglasbrown.html.
Scarry, Elaine. *The Body in Pain: The Making and Unmaking of the World*. Oxford UP, 1985.
Scott, Kevin Michael. 'The "Negro Touch" and the "Yankee Trick": William Sidney Mount and the Art of Race and Ethnicity'. *Visual Resources*, vol. 24, no. 3, 2008, pp. 233–52.
Scott, Lawrence. *Dangerous Freedom: Elizabeth d'Aviniere's Story*. Papillote Press, 2020.
Shakespeare, William. *Macbeth*. Edited by Nicholas Brooke, Oxford UP, 2008.

Shakespeare, William. *The Tempest*. Edited by Stephen Orgel, Oxford UP, 1987.

Shockley, Evie. 'Going Overboard: African American Poetic Innovation and the Middle Passage'. *Contemporary Literature*, vol. 52, no. 4, Winter 2011, pp. 791–817.

Skeehan, Danielle. 'Deadly Notes: Atlantic Soundscapes and the Writing of the Middle Passage'. *The Appendix*, vol. 1, no. 3, July 2013, the appendix.net/issues/2013/7/deadly-notes-atlantic-soundscapes-and-the-writing-of-the-middle-passage.

Slapkauskaite, Ruta. 'Intermedial Translation: The Gyrating Gaze in David Dabydeen's *Turner*'. *European Journal of English Studies*, vol. 18, no. 3, 2014, pp. 316–29.

Slauter, Eric. 'Looking for Scipio Moorhead: An "African Painter" in Revolutionary North America'. Lugo-Ortiz and Rosenthal, pp. 89–116.

Smiles, Sam. 'Turner and the Slave Trade: Speculation and Representation, 1805–40'. *British Art Journal*, vol. 8, no. 3, Winter 2007–8, pp. 47–54.

Smith, John Thomas. *Nollekens and His Times*. Edited by Edmund Gosse, London, 1895.

Smith, R. T. 'Turner's *Slave Ship*'. *Atlanta Review*, vol. 20, no. 2, 2014, pp. 104–5.

Smith, S. D. *Slavery, Family and Gentry Capitalism in the British Atlantic: The World of the Lascelles, 1648–1834*. Cambridge UP, 2006.

Sollors, Werner. *Neither Black nor White yet Both: Thematic Explorations of Interracial Literature*. Oxford UP, 1997.

Stauffer, John, Zoe Trodd and Celeste-Marie Bernier. *Picturing Frederick Douglass: An Illustrated Biography of the Nineteenth Century's Most Photographed American*. Liveright, 2015.

Steedman, Carolyn. 'Lord Mansfield's Women'. *Past & Present*, no. 176, Aug. 2002, pp. 105–43.

Stowe, Harriet Beecher. *Uncle Tom's Cabin; or, Life among the Lowly*. Edited by Elizabeth Ammons, Norton, 1994.

Tarantino, Quentin, director. *Django Unchained*. Columbia Pictures, 2012.

Tenac, Charles van. *Histoire Générale de la Marine*, Paris, 1847–8.

Thackeray, William Makepeace. 'A Pictorial Rhapsody'. *Fraser's Magazine for Town and Country*, June 1840, pp. 720–32.

Thomas, Hugh. *The Slave Trade: The History of the Atlantic Slave Trade: 1440–1870*. Picador, 1997.

Tlostanova, Madina. 'A Permanent Transit: Transgression and Metamorphoses in David Dabydeen's Art'. Karran and Macedo, pp. 86–105.

'To the Printer of *The Morning Chronicle*'. *The Morning Chronicle and London Advertiser*. 18 March 1783.

Trethewey, Eric. 'Her Swing'. *Prairie Schooner*, vol. 54, no. 3, Fall 1980, pp. 48–9.

Trethewey, Natasha. *Beyond Katrina: A Meditation on the Mississippi Gulf Coast*. U of Georgia P, 2010.

—. 'Blood'. *Thrall*, p. 34.
—. 'Enlightenment'. *Thrall*, pp. 68–71.
—. 'Knowledge'. *Thrall*, pp. 28–30.
—. *Thrall: Poems*. Houghton Mifflin Harcourt, 2012.
Trodd, Zoe, 'Am I Still Not a Man and a Brother? Protest Memory in Contemporary Antislavery Visual Culture'. *Slavery & Abolition*, vol. 34, no. 2, 2013, pp. 338–52.
Twain, Mark. *A Tramp Abroad*. Edited by Robert Gray Bruce and Hamlin Hill, Penguin Books, 1997.
Unsworth, Barry. *Sacred Hunger*. Hamish Hamilton, 1992.
Valenzeula-Mendoza, Eloisa. '"The Wages of Empire": American Inventions of Mixed-Race Identities and Natasha Trethewey's *Thrall* (2012)'. *African and Black Diaspora: An International Journal*, vol. 12, no. 3, 2019, pp. 337–54.
Virgil. *The Aeneid*. Translated and with an Introduction by David West. Rev. ed., Penguin Books, 2003.
—. *Virgil's Eclogues*. Translated by Len Krisak, U of Pennsylvania P, 2010.
Walcott, Derek. *Omeros*. Faber, 1990.
Walker, Andrew. 'From Private Sermon to Public Masterpiece: J. M. W. Turner's "The Slave Ship" in Boston, 1876–1899'. *Journal of the Museum of Fine Arts, Boston*, vol. 6, 1994, pp. 4–13.
Wallart, Kerry-Jane. 'Lines and Circles: Geometrical Horizons in David Dabydeen's *Turner*'. *Commonwealth*, vol. 33, no. 1, Autumn 2010, pp. 11–22.
Walters, Ronald G., *The Antislavery Appeal: American Abolitionism After 1830*. Johns Hopkins UP, 1976.
Walvin, James. *Slavery in Small Things: Slavery and Modern Cultural Habits*. Wiley Blackwell, 2017.
—. *The Zong: A Massacre, The Law and the End of Slavery*. Yale UP, 2011.
Ward, Abigail. '"Words Are All I Have Left of My Eyes": Blinded by the Past in J. M. W. Turner's *Slavers Throwing Overboard the Dead and Dying* and David Dabydeen's "Turner"'. *Journal of Commonwealth Literature*, vol. 42, no. 1, Mar. 2007, pp. 47–58.
Weisenburger, Steven. *Modern Medea: A Family Story of Slavery and Child-Murder from the Old South*. Hill and Wang, 1998.
West, Emily and R. J. Knight. 'Mothers' Milk: Slavery, Wet-Nursing, and Black and White Women in the Antebellum South'. *The Journal of Southern History*, vol. 83, no. 1, Feb. 2017, pp. 37–68.
Wheat. Ellen Harkins. *Jacob Lawrence: The* Frederick Douglass *and* Harriet Tubman *Series of 1938–40*. Hampton U Museum (in association with U of Washington P), 1991.
Wheatley, Phillis. 'To the Right Honourable WILLIAM, Earl of DARMOUTH, His Majesty's Principal Secretary of State for North-America, &c'. *Poems on Various Subjects, Religious and Moral*. London, 1773, pp. 73–4.

Wideman, John Edgar. 'Listening'. *Transforming Vision: Writers on Art*, edited by Edward Hirsch, Little, Brown and Company, 1994, pp. 67–8.

Wise, Steven M. *Though the Heavens May Fall: The Landmark Trial That Led to the End of Human Slavery*. Da Capo, 2005.

Wood, Marcus. *Black Milk: Imagining Slavery in the Visual Cultures of Brazil and America*. Oxford UP, 2013.

—. *Blind Memory: Visual Representations of Slavery in England and America, 1780–1865*. Manchester UP, 2000.

Wordsworth, William. *The Prelude: The Four Texts (1798, 1799, 1805, 1850)*. Edited by Jonathan Wordsworth, Penguin, 1995.

Yeats, W. B. 'Leda and the Swan'. *Yeats's Poems*, edited by A. Norman Jeffares, Macmillan, 1989, p. 322.

Young, Kevin. *Homage to Phillis Wheatley (1998–2010)*. *Blue Laws: Selected & Uncollected Poems, 1995–2015*, Alfred A. Knopf, 2016, pp. 311–32.

—. *To Repel Ghosts: Five Sides in B Minor*. Zoland Books, 2001.

Ziff, Jerrold. 'John Langhorne and Turner's "Fallacies of Hope"'. *Journal of the Warburg and Courtauld Institutes*, vol. 27, 1964, pp. 340–2.

Index

References to images are in italics; references to notes are indicated by n.

abolitionism, 5, 16, 48, 58, 72–3
  and Douglass, 167–8, 196–7, 199–201
  and Plampin, 89, 92
  and sugar, 81–2
Abraham, 143
Adam, Robert, 112
Aesop, 146
affinity, 131–3
Africa, 19, 22–3, 34–5, 47–8
  and Dido Elizabeth Belle, 102
  and Jeffers, 77–8
African Americans, 4, 5–7, 30, 163–4
  and publications, 197
  and suffrage, 187–8
  see also Douglass, Frederick; Hayes, Terrance; Komunyakaa, Yusef; Trethewey, Natasha; Wideman, John Edgar
Alexander, Elizabeth, 6, 66–7
  'Islands Number Four', 5, 67–76, 93
alienation, 131, 134, 164n1
Allen, Jeffrey Renard, 129
aloe, 191–2, 195, 197, 201
American Civil War, 1, 134–5
animals, 162, 186–7
Annunciation, 7, 170–2, 174, 187
antebellum South, 157, 159–63
anti-slave trade movement see abolitionism
Art Institute of Chicago, 129, 130, 131
artistic technique, 49–50, 52
Asante, Amma, 95–6
Audubon, John James, *Birds of America*, 162, *163*

Auld, Sophia, 203
Austen, Jane, *Sanditon*, 94n6

Bailey, Harriet, 171, 173–4, 178, 180, 193, 206n5
Baltimore, 201, 203–4
Basquiat, Jean-Michel, 205n3
beatings see violence
Belle (film), 95–6
Bernier, Celeste-Marie, 184, 188
Bible, the, 97–8, 100–2, 143, 170, 171–4, 177
birth see childbirth
blackface, 55, 64n7, 133
blackness see race
Blackwood's Edinburgh Magazine, 49–50
Bland, Sandra, 201
body parts, 51–2
Boime, Albert, 142, 144
Botticelli, Sandro, *Annunciation of Cestello*, 170, *172*, 173–4
Brady, Mathew B., *The Modern Medea – The Story of Margaret Garner*, 139, *140*, 141
Brathwaite, Edward Kamau, 14
Brito, Leonora, 113, 126
  'Dido Elizabeth Belle – A Narrative of Her Life (Extant)', 6, 96–108
Brontë, Charlotte, *Jane Eyre*, 94n5
Brookes (slaver), 1, 2, 53–5, 76–8; see also *Description of a Slave Ship*
Brown, F. Douglas, 164
  'Annunciation: Frederick Augustus Washington Bailey', 170–4

Brown, F. Douglas (*cont.*)
　'Begotten :: February, 1818', 174, 176–7
　'Daguerreotype c. 1841', 167–8, 169–70
　'Darkness, My Mother', 178, 180
　'The Flogging', 182, 184
　'Ghazal between Icons: An Imagined Conversation', 201, 203–4
　'Imagining Lawrence Imagine the 11th of August 1841', 197, 199–201
　'Mr Covey, Shall We Dance?', 186–9
　'A Slave Boy's Lullaby', 206n6
　'Un-Portrait of Frederick Douglass', 205n1
　'Why I Read: Partial Pecha', 189, 191–3, 195
　'Why I Write: Partial Kucha', 193, 195–7
Brown, Michael, 201
Bryant, Tisa, 'The Problem of Dido', 126n2
Burn, Andrew, 82
　'A Second Address', 91
Burney, Frances, *Evelina*, 112
Burns, Sarah, 149
Byrne, Paula, 112, 120, 121, 123

cannibalism metaphor, 82
Caribbean, 4, 5
caricature, 38, 164n1, 168
chain gangs, 38
child sacrifice, 141–7, 164n2
childbirth, 27–9, 32–4
children, 22–4, 34–5, 174, 176
　and paedophilia, 39–40
Christianity, 97–8, 100–2, 143
　and Douglass, 170, 171–4, 176–7, 187
Civil Rights Movement, 203
Clarkson, Thomas, 77
　The History of the Rise, Progress, and Accomplishment of the Abolition of the African Slave-Trade by the British Parliament, 72–3, 74
cleansing, 23–5
Clements, Elizabeth Rosina, 107–8

Cliff, Michelle, *Free Enterprise: A Novel of Mary Ellen Pleasant*, 5
clothing, 112, 120, 122, 169
Coffee after Dinner, Dean Hall Plantation, Berkeley County, South Carolina (anon), 157, *158*, 159–63
Cole, Willie, 9n9
Collingwood, Capt Luke, 14, 15, 59–60
community, 41
compassion, 32, 33
compensation, 15–16
containment, 119–20
coquettishness, 122–3
cotton, 169
Couture, Thomas, 135
Covey, Edward, 184, 186–9, 191
Cowley, Malcolm, 57
Cowper, William, 'Epigram', 91

Dabydeen, David, 6, 79
　Coolie Odyssey, 42n3
　A Harlot's Progress, 5, 42n3
　see also 'Turner' (Dabydeen)
D'Aguiar, Fred, *Feeding the Ghosts*, 5
Damballah, 102
dance, 56–8, 60, 64n7, 131–2, 133–4
Dawes, Kwame, *Requiem: A Lament for the Dead*, 9n9
dehumanisation, 160, 168
depersonalisation, 51–2
Description of a Slave Ship (anon), 1, 5, 53, *54*, 67
　and Alexander, 68–9, 70–1
　and reproductions, 71–3
　and written text, 73–4
Diana (goddess), 109, 115
Dibdin the Younger, Charles, *Christmas Gambols*, 55
Dido Elizabeth Belle, 6, 95–6, 126
　and Brito, 96–108
　and Donoghue, 108–19
　and Jeffers, 119–24
Dien Cai Dau (Komunyakaa), 135
diet, 59–60
Django Unchained (film), 164n3
Donoghue, Emma
　'Dido', 6, 96, 108–19, 126

Douglass, Frederick, 7, 10n11, 142, 166–70, 203–4
  and anti-slavery speeches, 197, 199–201, 205n4, 206n8
  and Christian imagery, 171–4, 177, 206n9
  and literacy, 189, 191–3, 195–7
  and mother, 177–8, 180
  My Bondage and My Freedom, 170–1, 174, 176
  'The Color Line', 139
  and violence, 181–2, 184, 186–9, 206n6
Dove, Rita, 3, 130
Drescher, Seymour, 16
drowning, 17
Du Bois, W. E. B., *The Souls of Black Folk*, 201

economics, 33, 35–6
ekphrasis, 1–8, 42n3, 68–71, 93–4
  and African Americans, 163–4
  and Dido Elizabeth Belle, 95–6
  and Donoghue, 109, 110–12
  and Hayes, 157, 159–63
  and Jeffers, 120–1, 122
  and Komunyakaa, 139, 141–2, 144–6
  and Plampin, 82–5, 87, 91–2
  and 'The Slave Ship' (Patrick), 50–63
  and Trethewey, 148–54
  and Wideman, 129–35
  see also *Frederick Douglass* series; Ruskin, John; 'Turner' (Dabydeen)
Elford, William, 71
Eliot, George, *Brother Jacob*, 94n5
Eliot, T. S., *The Waste Land*, 42n4
Emancipation Proclamation (1863), 197
Emery, Mary Lou, 5
empowerment, 117
England, 19–20, 29, 115–16; see also Harewood House; Kenwood House
entertainment, 55, 57, 64n7, 133
Equiano, Olaudah, 16
Euripides, *Medea*, 141
Evans, Mary, 9n9

Eve, 97–9
exploitation, 102–5

Fabre, Geneviève, 57
Falconbridge, Alexander, 73
  An Account of the Slave Trade on the Coast of Africa, 58, 59, 60
Fall, the, 97–8
falling, 97–9
Fanon, Frantz, *Black Skin, White Masks*, 37, 43n8, 128n15
father–daughter relationship, 154–7
father–son relationship, 142–7, 170–1
Feelings, Tom, *The Middle Passage: White Ships / Black Cargo*, 9n9
Fifteenth Amendment, 187–8
Finley, Cheryl, *Committed to Memory: The Art of the Slave Ship Icon*, 1, 5
Floyd, George, 8
Found Anew (anthology), 157, 163
Fox, William, 'An Address to the People of Great Britain, on the Propriety of Abstaining from West India Sugar and Rum', 82
Fra Angelico, *Cortona Altarpiece with the Annunciation*, 170, 171–3
Frederick Douglass series (Lawrence), 7
  Panel 1, 174, *175*, 176
  Panel 2, 178, *179*, 180
  Panel 3, 182, *183*, 184
  Panel 8, 189, *190*, 191, 193
  Panel 10, *185*, 186, 188
  Panel 18, 197, *198*, 199–201
  Panel 21, *194*, 196–7
  Panel 32, 201, *202*, 203, 204
freedom-within-slavery, 174, 176
Fugitive Slave Act (1850), 137
Fuller, George, *The Quadroon*, 148–52, 156
furniture, 160–3
Furth, Leslie, 138

Gabriel, 172–4
Gaines, Col Archibald Kinkead, 137, 138
Gainsborough, Thomas, *The Blue Boy*, 144, 164n3

Garner, Eric, 201
Garner, Margaret, 137–8; *see also* Brady, Mathew B.; Noble, Thomas Satterwhite
gender, 25–6, 43n9; *see also* women
ghazals, 201, 203
Girtin, Thomas, 79, 87, 88, 89–90
gold, 75, 142, 143
   and Annunciation, 170, 173, 176, 177
   and Dido Elizabeth Belle, 88, 103, 113–14
   and Douglass, 178, 180, 184, 193, 200–1
Grainger, William, 94n1
grammar, 46–7
Gray, Freddie, 201, 203–4
Great Britain, 6; *see also* England
guilt, 21–2, 23

hallucination, 20, 25
Hammond, James Henry, 169
hands, 22–3, 62–3
Harewood House, 67, 79, 80–1, 82–4, 87–9
Harlem Renaissance, 1
Hasselhorst, Johann Heinrich, 164n4
Hayden, Robert, 14, 130
   'Aunt Jemima of the Ocean Waves', 94n1
   'Middle Passage', 66, 73
Hayes, Terrance, 7, 129, 207n11
   'Antebellum House Party', 157, 159–63, 165n6
Heffernan, James A. W., *Museum of Words: The Poetics of Ekphrasis from Homer to Ashbery*, 2, 3, 4
Hemings, Sally, 152, 153, 154, 156–7
Hirsch, Edward, *Transforming Vision: Writers on Art*, 129–30
Hogarth, George, *The Songs of Charles Dibdin*, 55
Hogarth, William, *Scene from Shakespeare's* The Tempest, 43n6
Hughes, Langston, *Mulatto: A Play of the Deep South*, 146–7
hunting, 109
Hutchinson, Thomas, 105–6, 111, 118–19, 120, 121

identity, 78
illness, 58–9
In the Frame: Women's Ekphrastic Poetry from Marianne Moore to Susan Wheeler (collection), 2–3
infanticide *see* child sacrifice
invisibility, 19–20
Irish immigrants, 132–4
Irving, John B., *A Day on Cooper River*, 159
Isaac, 143
isolation, 99

Jeffers, Honorée Fanonne, 6, 66–7, 93–4
   The Age of Phillis, 5, 6
   'Illustration: "Stowage of the British Slave Ship 'Brookes' under the Regulated Slave Trade Act of 1788"', 76–8, 79
   'Portrait of Dido Elizabeth Belle Lindsay, Free Mulatto, and her White Cousin, the Lady Elizabeth Murray, Great-Nieces of William Murray, First Earl of Mansfield and Lord Chief Justice of the King's Bench', 96, 119–24, 126
Jefferson, Thomas, 121–2, 152–7
Johnson, Charles, 130
Johnston, John Taylor, 49
'Jump Jim Crow' (song-and-dance routine), 64n7, 133, 135

Kant, Immanuel, 155
Kearney, Douglas, '***SWIMCHANT FOR NIGGER MERFOLK (AN AQUABOOGIE SET IN LAPSIS)***', 65n9
Kelsall, James, 14, 59–60
Kenwood House, 95, 105–6, 108–9, 117, 127n3
'Kickeraboo', 53–5
King and I, The (musical), 186
Komunyakaa, Yusef, 7, 129, 135
   'Modern Medea', 139, 141–2, 164n2
   'The Price of Blood', 144–7

Lamb, Mrs (*Will & Tom*), 82, 84–5, 87–93, 94

Lamming, George, 14
Larsen, Nella, *Quicksand*, 128n13
Lascelles, Beau, 80, 81, 82, 89–90, 92–3
Lascelles, Edward, 80
Lawrence, Jacob, 10n11, 164, 166–7, 205n3; see also *Frederick Douglass* series
Levine, Robert S., *The Lives of Frederick Douglass*, 166
Levy, Andrea, *The Long Song*, 126n2
Lhamon, W. T., Jr, 55
Lindsay, Capt John, 95, 105–6
line style, 50–1
literacy, 189, 191–3, 195–7
Lloyd, Col Edward, 178, 182, 184, 189
Loizeaux, Elizabeth Bergmann, 4
London, 115–16
lynching, 3

Major, Clarence, 'The Slave Trade: View from the Middle Passage', 9n9
Mannix, Daniel P., 57
Mansfield, Lord, 15, 95, 114–15, 123, 127n8
 and Donoghue, 108–11, 113, 116–19
manual transgression, 22–3
Marshall, James, 137
Martin, Agnes, *Islands No. 4*, 68–71
Martin, David see *Portrait of Dido Elizabeth Belle and Lady Elizabeth Murray*
Mary, Virgin, 172–4
masculinity, 25–6
Master Paintings in the Art Institute of Chicago, 130, 131
Matthews, Lt John, *A Voyage to the River Sierra-Leone, on the Coast of Africa*, 47–8
memory, 19, 22–3, 25, 31–2, 34–5
menial labour, 132–3
Middle Passage, 24, 67–71, 72–3, 74–6
 and imagination, 93–4
 and Jeffers, 76–8
 and Plampin, 82–5
 and 'The Slave Ship' (Patrick), 51–63
 see also *Zong* massacre
Milton, John, *Paradise Lost*, 97–9, 100–2

minstrelsy, 55, 64n7, 133
mirrors, 110–11
miscegenation, 138, 147–8, 171
Mitchell, W. J. T., 'Ekphrasis and the Other', 2, 3, 4
mixed-race, 147–57, 164n4, 171
Modern Painters (Ruskin), 4, 11
Morrison, Toni, *Beloved*, 4, 14, 30–41, 137, 165n6
motherhood, 26–7, 28–9, 147–8, 160
 and *Beloved*, 30–1, 32–6, 38, 39–40
 and Dabydeen, 26–7, 28–9
 and Dido Elizabeth Belle, 102, 106–7, 113–14, 118, 123–4
 and *Margaret Garner*, 136–9
 see also Bailey, Harriet
Mount, William Sidney, *Bar-Room Scene*, 129–35
movement, 119–20
murder, 21–2
Murray, Lady Elizabeth, 97
 and Donoghue, 111, 112, 113, 115, 116
 and Jeffers, 6, 96, 120–1, 122, 124
Murray, Sean, 133
music, 55, 57–8; see also dance

nature, 97–105
naval prowess, 29–30
'Négrier Poursuivi, Jetant ses Nègres à la Mer' ('Slave Ship Being Pursued, Throwing its Blacks into the Sea') (anon), 5, 67, 86
Newton, John, *Thoughts upon the African Slave Trade*, 110
Noble, Thomas Satterwhite
 Margaret Garner, 135, 136–7, 138–9, 141–2, 164n2
 The Price of Blood: A Planter Selling His Son, 135, 142–6, 171
Nobles, Gregory, 162
Nollekens, Joseph, 107–8
North Star, The (newspaper), 189, 193, 195, 196–7

Obama, Barack Hussein, 203
oppression, 80–1, 114, 181
oxen, 186–7

paedophilia, 39–40
Palmetto State, 157
Patrick, William B., 16
   These Upraised Hands, 45, 63n1
   see also 'Slave Ship, The' (Patrick)
PechaKucha, 7, 189, 191–4, 201, 207n11
Phillis (slave ship), 76
photography, 167–70, 199
Pindell, Howardena, 9n9
Piper, Keith, 9n9
Pippin, Horace H., 205n3
Plampin, Matthew, *Will & Tom*, 5–6, 67, 79–93, 94
plantations, 42n2, 43n6, 60, 71, 80, 109, 150–1
   and *Beloved*, 32, 35
   and Hayes, 157, 159–63
   and Plampin, 89, 92, 94
police violence, 201, 204
Portrait of Dido Elizabeth Belle and Lady Elizabeth Murray (Martin), 6, 9n10, 95–6, 124, 126, 126n2
   and Brito, 96–8, 99, 105
   and Donoghue, 109, 111–13
   and Jeffers, 120–1, 122
'Portrait of Dido Elizabeth Belle Lindsay, Free Mulatto, and her White Cousin, the Lady Elizabeth Murray, Great-Nieces of William Murray, First Earl of Mansfield and Lord Chief Justice of the King's Bench' (Jeffers), 6
profit, 33
prophecies, 27–9
punctuation, 46–7, 49

quadroon see mixed-race

race, 3, 8, 19–20, 24–5
   and Dido Elizabeth Belle, 102–3, 108, 111, 112, 113, 116, 117, 120–1
   and Douglass, 200–1
   and equality, 203–4
   and Garner, 138–9
   and Jeffers, 78
   and Jefferson, 121–2
   and Komunyakaa, 146

   and photography, 168–9
   see also African Americans; mixed-race
Ramsay, Allan, 9n10
rape see sexual violence
Ray, Henrietta Cordelia, 'In Memoriam (Frederick Douglass)', 169
reading, 189, 191–3
Rediker, Marcus, 71
reflection, 17–18
rehumanisation, 168–9
repetition, 70, 71
Rice, Thomas Dartmouth 'Daddy', 64n7, 133, 134
Rowlandson, Thomas, 92
Royal Academy (London), 11
rum, 60
Ruskin, John, 16–18, 21–2, 50, 64n3
   'Of Water, as Painted by Turner', 4, 11, 13, 41

Saar, Betye, 9n9
sacrifice see child sacrifice
Scarry, Elaine, 133
Schumann, Robert, 'Auf Einer Burg' ('In a Castle'), 147
Scott, Kevin Michael, 132, 133
Scott, Lawrence, *Dangerous Freedom: Elizabeth d'Aviniere's Story*, 126n2
sea, 24–5; see also water
sexual violence, 36–40, 57, 138–9, 160
   and Dido Elizabeth Belle, 122–3
   and Douglass, 171, 173
sexuality, 102–4, 112–13
Shakespeare, William
   Macbeth, 4, 14, 21–30, 34, 41, 42n5
   The Tempest, 4, 14, 43n6
'Shall We Dance?' (song), 186
Sharp, Granville, 16, 21, 109
ships see Middle Passage
sixth-plate daguerreotype of Frederick Douglass, 167–8
skin colour see race
'Slave Ship, The' (Patrick), 5, 6, 13, 45, 46–7
   and Africa, 47–8
   and ekphrasis, 50–3
   and Middle Passage, 53–63

Slave Ship, The (Slavers Throwing Overboard the Dead and Dying – Typhon Coming On) (Turner), 4, 6, *12*, 64n2
  and Dido Elizabeth Belle, 95
  and ekphrasis, 49–50
  and Patrick, 45, 46
  and Ruskin, 17, 18, 19, 21–2
  and 'The Slave Ship' (Patrick), 50–3, 56–7, 60–3
  and 'Turner', 11, 13, 30
  and *Zong* massacre, 42n1
slave trade, 3, 6–7, 21–2, 109
  and *Beloved*, 30–1, 32–3, 36–8
  and caricatures, 133, 134
  and Dido Elizabeth Belle, 95, 113–15, 116–17, 120, 123–4
  and Fuller, 149–50, 151–2
  and Garner, 137–9, 141–2
  and Jefferson, 152–7
  and Komunyakaa, 144–7
  and Lascelles family, 80, 81, 82–4, 88–92
  and Mansfield, 105–6
  and Noble, 135–7, 138–9, 142–4
  and 'The Slave Ship' (Patrick), 46–8
  and Turner (artist), 42n2
  and 'Turner' (Dabydeen), 13, 35–6
  see also abolitionism; Douglass, Frederick; Middle Passage; plantations
Slavers Throwing Overboard the Dead and Dying – Typhon Coming On see *Slave Ship, The (Slavers Throwing Overboard the Dead and Dying – Typhon Coming On)*
Smith, John Thomas, 107–8
Smith, R. T., 'Turner's *Slave Ship*', 65n9
snakes, 102, 103–4, 105
Society for Effecting the Abolition of the Slave Trade, 16, 71
Somerset, James, 95, 109–10, 114–17, 118, 126
songs, 55, 57–8
staining, 23–5
stereotypes, 3, 20, 25, 78, 112
  and *Bar-Room Scene*, 132–3, 134
Stewart, Charles, 109
Stone, Lucy, 138

Stothard, Thomas, *Voyage of the Sable Venus, from Angola to the West Indies*, 94n1
Stowage of the British Slave Ship 'Brookes' under the Regulated Slave Trade Act of 1788 (anon), 5–6, 67, 75, 76–8
  and Plampin, 82–5, 87, 89, 91–2
  and written text, 73–4
Stowe, Harriet Beecher, *Uncle Tom's Cabin*, 137
Stuart, Gilbert, 'Edgehill' *Portrait of Thomas Jefferson*, 152–4
Stubbs, Robert, 14
sugar, 80, 81–2, 161
surgeons, 58–9, 60

Tarantino, Quentin, 164n3
Thackeray, William Makepeace, 49
Thames, River, 113–14, 115
Trethewey, Natasha, 7, 129
  'Blood', 147–9, 150–1, 151–2
  'Enlightenment', 147–8, 152–7
  'Knowledge', 164n4
Trotter, Thomas, 54–5, 58
Tubman, Harriet, 10n11
'Turner' (Dabydeen), 4, 5, 11, 13–14, 18–20, 46
  and *Beloved*, 30–41
  and *Macbeth*, 22–30, 42n5
Turner, J. M. W., 16–18, 42n2
  Hero and Leander, 17
  and Plampin, 67, 79, 80–1, 82–5, 87–90, 91–3
  Schloss Rosenau, 17, 19
  see also *Slave Ship, The (Slavers Throwing Overboard the Dead and Dying – Typhon Coming On)* (Turner)
Twain, Mark, 64n2
  A Tramp Abroad, 49, 128n11
typography, 50–1

Underground Railroad, 137
United States of America (USA) *see* African Americans; American Civil War
Unsworth, Barry, 14
  Sacred Hunger, 65n10

Valenzeula-Mendoza, Eloisa, 150
Van Tenac, Charles, *Histoire Générale de la Marine* (*General History of the Navy*), 5, 67
verbal association, 71
Vietnam War, 135
violence, 132–3, 134, 159–60
  and Douglass, 181–2, 184, 186–9
  see also police violence; sexual violence
visibility, 19–20
visual arts *see* ekphrasis

Walcott, Derek, *Omeros*, 4, 42n4
Walvin, James, 16
water, 17–19, 31
Weber, Joanna, 68
Weisenburger, Steven, 30
wet-nursing, 160, 165n5
Wheatley, Francis, *A Family Group in a Landscape*, 42n3
Wheatley, Phillis, 5, 76, 78, 106–7
  Phillis Wheatley, Negro Servant to Mr. Wheatley, of Boston, 125, 126
white gaze, 20, 36–9
whiteness *see* race
Wideman, John Edgar, 7
  'Listening', 129–35
Wilson, William J. ('Ethiop'), 164n1

Wombwell, George, 127n7
women, 2–3, 36–8, 147–51; *see also* Dido Elizabeth Belle; Garner, Margaret; motherhood; sexual violence
Wood, Marcus, 22
Words for Images: A Gallery of Poems, 67–8
World Anti-Slavery Convention, 11

Xanthus, 146

Yankees, 132, 134
Yeats, W. B., 'Leda and the Swan', 44n12, 44n15
yellow fever, 161

Zoffany, Johan Joseph, 111–13, 114, 115, 116
Zong massacre, 4, 11, 14–16, 21, 42n1, 43n7, 44n13
  and Alexander, 75
  and death toll, 65n8
  and Dido Elizabeth Belle, 99
  and Donoghue, 128n11, 128n16
  and Mansfield, 95
  and Plampin, 85, 87, 93
  and 'The Slave Ship' (Patrick), 47
  and Unsworth, 65n10
Zucchi, Antonio, 109, 115

EU representative:
Easy Access System Europe
Mustamäe tee 50, 10621 Tallinn, Estonia
Gpsr.requests@easproject.com

www.ingramcontent.com/pod-product-compliance
Lightning Source LLC
Chambersburg PA
CBHW071831230426
43672CB00013B/2815